THE HISTORY OF PHOTOGRAPHY

from 1839 to the present day · revised and enlarged edition · Beaumont Newhall

THE MUSEUM OF MODERN ART, NEW YORK

In collaboration with the George Eastman House, Rochester, New York
Distributed by New York Graphic Society, Boston, Massachusetts

All Rights Reserved
The Museum of Modern Art, 1964
11 West 53 Street, New York, New York 10019
Library of Congress Catalogue Card Number 64-15285
Cloth Binding ISBN 0-87070-0375-7
Paperbound ISBN 0-87070-374-9
Designed by Werner Brudi
Fourth edition, seventh printing, 1978

Foreword and Acknowledgments

Ever since 1839 photography has been a vital means of communication and expression. The growth of this contribution to the visual arts is the subject of this book. It is a history of a medium, rather than a technique, seen through the eyes of those who over the years have struggled to master it, to understand it, and to mold it to their vision.

Photography is at once a science and an art, and both aspects are inseparably linked throughout its astonishing rise from a substitute for skill of hand to an independent art form. The technology of photography is discussed in these pages in so far as it affects the photographer. No attempt, however, has been made to explain the scientific theory of the photographic process.

This is the fourth revised and expanded edition of the text first published in the illustrated catalogue of the exhibition *Photography 1839–1937,* which I organized for The Museum of Modern Art in 1937. In 1938 the text and illustrations were reprinted as *Photography: A Short Critical History.* In 1949, following a year of research made possible by a John Simon Guggenheim Memorial Foundation Fellowship, the book was entirely rewritten and appeared with the title *The History of Photography.*

For permission to reproduce copyrighted material I am indebted to the authors and publishers named in the notes. For permission to reproduce photographs I am indebted to the photographers, collectors, museums and historical societies named in the captions. Many of the photographs reproduced are in the collections of the Museum of Modern Art and the George Eastman House: these are indicated, respectively, by the letters MOMA and GEH.

I thank: The trustees and staff of The Museum of Modern Art and the George Eastman House for their support and constant help.

Ansel Adams, Jean Adhémar, Mlle. J. Boichard, Albert Boni, Edgar Breitenbach, Robert Bretz, Keast Burke, Josephine Cobb, Robert M. Doty, Helmut Gernsheim, L. E. Hallett, André Jammes, Nathan Lyons, Grace M. Mayer, A. Hyatt Mayor, Piero Racanicchi, John Szarkowski, D. B. Thomas, Monroe Wheeler, and Harold White.

Nancy Newhall, my wife and colleague, for encouragement, criticism, and for sharing with me the fruits of her research.

Beaumont Newhall

Contents

THE HISTORY OF PHOTOGRAPHY

Camera pictures have been made ever since the Renaissance. Artists turned to mathematics and optics for assistance in solving perspective problems, and they found the phenomenon of the *camera obscura* (literally "dark room") a mechanical aid of the greatest value. Leonardo da Vinci described the principle: light entering a minute hole in the wall of a darkened room forms on the opposite wall an inverted image of whatever lies outside. The first published account of the use of the camera as an aid to the draftsman appeared in Giovanni Battista della Porta's book, *Natural Magic*, of 1558. Ten years later Danielo Barbaro, professor at the University of Padua, and author of a treatise on perspective, showed that a more brilliant image could be produced by substituting a lens for the pinhole:

Close all the shutters and doors until no light enters the *camera* except through the lens, and opposite hold a sheet of paper, which you move forward and backward until the scene appears in the sharpest detail. There on the paper you will see the whole view as it really is, with its distances, its colors and shadows and motion, the clouds, the water twinkling, the birds flying. By holding the paper steady you can trace the whole perspective with a pen, shade it and delicately color it from nature.[1]

The camera, at first actually a room big enough for a man to enter, gradually grew smaller. The windows of sedan chairs were covered and the camera could be taken into the countryside. In the seventeenth and eighteenth centuries a lens was fitted into one end of a two-foot box, and the other end covered with a sheet of frosted or ground glass. The image cast on the ground glass by the lens could be seen outside of the camera. A perfected model, resembling the modern reflex camera, had the ground glass flush with the top of the box, the image being thrown upon it by a mirror placed at an angle of 45°. It had the advantage that the image was not upside down, and the artist could trace it by laying thin paper over the glass. Cameras became standard equipment for artists. Count Francesco Algarotti, in his *Essay on Painting* (1764), devotes a chapter to the camera: "The best modern painters among the Italians have availed themselves greatly of this contrivance; nor is it possible they should have otherwise represented things so much to life."

But the ancients had already observed that light not only forms images, but changes the nature of many substances. The chlorophyll of vegetation becomes green on exposure to it; colored fabrics fade. Among the substances radically altered by light are certain salts of silver, especially the halides. The combining element is liberated, leaving pure metallic silver which, because unpolished, is dark in tone. The light sensitivity of these salts was first scientifically established by the German physicist Johann Heinrich Schulze in 1727.

He filled a glass bottle with a mixture of chalk, silver, and nitric acid which, after he had thoroughly shaken it, combined to form whitish silver salts. When he put the bottle in bright sunlight, the mixture turned to a deep purple color. As exposure to the heat of a fire produced no such change, Schulze deduced that the reaction had been caused by the sun's light rather than by its heat. To prove his deduction, he pasted stencils of opaque paper on the flask. After exposure to light the stencil was removed, and images of the figures or writing which had been cut out of the paper were clearly visible on the surface of the mixture within the flask, traced by the dark color of metallic silver.

All unconsciously, Schulze had indicated a way to trap the elusive image of the camera. What we know as photography is the combined application of optical and chemical phenomena long known to man.

The incentive to work out a practical technique was stimulated by the unprecedented demand for pictures from the rising middle class of the late eighteenth century. Reproductions in quantity were in order: lithography was invented and wood engraving revived, so that pictures could be almost endlessly duplicated. The middle class wanted cheap portraits; mechanical devices to eliminate the need for lengthy artistic training were put in its hands, so that every man could become something of an artist. The *silhouette* required merely the ability to trace a cast shadow; the *physionotrace*, invented by Gilles Louis Chrétien in 1786, asked no more of the beginner, with the advantage that a miniature engraved copper plate was produced, from which duplicates could be printed. The sitter's profile was traced on a sheet of glass with a stylus connected by levers to an engraving tool which recorded in a reduced scale its every move-

A camera obscura; the image formed by the lens and reflected by the mirror on the ground glass is traced

ment on a copper plate. The instrument was immensely popular; six hundred physionotrace portraits were exhibited at the 1797 Paris Salon alone. Févret de St.-Mémin brought his physionotrace to America and made over eight hundred portraits, including a number of remarkable documents of the founding fathers.

Still another mechanical substitute for artistic skill was the *camera lucida*, invented by the Englishman William Hyde Wollaston in 1807. Drawing paper was laid flat. Over it a glass prism was suspended at eye level by a brass rod. Looking through a peephole centered over the edge of the prism, the operator saw at the same time both the subject and the drawing paper; his pencil was guided by the virtual image. The camera lucida, which resembled the camera only in name and function, could easily be carried about and was widely used by travelers. With it Basil Hall documented his American travels; in the preface to *Forty Etchings Made with the Camera Lucida in North America in 1827 and 1828* (Edinburgh, 1829) he praised the instrument which freed the amateur "from the triple misery of Perspective, Proportion and Form," and concluded that although Wollaston, its inventor, had not discovered the "Royal Road to Drawing," he had "at least succeeded in Macadamising the way already known."

But to many amateurs "Macadamising" was not enough. Even the camera lucida demanded a modicum of skill in drawing.

In all history the experimental amateur has not been the one to accept either his shortcomings or the difficulties which block the professional. The fever for reality was running high. The physical aid of camera obscura and camera lucida had drawn men so near to an exact copying of nature and the satisfaction of the current craving for reality that they could not abide the intrusion of the pencil of man to close the gap. Only the pencil of nature would do. The same idea burned in many at once, and the race for discovery was on: to make light itself fix the image in the camera without having to draw it by hand.

Before the camera lucida was developed, Thomas Wedgwood, son of the British potter, had already attempted to make permanent prints "by the agency of light." In the *Journal of the Royal Institution* for 1802[2] his friend Sir Humphry Davy described the process:

White paper, or white leather, moistened with solution of nitrate of silver, undergoes no change when kept in a dark place; but, on being exposed to day light, it speedily changes colour, and, after passing through different shades of grey and brown, becomes at length nearly black....

When a white surface, covered with solution of nitrate of silver, is placed behind a painting on glass exposed to the solar light; the rays transmitted through the differently painted surfaces produce distinct tints of brown or black, sensibly differing in intensity according to the shades of the picture, and where the light is unaltered, the colour of the nitrate becomes deepest.

When the shadow of any figure is thrown upon the prepared surface, the part concealed by it remains white, and the other parts speedily become dark.

For copying paintings on glass, the solution should be applied on leather; and, in this case, it is more readily acted upon than when paper is used.

Wedgwood was dismayed that his sun prints were not permanent. He found no way to desensitize the unexposed areas of the prepared paper or leather. Only by keeping his results in darkness could they be prevented from turning dark; he looked at them furtively by the weak light of a candle. His attempts to record the camera's image – "the first object of Mr. Wedgwood, in his researches on the subject," Davy wrote – were unsuccessful. Ill health forced him to abandon further experiments, and all that remains is the account by Davy, who concluded: "Nothing but a method of preventing the unshaded parts of the delineation from being coloured by exposure to the day is wanting, to render the process as useful as it is elegant."

Joseph Nicéphore Niépce of Chalon-sur-Saône, France, was more successful. Although the only example of his camera work that remains today appears to have been made in 1826, his letters and eye witness accounts leave no doubt that he had succeeded in permanently fixing the camera's image even earlier.

Nicéphore Niépce and his brother Claude were ardent inventors. They had patented a hot-air engine;

when lithography was introduced, Nicéphore turned his attention to it. He had no artistic skill, and first relied on others for the drawings which he reproduced. Soon he conceived the possibility of making them by means of light. On April 1, 1816, he wrote his brother:

The experiments I have thus far made lead me to believe that my process will succeed as far as the principal effect is concerned, but I must succeed in fixing the colors; this is what occupies me at the moment, and it is the most difficult.[3]

A few days later he described his camera as "a kind of artificial eye, simply a little box, each side six inches square, which will be fitted with a tube that can be lengthened carrying a lenticular glass."[4]

He broke the lens and had to make a new camera, smaller in size – about 1¼ inches on each side – because the only other lens he had was from his solar microscope.

I placed the apparatus in the room where I work, facing the birdhouse and the open casement. I made the experiment according to the process which you know [he wrote his brother on May 5, 1816] and I saw on the white paper all that part of the birdhouse which is seen from the window and a faint image of the casement which was less illuminated than the exterior objects.

This is but an imperfect trial.... The possibility of painting in this way seems to me almost demonstrated.... That which you have foreseen has happened. The background of the picture is black, and the objects white, that is, lighter than the background.[5]

This is an accurate description of a negative. The copies of natural objects and paintings upon glass which Wedgwood made by contact printing showed this same reversal of tone. Had Niépce only thought of making prints from these negatives he could have again inverted the tones so that they corresponded to the order of lights and shades in nature. But he wanted to secure pictures directly in the camera.

He began to search for a substance which light would bleach instead of darken. His experiments were fruitless until he found that a certain type of bitumen or asphalt, normally soluble in lavender oil, became insoluble in that chemical on exposure to light. At first, instead of trying to reproduce the infinite shades of light which form the camera's image, he attempted to fix simply the black and white contrasts of an engraving. Isidore, Niépce's son, recounts how his father

spread on a well-polished pewter plate bitumen of Judea dissolved in Dippel's oil. On this varnish he

Silhouette of George Washington, traced from a shadow on the wall by his ward, Eleanor Parke Custis, in 1798. The Metropolitan Museum of Art, New York

Physionotrace of Gilles-Louis Chrétien, inventor of the process, 1792. GEH

A camera lucida in use

placed the engraving to be reproduced, which had been made translucent, and exposed the whole to the light.... After a time he immersed the plate in a solvent which bit by bit brought out the image which until then had remained invisible; then he washed the plate and let it dry. After these different operations, for the purpose of etching it, he placed it in water more or less acidified.

My father sent this plate to [the engraver Augustin François] Lemaître, requesting him to contribute his talent in engraving the drawing still deeper. M. Lemaître acceded very courteously to my father's request. He pulled several proofs of this portrait of Cardinal d'Amboise....[6]

The printed lines of the engraving had held back the light; the white paper had permitted it to pass through. Thus most of the bitumen was rendered insoluble, but that which lay directly under the lines remained soluble and could be removed by lavender oil. The bared metal was then etched to form a printing plate. This process was a reproduction technique; it is the first of the photomechanical processes which were to revolutionize the graphic arts. Now Niépce went further. He attempted to fix in a similar manner the camera's image.

In January, 1826, Niépce received a letter from a stranger, Daguerre, who said he had been given Niépce's address by their mutual lens maker, Chevalier of Paris, and claimed he was working along similar lines.

Louis Jacques Mandé Daguerre was a painter who had specialized in producing stage sets for the Opéra and the popular theatres. At the time he wrote Niépce he was proprietor with Charles Marie Bouton of the *Diorama*, a theatre built for the display of great 45½ by 71½-foot paintings of the most illusionistic kind. Semi-transparent theatrical gauze was painted on both sides; by changing the lighting from top to back, one image dissolved while the other appeared, giving the illusion of lapse of time, or even motion. The Diorama had three prosceniums. The circular auditorium could be revolved, so that the audience saw one painting after the other. To produce these paintings, Daguerre and Bouton made frequent use of the camera obscura, and it was his familiarity with this instrument which led Daguerre towards photographic experimentation.

Jealous of his secret, Niépce sent a vague answer to Daguerre. More than a year passed before Daguerre wrote again. This second note led Niépce to ask his friend the engraver Lemaître: "Do you know one of the inventors of the Diorama, M. Daguerre?" He received an immediate reply:

...M. Daguerre, as a painter, has a fine talent for imitation, and an exquisite taste for the arrangement of his pictures. I believe he has an unusual understanding of stage machinery and lighting effects; the connoisseur, visiting his establishment, can easily convince himself of that. I know he has busied himself for a long time perfecting the camera obscura, but I do not know the object of his work.[7]

Daguerre sent Niépce something he called a "smoke drawing" (*dessin fumé*), and Niépce, in exchange, sent him a lightly etched plate which, he told Lemaître, "could in no way compromise the secret of my discovery." Still they were getting closer in a veiled correspondence in which each hinted at that which the other did not have but needed. On June 4, 1827, Niépce made his first positive approach to Daguerre for active collaboration. Nothing came of it.

Then Claude Niépce fell ill in England and his brother set off to visit him at the end of August. He was held up in Paris by passport difficulties and the advent of Charles X in Calais, which so jammed the stage coaches to the port that no seat was to be had. Niépce took advantage of the delay to meet Daguerre in person.

I have had many and very long interviews with M. Daguerre [he wrote his son on September 2–3, 1827]. He came to see us yesterday. His visit lasted for three hours... and the conversation on the subject which interests us is really endless.... I have seen nothing here that impressed me more, that gave me more pleasure, than the Diorama. We were taken through it by M. Daguerre and could contemplate at our ease the magnificent pictures which are exhibited there.... Nothing is superior to the two views painted by M. Daguerre: one of Edinburgh, taken by moonlight during a fire; the other of a Swiss village, taken at the end of a wide street, facing a mountain of tremendous height, covered with eternal snow. These representations are so real,

Camera lucida drawing by Sir John Herschel of the Temple of Juno, Girgenti, Sicily, 1824. The Science Museum, London

Camera lucida drawing by H. Fox Talbot of Lago Lecco, Italy, 1833. The Royal Photographic Society, London

DAGUERRE: Study for the Diorama *The Inauguration of Solomon's Temple*, 1836. Sepia drawing. GEH

NIÉPCE: View from his Window at Gras, 1826. Heliograph. Gernsheim Collection, University of Texas, Austin, Texas

"Though the image can clearly be seen by holding the plate at an angle against the light, or by reflecting light on it by means of a white cardboard to increase the contrast, the picture presented the greatest difficulty in reproduction, because the plate is as shiny as a mirror, and the image rather faint.... Our thanks are due to Mr. P. B. Watt of the Kodak Research Laboratory, who after many trials successfully overcame the difficult problem of reproducing the picture." H. & A. Gernsheim, *Photographic Journal*, May, 1952

even in their smallest detail, that one believes that he actually sees rural and primeval nature, with all the illusion with which the charm of color and the magic of chiaroscuro can endow it. The illusion is even so great that one attempts to leave one's box in order to wander out into the open and climb to the summit of the mountain. I assure you there is not the least exaggeration on my part, the objects are, or seem to be, of natural size.[8]

In England, Niépce met Francis Bauer, secretary of the Royal Society, who urged him to communicate his experiments to the Society. That learned body, however, refused to receive his communication because it was against its rules to discuss secret processes, and

Niépce declined to reveal his technique. He gave Bauer samples of his work; three of them, bearing Bauer's endorsement, are now in the Royal Photographic Society's collection in London. They are pewter plates made from engravings, but Bauer, in a letter to the *Literary Gazette*, February 27, 1839, stated that Niépce showed him in 1827 "his first successful experiment to fix the image of nature." This is without doubt the pewter plate found by Helmut and Alison Gernsheim, and identified by them as *View from his Window at Gras*, taken by Niépce in 1826, with an exposure of eight hours. While in England, Niépce wrote an instruction manual in French *On Heliography; or, A Means of Automatically Fixing, by the Action of Light, the Image Formed in the Camera Obscura*. It was left unpublished.

He came back to France in 1829 determined to concentrate on what he called "view points" (*points de vue*) with the "sole object to copy nature with the greatest fidelity." He reopened correspondence with Daguerre. The showman advised him to postpone his book: "As regards your intention of publishing your method, there should be found some way of getting a large profit out of it before publication, apart from the honor the invention will do you."[9] Lemaître criticized one of Niépce's "view points" for its contradictory shadows cast by the sun during the excessively long exposure time. Niépce replied:

Unfortunately I can't avoid it.... A camera as perfect as M. Daguerre's is needed, otherwise I shall be condemned to come more or less close to the goal without ever reaching it.... I am, therefore, hastening to reply to the gracious offer to be of service by proposing that he cooperate with me in perfecting my heliographic process.[10]

After nearly three years of polite distrust and trying each other out and leading each other on, Niépce and Daguerre joined articles of partnership, on December 4, 1829, to last ten years.

Only four had run their course when, in 1833, Niépce died in Chalon-sur-Saône.

In 1835 the magazine *Journal des artistes*, reviewing the Diorama *The Valley of Goldau*, noted that Daguerre

has found out a method of receiving, on a plate prepared by him, the image produced by the camera obscura, so that a portrait, a landscape or view of any kind, projected upon this plate by the ordinary camera obscura, *leaves* its impress there in light and shade, and thus makes the most perfect of drawings. A preparation applied to this image preserves it for an indefinite period. Physical science has, perhaps, never offered such a marvel.[1]

The announcement was somewhat premature, to judge from a letter to the editor published in the following year: "I doubt if M. Daguerre has reached the complete results attributed to him. If he had... it is very probable that he would have exhibited them...even if he had to make a night album, enclosing his results within black envelopes and displaying them only by moonlight."[2]

By 1837, however, Daguerre made a brilliant, detailed picture of a corner of his studio, using a modification of Niépce's invention which he considered sufficiently his own to name the *daguerreotype*. He persuaded Isidore Niépce, who had taken his father's place as Daguerre's partner, to agree to a revision in the contract. The process was to be made public jointly with heliography, the agreement stipulated, "in order that the name of M. J. Nicéphore Niépce may figure always, as it should, in this discovery."[3] The associates planned to market the process by subscription, but the public would have none of it. They were skeptical of Daguerre's claim that with his invention "anyone can take the most detailed views in a few minutes." They could not believe that the daguerreotype was "a chemical and physical process which gives Nature the ability to reproduce herself."[4]

Daguerre secretly demonstrated his invention to François Arago, director of the Paris Observatory. The famous scientist, himself an investigator of light, saw the potentialities of the daguerreotype, lectured on it to the Academy of Sciences, January 7, 1839, and proposed that if, on further investigation, the process was found practical and useful, he would recommend its purchase by the government. A few months later a bill was introduced into the Chamber of Deputies and the Chamber of Peers. After hearing reports by Arago for the Deputies and Joseph Louis Gay-Lussac for the Peers, both chambers passed the appropriation: Daguerre was to be granted an annuity of 6,000 francs and Isidore Niépce an annuity of 4,000 francs, in return for which they would "place in the hands of the Ministry of the Interior a sealed package containing the history and most detailed and exact description of the invention mentioned." For his extra 2,000 francs Daguerre was to divulge the processes of his Diorama. Arago was directed to make public the technical details at a joint open meeting of the Academy of Sciences and the Academy of Fine Arts, August 19, 1839.

The public's reaction to these negotiations was extraordinary. They marvelled over the daguerreotypes shown at the Chamber of Deputies:

In one, representing the Pont Marie, all the minutest indentations and divisions of the ground, or the building, the goods lying on the wharf, even the small stones under the water at the edge of the stream, and the different degrees of transparency given to the water, were all shown with the most incredible accuracy.[5]

The Leipzig *Anzeiger* – for the news spread rapidly throughout Europe – went so far as to brand the process sacrilegious. Excitement ran high; on the day set for formal publication, all Paris was tense.

Daguerre, although at the meeting, did not speak. He excused himself because of a sore throat, and the process was scientifically described, but not practically demonstrated, by Arago.

An eye witness – Marc Antoine Gaudin – relates that

the Palace of the Institute was stormed by a swarm of the curious at the memorable sitting on August 19, 1839, where the process was at long last divulged. Although I came two hours beforehand, like many others I was barred from the hall. I was on the watch with the crowd for everything that happened outside. At one moment an excited man comes out; he is surrounded, he is questioned, and he answers with a know-it-all air, that bitumen of Judea and lavender oil is the secret. Questions are multiplied, but as he knows nothing more, we are reduced to talking about bitumen of Judea and lavender oil. Soon the crowd surrounds a newcomer, more startled than the last. He tells us with no further comment that it is iodine and mercury. Finally the sitting is over, the secret is divulged....

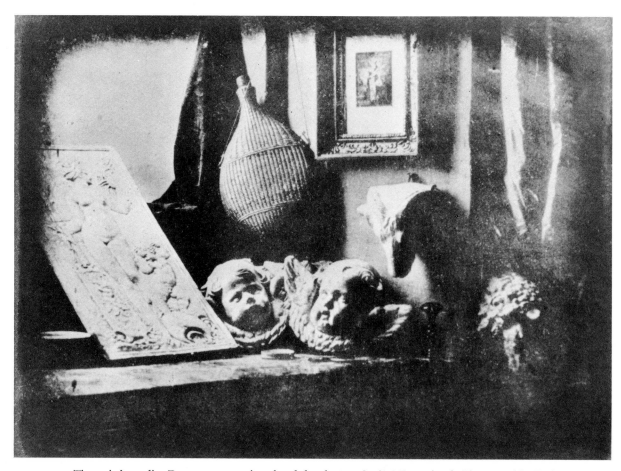

DAGUERRE: The artist's studio. Daguerreotype, signed and dated 1837. Société Française de Photographie, Paris

A few days later, opticians' shops were crowded with amateurs panting for daguerreotype apparatus, and everywhere cameras were trained on buildings. Everyone wanted to record the view from his window, and he was lucky who at first trial got a silhouette of roof tops against the sky. He went into ecstasies over chimneys, counted over and over roof tiles and chimney bricks, was astonished to see the very mortar between the bricks – in a word, the technique was so new that even the poorest proof gave him indescribable joy.[6]

Daguerre wrote a seventy-nine page booklet, *Histoire et description du procédé nommé le Daguerréotype*. It was illustrated with scale drawings of the camera and equipment, and the instructions were so complete that anyone could have the apparatus built by an instrument maker and could anticipate some sort of success if he followed the directions carefully. Within five months more than thirty editions, translations and summaries of the technical specifications had appeared; to list their places of publication is to plot the spread of the daguerreotype throughout the Western world: Barcelona, Berlin, Edinburgh, Genoa, Halle, Hamburg, Karlsruhe, Lon-

don, Madrid, Naples, New York, Paris, Philadelphia, Quedlinburg, Saint Gall, Saint Petersburg, Stockholm, Stuttgart.

But Parisians complained that the brochure was written in too scientific a language; the process seemed excessively complicated. In answer to this criticism the government ordered Daguerre to make daguerreotypes publicly, so that the simplicity of the process might become clear.

A special correspondent of *The New York Star* went to the demonstration of September 17 at the Grand Hotel on the Quai d'Orsay. He reported that Daguerre took a plate of copper plated with silver and rubbed the silver surface in a slight manner with very fine pumice powder and sweet oil, using small balls of cotton wool for this purpose. He thus completely dulled the surface, and I noticed that he rubbed first with a circular motion, and then with straight lines from top to bottom.

He then washed the plate thus dulled in a liquid consisting of: distilled water, 16 parts; nitric acid, 1 part. He then gave a slight heat to the plate by passing it over the flame of a lamp – the copper side being next to the flame and the silver surface uppermost. He then washed it a second time in dilute nitric acid.

The plate was now ready for a coating of iodine. The apartment was darkened, and the plate, fixed on a small board, was placed (with the silver part downwards) over an opening the size of the intended picture, in the lid of a box at the bottom of which the iodine was. Halfway down in the box was a slight wooden frame on which a piece of muslin was strained, and through this muslin, as the iodine evaporated, the fumes rose, and were thus equally received upon the silvered surface, there forming a coating of iodide of silver, having the yellow appearance of brass.

A camera obscura was now brought up. Its focus had previously been adjusted by trying the effect of the picture on a bit of ground glass. The plate prepared as above was placed in the camera. The view intended to be taken was the Tuileries, the Quay and the Seine in front of the window where the camera obscura was placed. It was there to remain until the action of the sun's rays on its surface was sufficient. This occupies a period of from five to forty minutes, according to the time of the year and state of the weather, and as the director (for I cannot call him the operator) cannot see by the plate how the process goes on, experience alone can tell him how to judge as to the advancement which the action of the light has made. In this instance the day was dull, and the plate remained fifteen minutes in the camera obscura. When it was taken out it appeared exactly the same as when it was put in, and the people looked very blank, I do assure you, at what looked like a failure; but indeed one could scarcely tell whether or not it had been marked, for the process requires that no light fall on it before finishing operations.

M. Daguerre took the plate and held it with the silver part downwards, and thus held it for half a minute, while three persons peered upon it and said, "Nothing has been traced upon it."

He fixed it then, at an angle of 45°, in a box at the bottom of which was an earthen pan holding two pounds of mercury. Under the pan was a lamp which heated the mercury to 62° Centigrade or 117° Fahrenheit, and as the mercury grew hot, its globules arising, combined with the prepared surface of the metal, *brought out the picture*. In front of the box is a glass spyhole, through which the process is watched, and the moment it was completed the plate was taken out and washed with distilled water saturated with common salt or with the hyposulphite of soda, heated to a degree below the boiling point. This finished it, and the picture thus literally executed by the sun, was handed about.

I never saw anything more perfect. When examined by the naked eye every object appeared minutely engraved, but when viewed through a magnifying glass the difference of grain in the separate flags of the *trottoir* [sidewalk] was visible, and the texture of everything, if I may use the phrase, was easily distinguishable.[7]

The *Star's* reporter was amazed that there was no trace of an image on the plate until it had been "brought out" by the mercury vapor. This *development* of the hidden or *latent* image enabled Daguerre to reduce the exposure time, and to succeed where earlier experimenters had failed. It is a principle followed ever since in most photographic processes. But still the exposures were minutes long. During those minutes vehicles and pedestrians moved about; they did not stay still in one place long enough for the plate to record their images. In only one of Daguerre's pictures does a man appear: by chance a pedestrian on the boulevard had stopped to have his shoes shined, and had held still during most of the exposure.

The daguerreotype had another disadvantage. Each picture was unique. It could be duplicated only by making a copy of it with a camera or by hand. Many engravings and lithographs after daguerreotypes were published; between 1840 and 1844 a hundred and fourteen travel views were issued in Paris as the series *Excursions Daguerriennes*. Daguerreotypes taken in Europe, Africa and America for the publisher, N. M. P. Lerebours, were painstakingly traced and transferred to copper plates by the aquatint process. Figures and traffic, imaginatively drawn in the romantic style, were added in an attempt to please the public who abhorred the depopulated aspect of the first daguerreotypes. Among the first to make these pictures for Lerebours was Frédéric Goupil-Fesquet, who was traveling in the Middle East with his uncle, the painter Horace Vernet. In November, 1839, they were two leagues outside Cairo "daguerreotyping like lions," Vernet wrote. On a boat going up the Nile Goupil-Fesquet, to his astonishment, met another cameraman also on assignment from Lerebours: Pierre Gustave Joly de Lotbinière, a Canadian. The two joined forces to produce the earliest photographic documentation of Egypt. Joly de Lotbinière went on to Greece. A view of Niagara Falls, surely the earliest photograph of that much-photographed landmark, is credited to H. L. Pattinson of Newcastle-on-Tyne; we know nothing more of him than a meagre note by Lerebours: "This distinguished amateur daguerreotypist is one of the first who busied himself with this art in America." Another cameraman, unknown by name, made a beautiful plate of the Kremlin under snow. Most of these daguerreotypes, like the names of so many of their makers, are now lost; they were undoubtedly destroyed by the engravers in tracing them, but the plates in the *Excursions Daguerriennes* retain the peculiar clarity and chiaroscuro of photographs. *The Edinburgh Review*, praising the publication in 1843, wrote that the pictures "actually give us the real impression of the different scenes and monuments at a particular instant of time, and under the existing lights of the sun and atmosphere."8

There were other travelers who recorded what they saw by daguerreotype. The French diplomat Baron Jean Baptiste Louis Gros made photographs in Bogotá, Colombia, in 1842 while he was chargé d'affaires there; when sent to Greece as French ambassador he continued to take daguerreotypes. Joseph Philibert Girault de Prangey took over a thousand plates of Arabic architecture in the Middle East from 1842–1844. On his second trip to Central America in 1841, John Lloyd Stephens took along a daguerreotype outfit, to supplement the pictorial documentation of the ancient ruins which George Catherwood was drawing with the help of the camera lucida.

Although daguerreotypes of the architecture and landscape of faraway places were popular, the public was disappointed that the invention did not reach the heights anticipated by its first announcement. "It has excited some surprise," we read in the London *Athenaeum* of October 26, 1839, "that, after the eager and natural curiosity of the public concerning the discovery

JOSEPH SAXTON: The Arsenal and cupola of the Philadelphia High School. Daguerreotype, 1839. Pennsylvania Historical Society, Philadelphia

DAGUERRE: A Parisian boulevard. Daguerreotype, c. 1838 Bayerische Nationalmuseum, Munich

Snow scene, Moscow, c. 1840. Aquatint engraving from a daguerreotype by an unknown photographer. Plate 51 of *Excursions Daguerriennes*, 1841. GEH

of M. Daguerre while it yet remained a secret, so little interest should now be taken in the subject." One reason was that, in spite of the apparently generous action of the French government in offering the daguerreotype "free to all the world (*à tout le monde*)," the inventor applied for and received a patent in England. Another, more important reason, was that the process did not at first fulfill the public's demand for portraits.

Daguerre himself despaired of ever securing portraits by his invention, on account of the length of the sitting, which led the satirical journal *Le Charivari* to propose in its August 30, 1839, edition:

You want to make a portrait of your wife. You fix her head in a temporary iron collar to get the indispensable immobility.... You point the lens of the camera at her face, and when you take the portrait it doesn't represent your wife; it is her parrot, her watering pot, or worse.

In October Alfred Donné showed the Academy of Sciences a portrait of a woman with her face powdered white. It could hardly have been successful, for in April, 1840, J. F. Soleil wrote that "hopes that had been held for obtaining portraits have not yet been realized... I know that up to now no portrait has been produced with the eyes open and the attitude and face natural." [9]

Samuel F. B. Morse, the American painter and inventor, tried to take portraits shortly after Daguerre's instructions arrived in New York. His wife and daughter sat "from ten to twenty minutes," he recollected, "out of doors, on the roof of a building, in the full sunlight, with the eyes closed." [10] This trial of patience took place, according to Morse, in September or October. He stated that his associate, John William Draper, was taking portraits "at about the same time." Alexander S. Wolcott and John Johnson claimed to have taken "profile miniatures" in New York in October, using a camera of their own invention, in which a concave mirror was substituted for a lens. The results were at first indeed miniatures, for the plates were but three-eighths of an inch square. A few months later they were taking them 2 by $2\frac{1}{2}$ inches, and opened a studio which the *New York Sun*, in its issue of March 4, 1840, called "the first daguerreotype gallery for portraits." Their example was followed in Philadelphia by Robert Cornelius, and in London by Richard Beard, who imported the Wolcott camera and patented it.

To increase the illumination, sunbeams were reflected into these first portrait studios by mirrors. Sitting was an ordeal, for the light, in spite of being intercepted by a rack of bottles filled with blue vitriol, was of blinding brilliance. One victim recollected that he sat

for eight minutes, with the strong sunlight shining on his face and tears trickling down his cheeks while... the operator promenaded the room with watch in hand, calling out the time every five seconds, till the fountains of his eyes were dry. [11]

So long as such heroics were demanded, portraitists could not hope for popular support. Radical improvements in technique were needed. Daguerre himself did little to perfect his invention. He took up again the scene painter's brush and painted an illusionary apse for the church at Bry-sur-Marne. He died in that village in 1851.

By the end of 1840 three substantial technical advances had been made.

First, an improved lens, which formed an image sixteen times more brilliant than Daguerre's simple meniscus, was constructed in Vienna in May, 1840, by Peter Friedrich Voigtländer. The lens, which by today's nomenclature would be rated as $f/3.6$,* was designed by Josef Max Petzval at the suggestion of Andreas Freiherr von Ettingshausen, professor of mathematics and physics at the University of Vienna, who was in Paris at the announcement of the daguerreotype, learned the process from Daguerre, and introduced it to Austria. The design at once became so popular in France that imitations were marketed as "German lenses," while in America unscrupulous dealers even engraved the name Voigtländer on "tubes" of domestic manufacture.

Second, the light sensitivity of the plate was increased by recoating the iodized surface with other halides. The thought had occurred to many and had been tried by many, but it is clear that the first to publish a practical method was John Frederick Goddard, lecturer on optics and natural philosophy at the Adelaide Gallery, London: after the silvered plate had been fumed with iodine, the operation was repeated with bromine, alone or in combination with chlorine. The use of such an *accelerator*, or in the vernacular of the daguerreotypists, *quickstuff*, in combination with the Petzval lens, made it entirely possible to take portraits regularly at exposures of less than a minute.

Third, the tones of the daguerreotype were softened and enriched by gilding the plate, the invention of Hippolyte Louis Fizeau. After the plate had been bathed with hypo it was heated, and a solution containing gold chloride was flowed over it, which toned the image deep purplish brown. This operation had the added advantage that the delicate surface of the daguerreotype – compared by Arago to a butterfly's wing – was rendered less fragile.

As soon as these improvements had been made,

portrait galleries were opened everywhere and the world rushed to them.

All kinds of people sat before the camera; thanks to the relative cheapness of production, financial distinctions mattered little. Celebrated men and distinguished ladies as well as peasants and workmen who otherwise would be forgotten have left their features on the silvered plate, which the American writer and physician, Oliver Wendell Holmes, called "the mirror with a memory." The best daguerreotype portraits are straightforward and penetrating, due partly to the complete absence of retouching, which, except for delicate tinting, the fragile surface did not allow. But perhaps of more importance is the apparent handicap of the long exposure time. It was hard work to be daguerreotyped; you had to cooperate with the operator, forcing yourself not only to sit still for at least half a minute, but also to assume a natural expression. If you moved, the picture was ruined; if you could not put yourself at ease in spite of the discomfort, the result was so forced that it was a failure.

A chapter of the illustrated book on Paris, *La Grande Ville* (1842), describes a daguerreotypist's studio which was so popular that people waited their turn for an hour. One sitter

who is naturally ugly, and finding herself still uglier in the doleful expression of the daguerreotype, insists that it is a failure, and goes out without taking it. After her there comes a man with a tic, who constantly twitches the corner of his mouth, and in spite of it wants to be daguerreotyped; then another who blinks his eyes rapidly, then an old lady who everlastingly shakes her head. All these people cannot understand that they will never have a portrait by this process.

Of all the countries, America adopted the daguerreotype with most enthusiasm, and excelled in its practice. After the first attempts of Morse and Draper to take portraits, the Frenchman François Gouraud brought to America daguerreotypes taken by Daguerre and by himself which he exhibited in New York, Boston, and Providence, R.I., during the winter of 1839–40. He gave demonstrations to packed audiences and sold apparatus; from him Americans learned Daguerre's technique. Within a few years there were "Daguerreian Galleries" in leading American cities, and traveling daguerreotypists visited outlying communities. When Edward Anthony and his partner J. R. Clark sent Daguerre some pictures taken in their New York gallery in 1847, the inventor replied:

It is with great satisfaction that I express all the pleasure that your daguerreotype portraits have given me. I cer-

---

* A number obtained by dividing the focal length of a lens by its effective diameter. All lenses with the same *f*-number form images of equal brilliance of the same subject. This system of lens marking, which originated in the nineteenth century, was adopted as an international standard at the International Congress of Photography held in Paris in 1900.

tify that these pictures, in execution, are among the most perfect I have ever seen.

I am very flattered to see my invention thus propagated by such artists in a foreign country; it brings me much honor.[12]

Yankee ingenuity brought mechanical improvements. The tedious task of buffing plates to a high polish was done by machinery. John Adams Whipple of Boston installed a steam engine in his gallery to run the buffing wheels, heat the mercury, fan the clients waiting their turn, and revolve a gilded sunburst outside his gallery. At the Great Exhibition in the London Crystal Palace, 1851, Americans won three of the five medals awarded for daguerreotypes.

Among the exhibits were eight whole-plate ($6\frac{1}{2}$ by $8\frac{1}{2}$ inch) views of Cincinnati, Ohio, taken by Charles Fontayne and William Southgate Porter in 1848. The daguerreotypes were framed end to end to form a panorama, showing the river front crowded with

Daguerreotype by unknown French photographer, c. 1845.
GEH

ALEXANDRE CLAUSEL: Landscape, probably near Troyes, France, c. 1855. Daguerreotype. GEH

Opposite page: JEAN-BAPTISTE SABATIER-BLOT: Portrait of Mme Sabatier-Blot, c. 1844. Daguerreotype. GEH

General Sir Hugh Gough. Daguerreotype by unknown English photographer, c. 1850. GEH

Opposite page: HAWES: Lemuel Shaw, Chief Justice of the Massachusetts Supreme Court. Daguerreotype, 1851. The Metropolitan Museum of Art, New York

Daguerreotype by unknown French photographer, c. 1845. GEH

steamboats, and the city climbing the heights above. Similar views were frequently made of other cities. The daguerreotype image is normally laterally reversed; the picture appears as in a mirror. In portraiture this reversal was not noticed; indeed, the sitter found the likeness identical to his own vision of himself, which he knew only from a looking glass. But the reversal was troublesome in views; landscapes did not appear natural, signboards read backwards. To overcome this defect, daguerreotypists commonly fitted a prism over the lens when working out of doors, despite the fact that exposure was thus increased.

By 1853 there were eighty-six portrait galleries in New York City. Each American city and most of the larger towns boasted of several daguerrean galleries apiece, many of which were magnificently fitted out. In the Boston gallery of Luther Holman Hale

the pianoforte, the music box, the singing of birds; the elegant drapery; the beautiful pictures; the expensive gallery of portraits; the struggling sunbeam peering through doors of stained glass; statuary, engravings; all, all seem to impress the visitor with the ideal of palace-like magnificence, and serve to soothe the troubled spirit, and calm the anxious brow, preparatory to the obtaining of a good picture.[13]

Daguerreotypists vied with one another for the privilege of making portraits of the famous. One of the largest collections was formed by Mathew B. Brady, a leather-case maker who opened a daguerreotype gallery in New York in 1844, and began to collect a *Gallery of Illustrious Americans*. Twelve of the portraits were published as lithographs by François d'Avignon in 1850. Later Edward Anthony, associated since 1852 with his brother Henry, issued quantities of photographic copies of the Brady collection in the size called cartes-de-visite. It must not be assumed that all of the portraits in the collection were actually made by Brady. For years he had three galleries – two in New York and one in Washington – and employed many "operators," as cameramen were called. He also constantly acquired, by purchase or exchange, portraits made in other galleries. The credit, "From a Daguerreotype by Brady," which appeared again and again beneath wood-engravings in the illustrated magazines of the fifties and under engraved frontispieces of biographies was a trademark, not the signature of an artist.

In Boston Albert Sands Southworth and Josiah Johnson Hawes, both pupils of Gouraud, produced portraits far removed from the conventional stiff poses so favored by the majority of their colleagues. When Chief Justice Lemuel Shaw of the Massachusetts Su-

Daguerreotype by unknown American photographer, c. 1850. Collection B. and N. Newhall, Rochester, N.Y.

Daguerreotype by unknown American photographer, c. 1850. GEH

preme Court came to their gallery he happened to stand in a beam of sunlight which brought out his rugged features with uncompromising force; the daguerreotypists took him as he stood. They went to the home of John Quincy Adams and there daguerreotyped him with spontaneous informality, sitting by the fireplace, a book-strewn table at his elbow. They even took a schoolroom full of girls. Hawes remained a photographer to his death in 1901, and although he gave up taking daguerreotypes commercially in the late fifties, turning to the production of the more popular paper prints, he never lost his love for the process, which he attempted to revive in the 1890's. Because Southworth and Hawes took many plates at each sitting a quantity of duplicates remained in the Hawes studio; the cream of this collection is now divided among the Metropolitan Museum of Art, New York; the Museum of Fine Arts, Boston; and the George Eastman House, Rochester, New York. In an advertisement in the 1852 *Massachusetts Register* they boasted:

One of the partners is a practical artist, and as we never employ *Operators*, customers receive our personal attention…. We will reserve and claim by right the name of our establishment. "The Artists' Daguerreotype Rooms." As no cheap work is done, we shall spend no time in bantering about prices; and we wish to have all understand that ours is a one price concern….

Without doubt the "practical artist" was Hawes, since some of the finest daguerreotypes were made between 1849 and 1851, when Southworth was in the gold fields of California, vainly seeking a fortune. He returned to Boston in such poor health that he could not work actively, and left Hawes in 1861.

The average price in most American daguerreotype galleries for a medium plate ($2\frac{3}{4}$ by $3\frac{1}{4}$ inches) complete with case was $2. Competition forced prices lower and lower, until by slap-dash methods daguerreotypes were made at two for twenty-five cents. In vain did the conscientious artists of the profession form protective societies, boycotting the "blue bosom boys" – so called because they were not craftsmen enough to record a white shirt front white.

The daguerreotype was doomed. It did not lend itself to ready duplication. It was fragile and had to be kept under glass in a bulky case. It was hard to look at because of the metallic glare. And it was expensive. When the rival paper process was perfected so that the public could buy a dozen prints for less than the price of one daguerreotype, the beautiful silver picture became obsolete.

FONTAYNE & PORTER: Cincinnati waterfront: Public Landing and Front Street. One of a series of eight daguerreotypes taken in 1848. Cincinnati Public Library

While Daguerre was perfecting Niépce's heliography in France, William Henry Fox Talbot, English scientist, mathematician and linguist, was busily conducting similar researches. Neither knew of each other's work until Arago's lecture to the Academy of Sciences on January 7, 1839, informed Talbot of the Frenchman's success and spurred him to prior publication.

Talbot had the idea of what came to be called photography six years earlier.

One of the first days of the month of October, 1833 [he later recollected], I was amusing myself on the lovely shores of the Lake of Como in Italy, taking sketches with Wollaston's *camera lucida*, or rather, I should say, attempting to take them: but with the smallest possible amount of success.... After various fruitless attempts I laid aside the instrument and came to the conclusion that its use required a previous knowledge of drawing which unfortunately I did not possess. I then thought of trying again a method which I had tried many years before. This method was, to take a *camera obscura* and to throw the image of the objects on a piece of paper in its focus – fairy pictures, creations of a moment, and destined as rapidly to fade away. It was during these thoughts that the idea occurred to me – how charming it would be if it were possible to cause these natural images to imprint themselves durably, and remain fixed upon the paper.[1]

That fall, as soon as he returned to England, Talbot began to experiment.

He bathed paper with a weak solution of common salt (sodium chloride) and then, after it had dried, with a strong solution of silver nitrate. These chemicals reacted to form silver chloride, a light-sensitive salt, insoluble in water, within the paper. He pressed a leaf, a feather, a piece of lace against this prepared paper under glass and exposed it to sunlight. Gradually the paper darkened wherever it was not protected from light by the opacity of the object in contact with its surface. Talbot then washed the paper either with a strong solution of common salt or with potassium iodide, a treatment which made the unaltered silver salts relatively, but not completely, insensitive to light. This change in property was due to the fact that silver salts differ greatly in their sensitivity to light according to the way they are produced. If a strong solution of silver nitrate is added to a weak solution of a halide salt, the silver halide which is precipitated is much more sensitive to light than one produced by a strong solution of the same halide salt, even though it is identical in chemical structure. Talbot's "preserving" technique was most unstable, and nearly all the early experiments fixed with strong halides have faded – some, indeed, so completely that only Talbot's signature in ink gives evidence that the blank sheet once carried an image. But at least his fixing process gave these "photogenic drawings" sufficient permanence so they could stand examination by daylight.

Talbot now began to use his invention to record the image of the camera obscura. His first camera was, he said, made "out of a large box, the image being thrown upon one end of it by a good object glass fixed in the opposite end."[2] An hour's exposure on a summer afternoon left only the impress of the highlights on the paper. But with small cameras, fitted with lenses of relatively large diameter, he had better success, obtaining "very perfect, but extremely small, pictures; such... as might be supposed to be the work of some Lilliputian artist." One of these is now preserved in the Science Museum, London. It is a negative, hardly an inch square, of a lattice window in his country house, Lacock Abbey, near Bath. He mounted it neatly on a card, and wrote beside it: "Latticed Window (with the Camera Obscura) August 1835 – When first made, the squares of glass about 200 in number could be counted, with help of a lens." He had a collection of box cameras – "little mouse traps," his wife called them – which, upon a summer day, he would train upon the Abbey. "After the lapse of half an hour [he wrote], I gathered them all up, and brought them within doors to open them. When opened, there was in each a miniature picture of the objects before which it had been placed."

In his researches, Talbot came upon the description of Wedgwood's work, but he later claimed that he was completely unaware of what Daguerre was doing, and Arago's lecture took him completely by surprise. "I was placed," he recollected, "in a very unusual dilemma (scarcely paralleled in the annals of science), for I

Opposite page: NÈGRE: Henry Le Secq at Notre Dame Cathedral, Paris. Print from the 1851 calotype negative in the Collection André Jammes, Paris.

DICKINS: Gordon Castle. Calotype negative, signed and dated 1854. GEH

was threatened with the loss of all my labours, in case M. Daguerre's process proved identical with mine."[3]

To establish priority he rushed samples of his work to the Royal Institution in London where, at the regular Friday evening meeting on January 25, 1839, Michael Faraday showed them to the members. They comprised

flowers and leaves; a pattern of laces; figures taken from painted glass; a view of Venice copied from an engraving; some images formed by the Solar Microscope [and] various pictures representing the architecture of my house in the country... made with the Camera Obscura in the summer of 1835....[4]

On January 31, 1839, Talbot's paper, "Some Account of the Art of Photogenic Drawing," was read at the Royal Society. It was a general description of the results he obtained. Technical details, specific enough to enable anyone to repeat his experiments, were given in a second paper read on February 20.

While both Talbot's and Daguerre's processes were still secret, the astronomer and scientist Sir John Herschel, with characteristic intellectual curiosity and vigor, set about solving the problem independently. In his notebook, now preserved in the Science Museum, London, he wrote: "Jan. 29. Experiments tried within the last few days since hearing of Daguerre's secret and that Fox Talbot has also got something of the same kind.... Three requisites: (1) Very susceptible paper; (2) Very perfect camera; (3) Means of arresting the further action." Like Talbot, he sensitized paper with silver salts. Of his camera we know nothing. His method of "arresting the further action [of light]" was an epochal contribution. He had discovered in 1819 that the hy-

posulphite of soda dissolved silver salts; now, in 1839, he recorded his successful attempt to use this chemical to fix his photographs.

Tried hyposulphite of soda to arrest action of light by washing away all the chloride of silver or other silvering salt. Succeeds perfectly. Papers $\frac{1}{2}$ acted on [and] $\frac{1}{2}$ guarded from light by covering with pasteboard, were when withdrawn from sunshine, sponged over with hyposulphite soda, then well washed in pure water – dried, and again exposed. The darkened half remained dark, the white half white, after any exposure, as if they had been painted in sepia.

This chemical is known today as *sodium thiosulfate*, but photographers still persist in calling it "hypo."

Talbot visited Herschel on February 1 and learned of this fixing technique. He described it, with Herschel's consent, in a letter published in the *Comptes rendus* of the French Academy of Sciences. Daguerre at once adopted it. Almost all subsequent photographic processes rely upon Herschel's discovery.

Talbot's first photogenic drawings were reversed. In presenting them to the Royal Institution, Faraday said: "All the lights are dark and all the shadows light."[5] It was also noted that the camera pictures were reversed in respect to right and left. In February Talbot pointed out how these defects could be remedied: "If the picture so obtained is first preserved so as to bear sunshine, it may be afterwards itself employed as an object to be copied; and by means of this second process the lights and shadows are brought back to their original disposition."[6] The original reversed picture Herschel named the *negative*. Its re-reversed copy he named the *positive*. These terms became international.

TALBOT: Lacock Abbey. Photogenic drawing, 1839. The Metropolitan Museum of Art, New York

TALBOT: Botanical specimens. Photogenic drawing, 1839. The Metropolitan Museum of Art, New York

With his invention of the negative-positive technique, Talbot had the advantage over Daguerre: from a single negative he could print any number of positives. This discovery changed the entire course of photographic history, for it made possible the mass printing and publication of photographs.

However, in point of excellence the photogenic drawing was eclipsed by the daguerreotype. Talbot's warmest supporters had to admit it: Herschel told Arago that "compared to the masterful daguerreotype, Talbot produces nothing but mistiness."[7] Furthermore it had already become apparent that fixing the photographs with sodium chloride or with potassium iodide was not reliable.

In the fall of 1840 Talbot invented a modification of his process so radical that he gave it a new name, the *calotype* (later, at the suggestion of friends, changed to *talbotype*). Previously he had allowed his sensitive paper to remain exposed to light in the camera until the image became visible. Now he found, as had Daguerre, that it was possible to give a much shorter exposure and yet secure a satisfactory image by after treatment. Although the paper was blank when taken from the camera, by *development* the image appeared as if by magic.

He prepared the paper by bathing it first in silver nitrate and then in potassium iodide. The relatively stable silver iodide which was formed became, he found, highly light sensitive when he washed the paper with a mixture of gallic acid and silver nitrate, a solution he named "gallo-nitrate of silver." After exposure the paper was bathed again in the same solution which, acting as a physical developer, gradually brought out the image. To fix these negatives Talbot used at first potassium bromide and later a hot solution of hypo. He printed them with his silver chloride paper.

Late in the spring of 1844 Talbot began the publication of a handsome quarto, *The Pencil of Nature*. On the title page he put a Latin verse from Virgil's *Georgics*: "It is a joyous thing to be the first to cross a mountain." It was a show book, an account of the history of the invention, and a demonstration of its accomplishments in the form of twenty-four actual photographs. He wanted to put on record "some of the early beginnings of a new art, before the period, which we trust is approaching, of its being brought to maturity by the aid of British talent." The photographs were mostly of architecture, still-life arrangements, or works of art. Accompanying each was a page or two of text explaining the significance of the picture and occasionally offering predictions not realized for decades.

TALBOT: The Open Door. Calotype: Plate VI of *The Pencil of Nature*, 1844. GEH

The most interesting plates show scenes of daily life around Lacock Abbey. Talbot said:

We have sufficient authority in the Dutch School of art for taking as subjects of representation scenes of daily and familiar occurrence. A painter's eye will often be arrested where ordinary people see nothing remarkable. A casual gleam of sunshine, or a shadow thrown across his path, a time-withered oak, or a moss-covered stone may awaken a train of thoughts and feelings, and picturesque imaginings.

The *Art Union*, reviewing the book, spoke particularly of Plate VI, *The Open Door*: "It is, of course, an effect of sunshine, and the microscopic execution sets at nought the work of human hands."[8]

Eleven years after his unsuccessful attempts to sketch Lake Como, Talbot could write:

there is, assuredly, a royal road to *Drawing*; and one of these days, when more known and better explored, it will probably be much frequented. Already sundry amateurs have laid down the pencil and armed themselves with chemical solutions and with *camerae obscurae*. These amateurs especially, and they are not a few, who find the rules of *perspective* difficult to learn and to apply – and who, moreover, have the misfortune to be lazy – prefer to use a method which dispenses with all trouble.[9]

The talbotype, however, was not free for all to use, for in 1841 Talbot had secured for it Her Majesty's Royal Letters Patent No. 8842. This action, so out of keeping with the open and unrestricted publication of

A. F. J. CLAUDET: Portrait, c. 1844. From the original calotype negative in the Science Museum, London

TALBOT: Sailing craft, c. 1845. From the original calotype negative in the Science Museum, London

his original process, was perhaps suggested to Talbot by the example of Daguerre in taking out a patent for his invention in England. Talbot had received no recompense and but little recognition for his work; Daguerre, on the other hand, had been rewarded with a life-long pension, was receiving income from the sale of licenses in England, and had won international fame. Talbot saw others making a commercial success with photography, and felt entitled to exact royalties from those using his invention.

He vigilantly controlled the patent, prosecuting those who infringed it. Amateurs and professionals felt hampered, and the Presidents of the Royal Academy and of the Royal Society jointly appealed to Talbot to relax his grip. In a letter published in *The Times*, August 13, 1852, he relinquished all control of his invention except its use for taking portraits for profit.

The exception was significant, for portraiture was the most lucrative use of photography. Fortunes had been made: in one year Richard Beard realized £40,000 from the chain of daguerreotype portrait galleries which he owned and managed in cities throughout the British Isles. By far the greater number of professional portraitists used the daguerreotype, which was more suited than the talbotype for the rapid production methods essential to commercial success, and which, by its shorter exposure time, was less of a tax on the sitter's patience. But with the introduction of the collodion process in 1851 both the daguerreotype and the talbotype were dropped almost at once. Like the talbotype, the new process was negative-positive. But the negatives were on glass instead of on paper, they were developed in pyrogallic acid instead of "gallo-nitrate of silver," and the exposures were shorter. This technique seemed to Talbot identical in principle to his patent; indeed, he considered it an outright infringement and sued a professional portraitist, Martin Laroche, for working it without a license.

Laroche, supported by colleagues, took the case to court in 1854. The defense attempted to show that

TALBOT: Sailing craft, c. 1845. From the original calotype negative in the Science Museum, London

Talbot was not entitled to the patent which he held and, secondly, even if he was, the collodion process was so dissimilar and distinct from the talbotype that no infringement could be claimed. To support the first argument, evidence was submitted that Talbot had been preceded in the use of gallic acid by the Reverend Joseph Bancroft Reade. The intricacies of photochemistry perplexed the judge, who said to the jury, "It is already sufficiently difficult to understand the subject, particularly as you and I know nothing at all about it.... I am sorry to say the case kept me awake all last night." He was able, however, to reduce the second charge to a technicality which he summed up to the jury:

Is pyrogallic acid, though it may differ in its shape, in its action with reagents, in its composition, is it or is it not a chemical equivalent with gallo-nitrate of silver? If it is, the defendant is guilty; if it is not, he is not guilty.[10]

After an hour's deliberation the jury brought in a double verdict. They found the defendant, Laroche, not guilty. They also found that Talbot was the first and true inventor of the talbotype "within the meaning of the Patent Laws: that is, the first person who disclosed it to the public."

The first painter to realize the artistic potentials of Fox Talbot's process was David Octavius Hill, of Edinburgh. He was secretary of the Scottish Academy of Painting, and author of a book of steel engravings from his landscapes, *The Land of Burns*. In 1843 he set himself a difficult task: to portray, on one canvas, all four hundred and fifty delegates to the convention at which the Free Church of Scotland was founded. To secure likenesses of each of these Scottish worthies was a Herculean task. Sir David Brewster, who had learned the process from Talbot, showed him some examples of photographic portraiture and as a result Hill secured the assistance of Robert Adamson, who had been taught to calotype by Sir David himself, and who was practicing professionally in Edinburgh.

Hill and Adamson collaborated until 1848, when

Adamson died at the age of twenty-seven. They did not limit their work to making memoranda for Hill's *Disruption* picture: all kinds of sitters found their way to the outdoor studio on Calton Hill, or were photographed among the baroque monuments of the Greyfriars Cemetery. The part which Adamson played appears to have been more than that of technician, for on his death Hill ceased to make photographs until he again found a collaborator, and these later pictures do not compare with the work he did with Adamson.

They posed their sitters outdoors, usually singly. The strong shadows cast by the direct sunlight were softened by reflecting light into them with a concave mirror; the exposures were often minutes long. They saw their subjects broadly, and composed in simple masses of light and shade, for they had an intuitive respect for the medium. In 1848 Hill wrote:

The rough surface, and unequal texture throughout of the paper is the main cause of the Calotype failing in details, before the process of Daguerreotypy – and this is the very life of it. They look like the imperfect work of a man – and not the much diminished perfect work of God.[11]

It is not surprising that the influence of painting is strong in the photographs of these Scottish pioneers. Hugh Miller, the geologist, had compared their portraits with Raeburn's, and some of their genre studies of ladies clothed in glistening gowns of rich silk remind one of Dutch seventeenth-century paintings. But we remember Hill and Adamson for the dignity and depth of their perception, and for their awareness of individual character. A collection of their calotypes received Honorable Mention at the Great Exhibition of 1851 in the London Crystal Palace; during the next decade they were widely shown. Then they were almost forgotten until in 1890 J. Craig Annan made modern prints from the old negatives which delighted connoisseurs. The painter, James Abbott McNeill Whistler, among others, praised them; they were recognized as incunabula of portrait photography. Hill's paintings have long since been forgotten. He did not complete the great canvas which had led him into photographic work until 1866, four years before his death.

The chief use of the calotype, however, was not for portraiture, but for recording architecture and landscapes. There was much activity in this field by British amateurs: Thomas Keith, famous as a surgeon, made a number of excellent calotypes of Edinburgh; C. S. S. Dickins recorded country estates; John Shaw Smith, traveling in the Mediterranean area from 1850 to 1852, came back with several hundred paper negatives.

Although Talbot had taken out a French patent, he does not appear to have enforced it, and the calotype was widely used in France, especially for the documentation of architecture for governmental surveys. Louis Désiré Blanquart-Evrard, who worked out many improvements, was accused by his own countrymen of having appropriated Talbot's invention without even the courtesy of a credit. In 1850 he invented a new kind of sensitive paper which at once, under the name *albumen paper*, was universally adopted and became the standard method of making prints throughout the century. He coated paper with egg-white in which was dissolved potassium iodide and potassium bromide. The albumen dried to form a smooth surface. Paper thus prepared was sensitized before use by floating it on a solution of silver nitrate to which had been added acetic acid. After exposure to the sun beneath a negative, the image was toned to a pleasing brown by the same gold chloride formula which daguerreotypists used, then fixed, washed, and dried.

HILL & ADAMSON: Rev. Thomas Henshaw Jones. Calotype, c. 1845. GEH

HILL & ADAMSON: Thomas Duncan and his brother. Calotype, 1845 or earlier. Modern print from the calotype negative. GEH

Opposite page: HILL & ADAMSON: Mrs. Anne Rigby and her daughter Elizabeth (later Lady Eastlake). Calotype, c. 1844. GEH

KEITH: Castle Hill, Edinburgh. Gum platinum print by A. L. Coburn from the original calotype negative, c. 1855. GEH (A. L. Coburn Coll.)

Blanquart-Evrard was dissatisfied with this printing method, because the printing time was too great to permit mass production. By using for positives a slight modification of Talbot's calotype negative paper a much shorter exposure, measured in seconds instead of minutes, could be given. The latent image was developed, and the olive-green color of the image was changed to a rich slate tone by acidifying the hypo-fixing bath.

This innovation enabled Blanquart-Evrard to produce photographs in bulk. In the summer of 1851 he published the first number of the *Album photographique*, a portfolio of single prints of architectural and landscape subjects in the style of romantic lithographs.

HILL & ADAMSON: The McCandlish children. Calotype, c. 1845. MOMA GEH

Thomas Sutton, editor of *Photographic Notes*, wrote in 1857 that

the proofs are permanent, they have not faded. They are also beautifully artistic: vigorous, without being glazed, and superb in color, particularly in the lights. A vast number of copies of this *Album* were sold, and it became necessary for him in 1852 to enlarge his printing establishment. A huge building, resembling a manufactory, was then erected in the grounds of a chateau, belonging to a friend, situated three miles from Lille. Blanquart-Evrard being a man of fortune, handed over the concern to his friend, who had been connected with chemical and dyeing operations, and who speedily mastered the details of Photographic Printing. A staff of thirty or forty assistants, mostly girls, were then instructed, each in a particular branch of the process, and operations commenced on a large scale. About a hundred thousand prints have been issued from that establishment.[12]

An important use for these mass produced prints was for the illustration of books. The first production of the establishment was a handsome folio volume, *Egypte, Nubie, Palestine et Syrie*, with 125 prints from paper negatives taken by Maxime Du Camp, a writer who learned photography in order to document the trip he made to the Middle East with Gustave Flaubert from 1849 to 1851. Blanquart-Evrard later opened in partnership with Thomas Sutton an "Establishment for Permanent Positive Printing" at St. Brelade's Bay, on the Isle of Jersey in 1855.

Prints made by Blanquart-Evrard have stood the test of time most remarkably; those that have come down to us have retained their original brilliance and clarity. Strangely, the technique never became popular, and it was four decades before a developing-out paper was again adopted.

Henry Le Secq, whose negatives Blanquart-Evrard printed, specialized in architectural views; he had been appointed photographer to the Historical Monuments Commission, the government bureau charged with the preservation and restoration of cathedrals. So sympa-

Page 42: MARVILLE: Cathedral of Notre Dame, Paris. Calotype taken in 1852 and printed by Blanquart-Evrard. GEH

DU CAMP: Colossus of Abu Simbel, Egypt. Calotype negative taken in 1850 and printed by Blanquart-Evrard for the album
Egypte, Nubie, Palestine et Syrie, Paris, 1852. MOMA GEH

NÈGRE: Chimney Sweeps, Paris. Print from the 1852 calotype negative in the Collection André Jammes, Paris

thetic and informative were his photographs that one critic went so far as to say that the sculptured portal of Rheims Cathedral could be studied better in them than on the spot, where the eye is overwhelmed by the great scale and wealth of detail. Le Secq's 11 by 14-inch paper negatives, signed and dated 1852, still yield brilliant prints. His contemporary Charles Nègre made even larger negatives: some of his photographs of Chartres Cathedral measure 20 by 29 inches.

An attempt was made to popularize the talbotype in the United States. William Langenheim visited Talbot in 1849 at Lacock Abbey and paid him £1000 for the rights to his American patent. He and his brother Frederick tried to sell licenses. They pointed out in a broadside addressed to daguerreotypists that paper portraits and views were "devoid of all metallic glare," and could be multiplied "to an unlimited extent with very little expense and labor." Their appeal met with little response. They failed, partly because their results could not be compared with the brilliant and precisely defined daguerreotypes which delighted the American public, and partly because American photographers rebelled at paying a license fee to anybody.

Although Talbot's technique proved to be the first successful way of making paper photographs, his was not the only method. No sooner had he described

photogenic drawing than others broke into public print with ingenious alternative techniques in which the light sensitivity of other metals – iron, platinum, potassium – were employed. In May, 1839, the editor of the *Magazine of Science* noted that the "periodicals still teem with fresh experiments and receipts relative to this art."

The most luckless pioneer was Hippolyte Bayard, who exhibited thirty photographs in Paris on June 24, 1839. His method was original: silver chloride paper was held to the light until it had turned dark. It was then plunged into potassium iodide solution and exposed in the camera. The light now bleached the paper, in proportion to its strength, and he thus obtained direct positives, each unique.

But in the spectacular publication of the daguerreotype the work of Bayard was completely overlooked. He commented on his misfortune in a photograph, dated 1840. He showed himself half naked, propped up against a wall as if dead. On the back of the print he wrote:

The body you see is that of Monsieur Bayard.... The Academy, the King, and all who have seen his pictures admired them, just as you do. Admiration brought him prestige, but not a sou. The Government which gave M. Daguerre too much, said it could do nothing for M. Bayard at all, and the wretch drowned himself.[13]

BAYARD: Still life, 1839. Société Française de photographie, Paris

<small>HESLER</small>: President Abraham Lincoln, 1860. <small>GEH</small>

The demand for cheap portraits became so great in the fifties that the daguerreotypists and calotypists could hardly keep up with it. In a price war operators offered the public daguerreotypes at 50 cents, at 25 cents and finally at 12½ cents – made "two at a pop" with a double lens camera. In picture factories division of labor was said to have speeded up the work to a production of "300, 500 and even 1000 daily."[1] The sitter bought a ticket and was posed by an operator who never left the camera. A plate, already prepared by the polisher and the coater, was brought to him, and he passed it on exposed, in its protective shield, to the mercuralizer who developed it, to the gilder who enriched it, and to the artist who tinted it: fifteen minutes later the customer exchanged his ticket for the finished likeness. Such hastily made portraits were seldom satisfactory; many were left behind by disappointed customers; but prospects streamed up the stairs to the skylight and the cash rolled in.

Then the perfection of new techniques brought prices even lower and quantities even higher. The collodion process, invented by Frederick Scott Archer in England in 1851, almost at once replaced the calotype. Three times, in three guises, it threatened the daguerreotype, and finally triumphed.

Like the calotype, the process was primarily a method of making negatives. Collodion, discovered in 1847 as a means of protecting wounds, is a mixture of guncotton in alcohol and ether; flowed on a surface it dries to form a tough, skin-like film. Archer first used it to save glass plates. The imperfection of the talbotype negative because of the fibrous texture of paper had early suggested the use of glass as a support for light sensitive emulsion. To attach the silver salts to glass various substances had been tried, even the gluey slime exuded by snails, until partial success came with the use of egg white. These albumen plates – invented by Claude Félix Abel Niepce de St. Victor in 1847 – gave excellent negatives, of a brilliance and fineness of detail far surpassing the calotype. They could be prepared in advance; Felice Beato, a naturalized Englishman who photographed the Indian Mutiny in 1857, coated plates in Athens and exposed them months later in India. The chief drawback of albumen plates was their low sensitivity. Beato at first gave exposures of three hours, but he was able to reduce the time to four seconds by a special developing technique, the secret of which he jealously guarded and did not disclose until 1886, long after the process was obsolete. It never became popular, partly because most photographers were not able to shorten the exposure and partly because they were used to carrying around light-weight sheets of inexpensive paper, and found glass plates heavy and dear.

Archer's collodion process, as he originally described it in *The Chemist* for March, 1851, was an ingenious method of overcoming this problem. Glass was coated with collodion in which potassium iodide had been dissolved. It was then dipped in silver nitrate, and exposed while wet. After development in pyrogallic acid, the film of collodion bearing the negative image was stripped from the plate, rolled up with paper around a glass rod, and carried home to be fixed and washed. "Thus one piece of glass," he wrote, "will be sufficient to make any number of drawings upon, the above operations being repeated for each picture."

As finally perfected, a separate piece of glass was used for each negative. The seven following steps were carried out:

1. A piece of glass was placed in a vise and thoroughly cleaned and polished.

2. Holding the cleaned glass by one corner, enough of the viscous collodion (to which an iodide and often a bromide had been added) was skilfully flowed over the surface to form a smooth, even coating.

3. In the subdued orange light of the darkroom the coated plate, while still tacky, was *excited*, or made light sensitive, by soaking it for about five minutes in a bath of silver nitrate. When it had become creamy-yellow it was taken out, drained and put, *still wet*, into a light-tight plate holder, or shield.

4. "Place the cap on the lens [the beginner was directed by John Towler in his handbook, *The Silver Sunbeam*]; let the eye of the sitter be directed to a given point; withdraw the ground-glass slide; insert the plate-holder; raise or remove its slide: attention. One, two, three, four, five, six! (slowly and deliberately pronounced in as many seconds, either aloud or in spirit). Cover the lens. Down with the slide gently but with firmness. With-

Polishing the plate

Coating the plate

Sensitizing the plate

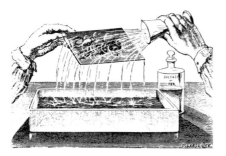

Developing the plate

draw the plate-holder and yourself into the darkroom, and shut the door."

5. The plate was removed from its holder and over its surface a solution of pyrogallic acid or protosulphate of iron was poured. In a few seconds the image began to appear, increasing rapidly in brilliance. When it was judged to be fully developed, the plate was rinsed in clean water.

6. Hypo or potassium cyanide in solution was now poured over the developed plate to dissolve the remaining unaltered silver salts. The plate was then well washed under running water.

7. Over a gentle flame the fixed plate, held between thumb and forefinger, was rapidly moved until dry; while still warm it was varnished.

The process required experience and skill of hand; a mistake in any one operation spelled failure. The photographer was chained to his darkroom, for all these operations had to be done rapidly, before the collodion dried or else excess silver nitrate would crystallize out and spoil the image. Because the plate had to be kept continually moist from preparation through development, the process came to be called "wet plate."

Although invented for making negatives, Archer described the application of his technique to the production of positives. A wet-plate negative could be viewed as a positive simply by placing it against a piece of dark material or by painting the back black. The highlights were represented by the grayish-white tone of the developed collodion emulsion; the shadows, being more or less transparent, revealed the black background. Like the daguerreotype, each such picture was unique; the very glass plate exposed in the camera was itself the final product. Thus Archer's modification lacked the power of duplication, but it had the advantage of speed; the sitter could take the finished picture with him almost immediately.

These glass positives, because of their similarity to the daguerreotype, both in appearance and in manner of production, were especially popular in America. Scott Archer's invention, which he had published without restrictions of any kind, was patented by James Ambrose Cutting of Boston in 1854. Marcus A. Root, a Philadelphian writing master turned daguerreotypist, named the pictures *ambrotypes*. Like the daguerreotypes, which they imitated, they were commonly enclosed in leather or composition cases.

The familiar *tintype* is a modification, the support for the light-sensitive collodion emulsion being, instead of glass, thin metal plates japanned black or chocolate color. The inventor, Hamilton L. Smith,

assigned his 1856 patent to Peter Neff and Peter Neff, Jr.
The manufacture of plates was begun in 1856 by the
Neffs, who named the process *melainotype*, and by Victor M. Griswold, who chose the name *ferrotype*. The
more popular word *tintype* was introduced later.

Because the surfaces of tintypes were not fragile they
could be sent through the mail, carried in the pocket,
and mounted in albums. They were processed while
the customer waited. They were cheap, not only because the materials were cheap, but also because, using
a multilens camera, several images could be secured
with one operation. After processing, the plate was cut
into single pictures with tin snips.

Tintyping was usually casual; when the results have
charm it is due to the lack of sophistication and to the
naïve directness characteristic of folk art. Records of
outings, mementos of friendships, stiffly posed portraits of country folk against painted backgrounds are
common: views are few. The process lingered in the
backwaters of photography as the direct descendant of
the daguerreotype. Tintypes were enormously popular:
"It is impossible to compute the number of quantities
which have been made and sold since 1860," wrote
Edward M. Estabrooke in his standard handbook, *The
Ferrotype and How to Make It*, and concluded, "I suppose it would exceed that of all other pictures put
together."

Despite the competition of direct imitation, neither
the tintype nor the ambrotype dealt the death blow to
the daguerreotype. That was left to a third application
of the collodion technique, the *carte-de-visite* photograph, patented in France by Adolphe-Eugène Disdéri
in 1854. The name refers to its similarity to a common
visiting card in size, for it was a paper print pasted on
a mount measuring 4 by 2½ inches. To take these small
portraits, Disdéri first made a wet-plate negative with
a special camera that had several lenses and a plate-
holder which moved. Eight or a dozen poses could be
taken on one negative. A single print from this negative
could then be cut up into eight or more separate portraits. Unskilled labor was used for this work; the production of the cameraman and printer was thus increased eightfold or more.

Disdéri, a brilliant showman, made this system of
mass production portraiture world famous. Napoleon
III halted a column of troops he was leading out of
Paris on their way to Italy in front of Disdéri's studio
while he had his portrait taken. So great was the publicity that all Paris, it seems, wanted portraits. Disdéri's
studio became, in the eyes of a German visitor, "really
the Temple of Photography – a place unique in its

The hunter, c. 1856. Ambrotype by unknown American
photographer. Collection Zelda P. Mackay, San Francisco

Carriage party, c. 1885. Tintype by unknown American
photographer. Collection B. & N. Newhall, Rochester, N.Y.

Civil War soldier, c. 1862. Tintype by unknown American photographer. Chicago Historical Society

luxury and elegance. Daily he sells three to four thousand francs' worth of portraits."[2]

Blind, penniless and deaf, Disdéri, whose fortune had once been the talk of Paris, died in a public hospital in Nice. He was a victim of his own invention. The system which he popularized was so easy to imitate that all over the world cartes-de-visite were being made in a mechanical, routine way by photographers who were hardly more than technicians.

The "cardomania"[3] jumped to England (70,000 portraits of the Prince Consort were sold during the week following his death) and to America (1,000 prints a day were sold of Major Robert Anderson, the popular hero of Fort Sumter).

At first sitters were invariably taken at full length. To Americans, the first carte-de-visite imported from France seemed comical. Abraham Bogardus, a veteran New York daguerreotypist, recollected that "it was a little thing; a man standing by a fluted column, full length, the head about twice the size of a pin. I laughed at that, little thinking I should at a day not far distant be making them at the rate of a thousand a day."[4]

As portraits, most cartes-de-visite are of little esthetic value. No effort was made to bring out the character of the sitter by subtleties of lighting, or by choice of attitude and expression. The images were so small that the faces could hardly be studied, and the posing was done too quickly to permit individual attention. To accommodate card photographs of relatives, friends and celebrities, elaborately bound albums were introduced around 1860. The cards, of uniform size the world over, could readily be slipped into cut-out openings. The family album became a fixture in the Victorian home, and as a consequence, quantities of cartes-de-visite have survived. As documents of an era, they are often of great charm and interest.

It is to the more serious photographers, who worked with a larger format, that we must turn for the finest portraits of the mid-century. Especially in France a school of photographers developed a bold and vigorous style well suited to interpreting those highly individualistic personalities who made Paris the center of the literary and artistic world.

The most prominent of these photographers had for the most part been Young Romantics of the Latin Quarter, living the *Vie de Bohème* as second-rate painters, caricaturists and writers. Nadar, whose real name was Gaspard Félix Tournachon, contributed sketches and articles to comic magazines and founded a new one, *La Revue comique*. He planned a vast series of caricatures, the *Panthéon-Nadar*, of everybody prominent in Paris;

to gather documents for the hundreds of sketches to be included, he turned to photography. One lithograph only was published; it measured 32 by 42 inches and contained two hundred and seventy portraits.

In 1853 Nadar opened a photographic studio in Paris with his brother Adrian. He quickly became a master of the collodion process and, using large plates, began to record the famous people who flocked to his studio, which had become a favorite meeting place. His portrait style was simple and straightforward: he took his friends usually three-quarter length standing under a high skylight against a plain background. The posing was subdued; the faces are seen with a directness and penetration due partly to the fact that he knew most of the sitters intimately, but more to the power of his vision. In 1859 a critic, reviewing an exhibition of Nadar's photographs, wrote in the *Gazette des Beaux-Arts*:

All the artistic, dramatic, political galaxy – in a word the intelligentsia – of Paris has passed through his studio. The series of portraits that he exhibits is the *Panthéon* – serious this time – of our generation. Daumier meditates on his epic Robert Macaire – M. Guizot stands, his hand in his waistcoat, as severe and cold as if he were waiting for silence in the court before launching into a thundering rebuttal – Corot smiles as someone asks him why doesn't he *finish* his landscapes. These photographs are broadly seen.... The photographer has the right to be called an artist.[5]

He was a ceaseless worker. While still taking portraits, he continued to illustrate books and to write novels. He was an experimenter. He was among the first to photograph by electric light. His photographs taken from a balloon in 1858 are the world's first. Aeronautics became an obsession. He built one of the largest balloons in the world, *Le Géant*, "The Giant."

Civil War soldier on horseback, c. 1862. Tintype by unknown American photographer. GEH

MAYALL: Queen Victoria. Carte-de-visite, signed and dated Mar. 1, 1861. GEH

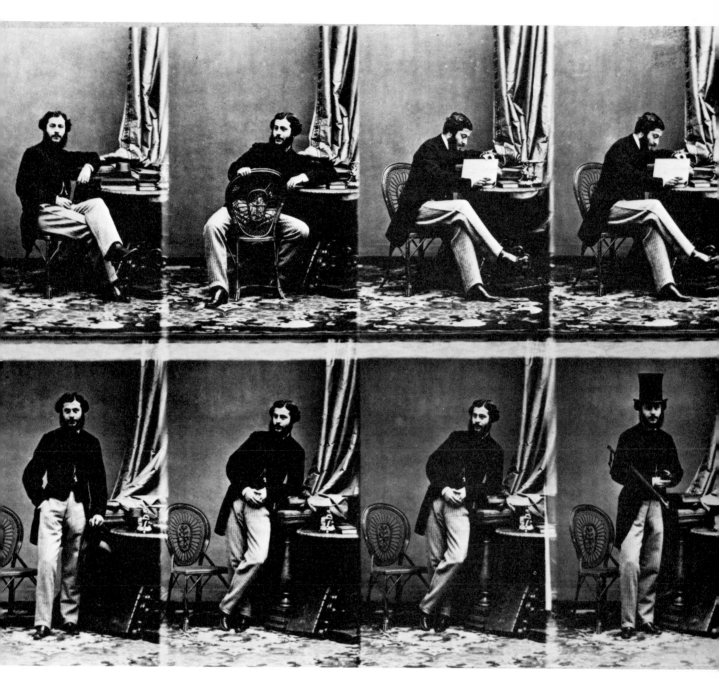

DISDÉRI: Uncut print from a carte-de-visite negative, c. 1860. GEH

CARJAT: Charles Baudelaire, c. 1863. Woodburytype from *Galerie contemporaine*, 1870. MOMA GEH

NADAR: Sarah Bernhardt, 1859. Print by Daniel Masclet from the collodion negative in the Bibliothèque Nationale, Paris

NADAR: François Guizot, 1857. Print by D. Masclet from the collodion negative in the Bibliothèque Nationale, Paris

On its second ascension the balloon, with its two-story nacelle, was carried to Germany; the descent was made near Hanover. At the last moment control of the balloon was lost, and the luckless passengers were banged and dragged some twenty-five miles over open country before they finally came to rest. In 1870 Nadar was one of those who organized the balloon service by which the inhabitants of besieged Paris were able to maintain contact with the world.

His aeronautical ventures proved to be a financial failure, and he took up photography again, this time to make money. In the meanwhile competition had become enormous. "The appearance of Disdéri and the carte-de-visite," he wrote in his autobiographical *Quand j'étais photographe*, "spelled disaster. Either you had to succumb – that is to say, follow the trend – or resign." And he went on to tell of his friend Gustave Le Gray who had taken up photography because of his "preoccupation with art" and who, rather than change his studio into a factory, abandoned the camera and spent the rest of his life in Egypt as an art professor.

Nadar, who lived on into the twentieth century, never again achieved the brilliance of his earlier work. In 1880 the business was taken over by his son Paul, who used the bold signature of his father as a trademark for the somewhat routine products of his studio. Nadar fils was for some years the Paris agent for George Eastman who, with his newly invented Kodak camera, photographed him one morning in 1890 standing top-hatted in the Place de l'Opéra.

There were other contemporaries: Etienne Carjat, Pierre Petit, Antony Samuel Adam-Salomon. The work of these members of the great school of French portrait photographers, along with Nadar, is best seen in the magnificent reproductions in the seven volumes of the *Galerie des Contemporains*.

Largely through the portraits of these photographers we have molded our vision of the life of the Second Empire. Sir Kenneth Clark has compared them to the images of the courts of Henry VIII and Charles I left us by Holbein and Van Dyck.[6]

In America the finest portraits were taken by former daguerreotypists. Brady, Charles Fredricks, Jeremiah Gurney, and Alexander Hesler applied the same direct, uncompromising approach they had developed as daguerreotypists to the wet plate. Hesler's portrait of Abraham Lincoln is a noble interpretation of the much photographed president, who once said that his Cooper Union speech and Brady's photographs put him in office.

The demand for publicity photographs by actors and actresses led to specialization in this work. The most popular style was the *cabinet photograph*, a print 5½ by 4 inches on a mount 6½ by 4½ inches, introduced first in England in 1866. Most theatrical photographs owed their effect to the actor. The stage settings were imitated in the studio, and the actor played out his role before the camera; the success of the photograph was largely due to the sitter's power to project his personality.

One of the most colorful theatrical photographers was Napoleon Sarony, born in Canada in 1821, the year his famous namesake died. In 1846 he joined Henry B. Major to found the lithographic firm of Sarony & Major in New York City. In 1856 he visited his brother, Oliver Francis Xavier Sarony, who was a photographer in England, with the result that he opened his own studio in Birmingham. He returned to New York in 1864; his studio, marked by his flowing signature, became famous. He posed his sitters and directed them, bringing out by flattery, threat, mimicry, their histrionic powers. He left the photography to his cameraman, Benjamin Richardson. "If I make a position," he told an interviewer, "and his camera is right, my longtime assistant here, Richardson, is able to catch my ideas as deftly and quickly as necessary."[7] The cameraman recollected:

Sometimes when things were quiet under the skylight suddenly his step would be heard on the stairs followed by half a dozen sitters. "Put in a plate my boy;" answer would go back, "Hi, hi, your honor!" and then things were quite lively for a time. When he photographed Jim Mace, the pugilist, on his first visit to this country, he danced around him, slapping him on his chest and in the ribs in a way which fairly astonished the champion, who enjoyed it hugely.[8]

Sarony complained at the rush of business: "Think what I must suffer... fancy my despair. All day long I must pose and arrange for those eternal photographs. They *will* have me. Nobody but me will do; while I burn, I ache, I die, for something that is truly art. All my art in the photograph I value as nothing. I want to make pictures out of myself, to group a thousand shapes that crowd my imagination. This relieves me, the other oppresses me."[9] And so he spent his few odd moments in what he called his "den," drawing in charcoal such subjects as *Venus in the Bath* and *The Vestal Virgin*.

There were other photographers who felt that the camera offered them the opportunity to rival the painter, and they set about emulating the older art, largely by imitation.

SARONY: Joe Jefferson as Rip van Winkle, 1869. GEH

CAMERON: The Kiss of Peace — G. F. Watts and children, c. 1867. GEH (A. L. Coburn Coll.)

In 1861 an English critic, in an article "On Art-Photography," wrote: "Hitherto photography has been principally content with representing Truth. Can its sphere not be enlarged? And may it not aspire to delineate Beauty, too?" He encouraged photographers to produce pictures "whose aim is not merely to amuse, but to instruct, purify and ennoble."[1]

Allegories had been attempted. In 1843 John Edwin Mayall of Philadelphia made ten daguerreotypes to illustrate the Lord's Prayer; they were acclaimed by the British art press when he showed them a few years later in his London studio. In 1848 he produced six plates based on Thomas Campbell's poem *The Soldier's Dream*. At the Great Exhibition of 1851 in the London Crystal Palace other American daguerreotypists exhibited allegorical pictures: Martin M. Lawrence, for example, showed a 13 by 17 inch plate of three models facing left, front and right, which he titled *Past, Present, and Future;* it was, he said, inspired by Edwin Greene Malbone's miniature painting, *The Hours*. This daguerreotype was one of several which won for Lawrence a prize medal, but they were made by Gabriel Harrison, then his cameraman, who later protested: "Why not," he asked in a letter published in the *Photographic Art Journal* for September 1853, "give the name of the operator *by whom they were taken?*"

In the work of Hill and Adamson are many calotypes of friends dressed up in armor and monk's garb, acting out historic scenes. These pictures, and the allegorical daguerreotypes, relied for their effect upon the choice, costuming and posing of models; they were records of *tableaux vivants*, or amateur theatricals. In lighting and in technique they were routine, and foreshadowed theatrical photography.

With the perfection of the collodion process an increasing number of amateurs were attracted to photography, and they brought with them a broader view of artistic matters than the average professional possessed. In 1853 the Photographic Society of London (since 1894 the Royal Photographic Society of Great Britain) was founded; its first president, Sir Charles Eastlake, was himself an amateur; although the membership was divided between those who practised photography as an avocation and as a profession, the amateurs were

more often heard. At the first meeting Sir William Newton, miniature painter to the court, addressed the members "Upon Photography in an Artistic View." He denied photography's position as an independent art, and urged photographers who were taking studies to be used by painters to put the image slightly out of focus.

The concept was not new. In 1843 daguerreotypists were instructed to use a relatively large lens opening when taking a portrait of a person with wrinkled features to "obtain one of those soft and rather vague likenesses which painters call *'flous'*."[2] But Sir William's recommendation led to such a heated controversy that, at a later meeting, he reminded the members that he was referring to photographs taken *for the use of artists*: when making record photographs, the sharper the focus the better, he said.

Up to the introduction of the collodion process, the photographic image had largely been respected. Daguerreotypes were commonly tinted with dry pigment laid on with the fine point of a dry brush, but they could not be successfully retouched. Large expanses of sky in calotype negatives were commonly painted black so that they would print a uniform tone. D. O. Hill had even painted in a complete waterfall on a paper negative, but this was an exception. In the desire to compete with painting, photographers began to manipulate the image and to retouch negatives and even paint over the print.

Collodion emulsion was overly sensitive to blue light. As a result when an exposure had been given that was long enough to record the landscape, the blue sky above was recorded on the negative as a solid tone: the print consequently appeared with a white, cloudless, sky. This was intolerable to photographers who were emulating painters, and to remedy this shortcoming two negatives were often taken – one a short exposure to record the sky, the other longer, to record the landscape. The two negatives were masked; part of the print was made from one, and part from the other.

This technique of using several negatives to make one picture was called *combination printing*. It was used by Oscar G. Rejlander, a Swede working in Wolverhampton, England, for making allegorical composi-

REJLANDER: The Two Ways of Life, 1857. The Royal
Photographic Society, London

ROBINSON: Fading Away, 1858. The Royal Photographic
Society, London

tions. He conceived a vast stage, on which was acted
out by twenty-five models an allegory

representing a venerable sage introducing two young
men into life – the one, calm and placid, turns towards
Religion, Charity and Industry, and the other virtues,
while the other rushes madly from his guide into the
pleasures of the world, typified by various figures,
representing Gambling, Wine, Licentiousness and other
vices, ending in Suicide, Insanity and Death. The center
of the picture, in front, between the two parties, is a
splendid figure symbolizing Repentance, with the
emblem of Hope.[3]

He would have needed a huge studio and many models
to take this picture with a single negative. He enlisted
the services of a troupe of strolling players, and photographed them in groups at scales appropriate to the
distance at which they were to appear from the spectator. On separate negatives he photographed models of
the stage sets. Then, painstakingly masking the paper,
he printed the negatives one by one in the appropriate
positions. The final print, which measured 31 by 16
inches, he entered in the Manchester Art Treasures
Exhibition of 1857, where it was purchased by Queen
Victoria, herself an amateur photographer.

The Two Ways of Life was hailed as "a magnificent
picture, decidedly the finest photograph of its class ever
produced."[4] Rejlander considered it an example of
the camera's usefulness to artists, in making a first
sketch for an elaborate composition, and said that he
could think of no other subject which would enable
him better to portray "various draped figures as well as
exhibit the beautiful lines of the human form."[5] The
nudity was not universally accepted; only the righteous
half of the photograph was shown at the annual exhibition of the Edinburgh Photographic Society.

Henry Peach Robinson made an equally famous
picture, *Fading Away*, a year later from five negatives.
The photograph shows a dying girl attended by grief-
stricken parents. On the mat was written:

> Must, then, that peerless form
> Which love and admiration cannot view
> Without a beating heart; those azure veins,
> Which steal like streams along a field of snow,
> That lovely outline, which is fair
> As breathing marble, perish?
> – *Shelley*

Robinson stated that the principal model "had three
years practice in expression for photography before a
satisfactory picture was taken."[6] Contemporaries were
shocked by the subject; it was felt to be poor taste to
represent so painful a scene. Though the criticism
seems ridiculous, we should not ignore it as Victorian

sentimentality. Far more painful subjects were painted in those days. But the very fact it was a *photograph* implied that it was a truthful representation, and so the scene was viewed literally. Its artificiality did not escape criticism. "Look steadily at it a minute," the *Literary Gazette* told its readers, "and all reality will 'fade away' as the make-up forces itself more and more on the attention."[7] Such criticism, which was widespread, was discouraging. Rejlander wrote Robinson in 1859:

I am tired of Photography for the public, particularly composite photos, for there *can be no gain* and there is no honor but cavil and misrepresentation. The next Exhibition must, then, only contain Ivied Ruins and landscapes forever besides portraits – and then stop.[8]

But Robinson produced quantities of art-photographs: he published one every year. His influence was even more strongly felt through his prolific writing. His *Pictorial Effect in Photography*, 1869, went through edition after edition, and was translated into French and German. The book, a handy manual for the production of art-photographs, was based on academic rules of composition. Robinson illustrated his text with reduced photographs of his own work and with crude woodcuts of paintings, particularly those of David Wilkie, whose "pyramidal" structures he analyzed for his readers. "As the science of photography has its formulae," he wrote,[9] "so has the art of picture-making, in whatever material, its rules." This regimentation of photographic esthetics and confusion of media caused damage still felt.

Not only did Robinson popularize the emulation of paintings, but he encouraged artificiality. At the very time when painters were moving their easels outdoors, Robinson was building nature under the skylight: shrubbery was mounted on a rolling platform; a brook was improvised from the darkroom drain; clouds were painted on backdrops. He told the beginning photographer that

Any "dodge, trick, and conjuration" of any kind is open to the photographer's use....It is his imperative duty to avoid the mean, the bare and the ugly, and to aim to elevate his subject, to avoid awkward forms, and to correct the unpicturesque....A great deal can be done and very beautiful pictures made, by a mixture of the real and the artificial in a picture.[10]

The professional artist's approach was brought to photography by the French sculptor Antony Samuel Adam-Salomon. He posed his models under the high side light which has ever since been called "Rembrandt lighting." He swathed them with velvet drapery to make the effect more painterly. And he mounted his prints on blue cards printed with the legend "composed

LEWIS CARROLL: Alice Liddell, the original *Alice in Wonderland*, c. 1859. GEH (A. L. Coburn Coll.)

and photographed by the sculptor Adam-Salomon." Alphonse de Lamartine, who had once called photography "a plagiarism of nature." confessed that

After admiring the portraits caught in a burst of sunlight by Adam-Salomon, the emotional sculptor who has given up painting, we no longer claim that photography is a trade – it is an art, it is more than an art, it is a solar phenomenon, where the artist collaborates with the sun.[11]

When some prints of Adam-Salomon's were shown at the Edinburgh Photographic Society, an argument broke out: was the effect due to retouching? It was settled only by a microscopic examination of the prints: Adam-Salomon had indeed retouched them.

Retouching had become controversial ever since Franz Hanfstaengl of Munich showed at the 1855 Exposition Universelle in Paris a retouched negative with a print made from it before and after retouching. It was, Nadar recollected, the beginning of a new era in photography. So difficult was it to believe that modifications had been made to the negative rather than to the print that one of Hanfstaengl's prints was even tested by the somewhat extreme method of bleaching out the silver image entirely with potassium cyanide; no trace of India ink was found.

Not all the work of these self-styled artist-photographers was artificial, sentimental and pretentious.

CAMERON: Mrs. Herbert Duckworth (later Mrs. Leslie Stephen), mother of Virginia Woolf, 1867. Collection B. and N. Newhall, Albuquerque, New Mexico

CAMERON: Sir John Herschel, 1867. MOMA GEH

F. C. CURRY: The Heron, c. 1865. GEH

Robinson produced charming genre scenes, such as the simple study of two little girls reading a book, used as a frontispiece to *Pictorial Effect*. Rejlander pioneered in instantaneous photography with a series of photographs showing the most fleeting facial expression for Charles Darwin's *Expression of the Emotions* (1872).

There was a curious duality apparent in the writings and work of artist-photographers. Robinson on one page wrote that beautiful photographs could be made "by the mixture of the real and the artificial,"[12] and on another page praised "this perfect truth, this absolute rendering of light and shade and form... beyond the reach of the painter and sculptor."[13] Jabez Hughes, while praising Rejlander's and Robinson's work, strongly rebelled against combination printing.

When an artist conceives a brilliant thought, and hastens to put it on canvas, how he sighs that he is obliged to work piecemeal – that he cannot, with one sweep of his brush, realize the thought in his mind. It is the proud boast of photography that it can do this.[14]

This ambivalence is characteristic of the photographs of Julia Margaret Cameron. Her dynamic portraits are among the most noble and impressive yet produced by means of the camera; her genre pictures, on the other hand, drip with sentimentality and lie within the stylistic idiom of the Pre-Raphaelite painters.

At Freshwater Bay, in the Isle of Wight, Mrs. Cameron, whose husband was a British civil servant, entertained illustrious friends: Tennyson, Herschel, Carlyle, Darwin, Browning, Longfellow. She took up photography in middle age: a portrait titled *Annie, My First Success* is dated 1864. She trained her camera on her friends; by the sheer force of her personality she seems to have intimidated them into coöperation. In her autobiographic *Annals of My Glass House* she describes the intensity she brought to portraiture.

When I have had such men before my camera my whole soul has endeavored to do its duty towards them in recording faithfully the greatness of the inner as well as the features of the outer man. The photograph thus taken has been almost the embodiment of a prayer.[15]

She blundered her way through technique, resorting to any means to get desired effects. It did not matter if the subject moved – she wanted that spirit which defines a personality, not accidental details. She used badly made lenses to destroy detail, and appears to have been the first to have them specially built to give poor definition and soft focus.

By accident or design, Mrs. Cameron gave her photographs that breadth and simplicity which was characteristic of early calotypes. Her compositions, undoubtedly inspired by her friendship with the painter

George Frederick Watts, are for the most part costume pieces. She admired the work of Rejlander and invited him to Freshwater Bay "to help her with his great experience." Tennyson tells of the tedious hours of posing for the *Mad Monk*; her children are seen in such pictures as *Venus Chiding Cupid and Removing his Wings*. Without the challenge of interpreting great personalities, her work tended to become lost in sentiment and to echo painting.

More and more laymen found photography a stimulating avocation. Writers seem to have been especially attracted: Charles Dodgson ("Lewis Carroll"), Charles Kingsley, Samuel Butler, Oliver Wendell Holmes were all amateurs. The French poet Auguste Vacquerie accompanied Victor Hugo to Jersey and, with Charles and François Hugo, produced in 1852 an album documenting the poet's life in exile. An eerie romanticism pervades these pictures; details seem selected for their symbolism: the gnarled logs of the breakwater, Hugo's resting place under the flowering vines of the conservatory, Vacquerie on a grassy bank. A series of hands alone – Hugo's and his wife's – appear, a novel idea in photography, and a portent of the close-up.

Perhaps the excellence of the work of these amateurs is due to the very difficulties which must have intimidated all but the more intrepid. They rebelled against the handicaps, against sensitizing their own plates on the spot, against lugging about the heavy equipment for immediate development, and against the caustic silver nitrate which blackened their fingers and ate into their clothes. Lady Eastlake seems to have written from personal experience in 1857:

Every sanguine little couple who set up a glass-house at the commencement of summer, call their friends about them, and toil alternately in broiling light and stifling gloom, have said before long, in their hearts, "Photography, thy name is disappointment!" But the photographic back is fitted to the burden.[16]

Yet, when a less messy process was invented, many looked back on the good old days. They missed the intimate sense of material and the craftsmanship of the obsolete process. As late as 1906 R. Child Bayley wrote:

The very smell of the ether has a fascination. The wet plate photographer cleans his glass and dirts his fingers, coats his plate, sensitizes it, develops it and dries or smashes it as he may think fit, and all within an hour.... There is no such feeling of "alone I did it" to be obtained by the user of the dry plate of commerce....[17]

Lewis Carroll would have nothing to do with the new process. He considered it unfit for "artistic effect," and sent his negatives to be printed by H. P. Robinson.

ADOLPHE BRAUN: Flower piece, c. 1856. GEH
"The first thing that drew attention to Braun was a number of pictures of flowers and garlands, photographed natural size on sheets of twenty inches; these pictures appeared about twelve years ago but, up to this day, they are unique. They excited the admiration of the profession, as well as the artist, and the men of science; King Frederick William sent him, in acknowledgment, a golden snuff box.... They were taken in direct sunlight with landscape lenses and very small stops, requiring sometimes an exposure of half an hour; in order to prevent the withering of the leaves in the heat of the sun the flowers were placed for a few hours in lime-water."
—H. W. Vogel, *Philadelphia Photographer*, Feb., 1868.

FENTON: Balaklava, 1855. Art Institute of Chicago

In the winter of 1855 Roger Fenton sailed from England on the ship *Hecla* for the theatre of the Crimean War as an accredited war photographer. He was backed by Agnew Brothers, picture dealers of Manchester, who knew his accomplished architectural, landscape and portrait photographs. He had studied painting with Paul Delaroche, and as the first secretary of the Photographic Society of London he was a friend of Rejlander, Robinson and other artist-photographers.

Documentation of battle was a new application of photography. Daguerreotypes had been taken during the Mexican War showing officers and men, but there is no evidence that they were taken during combat. Fenton photographed the battlefields under fire.

He took with him a wagon, fitted out as a darkroom, for he was using the wet collodion process. Five cameras, seven hundred glass plates, chemicals, rations, harnesses and tools made up his equipment. At Gibraltar he bought four horses.

The "Photographic Van" was unloaded at Balaklava in March, 1855. In a month he was at the front with his assistant, Marcus Sparling. Once a piece of the van roof was torn off by enemy shell fire, but he was more bothered by demands to take portraits. "If I refuse to take them, I get no facilities for conveying my van from one locality to another," he complained.[1] The heat was excessive. "When my van door is closed before the plate is prepared, perspiration is running down my face, and dropping like tears.... The developing water is so hot I can hardly bear my hands in it."[2] He returned from the Crimea in July with over three hundred negatives. Exhibitions were held in London and in Paris; wood engravings of the more interesting scenes were printed in *The Illustrated London News*. The subjects were landscapes and portraits – battlefields and fortifications, officers and men. There were no scenes of action; to record them was then beyond the power of the camera. "The photographer who follows in the wake of modern armies must be content with conditions of repose and with the still life which remains when the fighting is over," *The Times* wrote about Fenton's work.[3] To a public used to the conventional fantasies of romantic battle painters, these photographs seemed dull, yet they recognized in them the virtue of the camera as a faithful witness. "Whatever he represents from the field must be real," *The Times* admitted, "and the private soldier has just as good a likeness as the general."

War has ever been an ungrateful subject for the photographer. The battlefields of the Crimea appear deserted; officers and men stand in bored groups. Even those scenes taken under direct shellfire show nothing of the menace which the photographer felt. But to the soldiers in their unshapely battle dress and to the generals in their smart uniforms, these photographs must have carried an authentic stamp which no other kind of picture could convey.

The fall of Sebastopol was photographed by James Robertson, then chief engraver to the Imperial Mint in Constantinople; in 1857 he was official photographer to the British military force sent to India to quell the Bengal-Sepoy Mutiny. He worked in India with Felice Beato; their photographs of the aftermath of the siege of Lucknow, 1858, are among the most terrifying documents of the ravages of war: amidst shattered ruins of architectural splendor lie sun-bleached skeletons of the luckless defenders.

When war broke out in America between the States in 1861, the photographic fraternity took the news lightly. "A battle scene is a fine subject for an artist – painter, historian or photographer," declared the editor of the *American Journal of Photography*.[4] "We hope to see a photograph of the next battle.... There will be little danger in the active duties, for the photographer must be beyond the smell of gunpowder or his chemicals will not work."

How greatly the dangers and difficulties of combat photography had been underestimated was soon found out by Brady, the former daguerreotypist. He already had shown his interest in history in the publication of *The Gallery of Illustrious Americans*. This sense of photographic documentation impelled him to undertake the recording of the Civil War; his close friendship with influential government leaders enabled him to secure the necessary authorization to enter combat zones; and he had skilled cameramen in his employ.

With his cameramen he hurried to the front, where his photographic buggy became a familiar sight to the

ROBERTSON: Balaklava, 1855. GEH

soldiers, who called it the "What-is-it?" wagon, and spoke of Brady as "that grand picture maker." It must have required no little zeal and intrepidity to remain crouched for minutes on end in the darkness of that fragile darkroom, going through the delicate manipulations of preparing and processing the glass plates while the din of battle shook the ground. Unarmed, knowing that the wagon itself was a suspicious-looking target, the photographers were exposed to the hazards of war. They risked their lives to save their plates. Brady was almost killed at Bull Run. Lost for three days, he finally turned up in Washington, haggard and hungry, still in his long linen duster, from which protruded a sword given him by a Zouave. He purchased new equipment, rounded up his assistants, and rushed back to the battlefields. The *New York World* wrote:

Mr. Brady's "Scenes and Incidents"... are inestimable chroniclers of this tempestuous epoch, exquisite in beauty, truthful as the records of heaven.... Their projector has gone to his work with a conscientious largeness becoming the acknowledged leader of his profession in America.... "Brady's Photographic Corps," heartily welcomed in each of our armies, has been a feature as distinct and omnipresent as the corps of balloon, telegraph, and signal operators. They have threaded the weary stadia of every march; have hung on the skirts of every battle-scene; have caught the compassion of the hospital, the romance of the bivouac, the pomp and panoply of the field-review – aye, even the cloud of conflict, the flash of the battery, the after-wreck and anguish of the hard-won field.[5]

Brady's men photographed every phase of the war which their technique could encompass: battlefields, ruins, officers, men, artillery, corpses, ships, railroads. There were over seven thousand negatives when peace was declared; the majority of them are now preserved in the National Archives and the Library of Congress.

Brady appears to have been the first to undertake the photographic documentation of the Civil War, for the editor of *Humphrey's Journal of Photography* remarked in the issue of September 15, 1861, that Brady was planning to return to the front and was amazed that others had not followed his example. Soon cameramen by the score went to the battlefields. Most of them are unremembered, and their work has not been identified. Recently, in a painstaking search of War Department records, Miss Josephine Cobb of the National Archives has found the names of some three hundred photographers who were issued passes by the Army of the Potomac, together with the names of their employers.[6] Not all of them were combat cameramen, for there was a large business taking portraits. But we find the following employees of Brady: N. Addison, A. Berger, T. Brown, James E. Burke, A. B. Foons, R. Meyers, T. C. Roche, James Wright. The fact that Brady did not give personal credit to his employees led one of them, Alexander Gardner, who had been in charge of his Washington gallery since 1858, to break with him and to form his own photographic corps in 1863.

Brady felt that he was entitled to copyright in his own name all photographs taken by his employees, including those taken on their own time and with their own equipment. Gardner felt that the photographers should have credit as well as profit for their independent, personal work. He took with him many of Brady's best cameramen. His *Photographic Sketch Book of the War*, a hundred actual photographic prints mounted in two folio volumes, includes some of the finest photographs of the conflict. The names of the makers of the negatives and prints are meticulously recorded: Timothy H. O'Sullivan, George N. Barnard, Wood & Gibson, and others.

Perhaps the most poignant of these Civil War photographs are the inhumanly objective records of ruins – architecture and men. The bleak and ravaged fields, shattered houses, stiff and gruesome corpses, the pathetically homely pictures of camp life, overreach in their intensity mere records. They may be compared to another great documentation of the war – Winslow Homer's drawings in *Harper's Weekly*. But while we admire Homer's sketch of a sharpshooter in a tree, we do not necessarily believe in his existence. The

BRADY: The James River at City Point, Virginia, 1864. Modern print from the collodion negative in The National Archives, Washington, D.C.

BRADY: Ruins of the Gallego Flour Mills, Richmond, Virginia, burned during the evacuation of April 23, 1865. MOMA

Opposite page: GARDNER: "Home of a Rebel Sharpshooter," Gettysburg, Pennsylvania, 1863. Plate 41 of Gardner's *Photographic Sketch Book of the War.* MOMA GEH

BARNARD: Ruins of the Railroad Depot, Charleston, South Carolina, 1865. GEH

sharpshooter may actually have been there, or he may have been a figment of Homer's imagination, or a mixture of the two. We have no way of telling beyond the assurance given to us by the credit line which the editors felt necessary, "Drawn from life by our special artist."

But Gardner's dead sharpshooter, his long rifle gleaming by his side, is not imagined. This man lived; this is the spot where he fell; this is how he looked in death. There lies the great psychological difference between photography and the other graphic arts; this is the quality which photography can impart more strongly than any other picture making. As Oliver Wendell Holmes put it:

The very things which an artist would leave out, or render imperfectly, the photograph takes infinite care with, and so renders its illusions perfect. What is the picture of a drum without the marks on its head where the beating of the sticks has darkened the parchment?[7]

The camera records what is focused upon the ground glass. If we had been there, we would have seen it so. We could have touched it, counted the pebbles, noted the wrinkles, no more, no less. We have been shown again and again that this is pure illusion. Subjects can be misrepresented, distorted, faked. We now know it, and even delight in it occasionally, but the knowledge still cannot shake our implicit faith in the truth of a photographic record. A picture book called *Paris under the Commune* is subtitled "By a Faithful Witness, Photography."

The fundamental belief in the authenticity of photographs explains why photographs of people no longer living and of vanished architecture are so melancholy. Neither words nor yet the most detailed painting can evoke a moment of vanished time so powerfully and so completely as a good photograph.

Old Paris, medieval Paris, lives for us in the brilliant photographs of the condemned areas which Charles Marville recorded for the government before Napoleon III had the great boulevards cut through the city. Marville's camera was not an impersonal lens, for documentary photography is a personal matter. It is not enough to set up the camera and record unthinkingly that which lies before it; choice of stance, choice of time of day, choice of details to emphasize or to subdue are subjective matters. Marville's pictures of streets and houses, worn by human use but emptied of people, have the melancholy beauty of a vanished past.

In America, in the unsettled days which followed the cessation of hostilities, many war photographers followed the building of the transcontinental railroad and joined the semi-military survey parties of the army engineers. Combat photography had not only toughened them for the rigors of frontier travel but it had also trained them to handle the difficult wet collodion technique under unfavorable conditions.

Alexander Gardner drove his photographic buggy into the Kansas wheatfields in 1867 when the Eastern Division of the Union Pacific Railroad was being thrown across the plains at the rate of two miles or more a day. He made a hundred and fifty views of the country and of the construction gangs at work. For this record he used a stereoscopic, twin-lens camera.

The paired prints of the stereograph give a startling illusion of relief when viewed through the apparatus called the stereoscope. In many ways stereoscopic photography is the ideal technique for the historian, for the power of the camera to convince is greatly intensified by the three-dimensional effect. Oliver Wendell Holmes, who was not only an enthusiastic collector of stereoscopic views but who also devised the skeleton-type viewer which joined the brass-clasped photograph album in the Victorian parlor, found the twin pictures of inexhaustible interest. He revelled in the wealth of detail which they contained, and found their illusion of nature identical to nature herself. Of Brady's Civil War stereographs he wrote:

Top left: O'SULLIVAN: General U. S. Grant and staff officers, Massapomax Church, Virginia, May 21, 1864. Modern print from stereoscopic collodion negative in The Library of Congress, Washington, D.C.

Left: ROBERT HOWLETT: Isambard Kingdom Brunel, builder of the steamship *Great Eastern*, against anchor chains, 1857. GEH

MARVILLE: Rue Glatigny, Paris, 1865. Collection V. Barthélemy, Paris

It is so nearly like visiting the battlefields to look over these views that all the emotions excited by the actual sight of the stained and sordid scene, strewed with rags and wrecks, came back to us, and we buried them in the recesses of our cabinet as we would have buried the mutilated remains of the dead they too vividly represented.[8]

The stereograph creates its dramatic effect because it reproduces binocular vision. Normally we see the world with both of our eyes. The image of each eye is slightly different: the fusion of the two in our mind is our most important method of depth perception. Charles Wheatstone maintained in 1838 that if two perspective drawings were made, reproducing exactly the image created in each eye, and were looked at by each eye simultaneously yet independently, depth perception would be re-created.

Attempts were made to draw pairs of pictures by hand so exactly that they could be fused into a three-dimensional unity, but the process was so exacting and so laborious it was not practical. It meant that the artist had to calculate the true perspective from viewpoints separated only by the distance between the eyes – about

HILLERS: John Wesley Powell, first to navigate the Grand Canyon of the Colorado, with Tau-Gu, Great Chief of the Pai-Utes, c. 1872. Stereograph. MOMA GEH

2½ inches. But the camera gave exact perspective automatically; it was simply necessary to make one exposure, move the camera laterally 2½ inches, and make a second exposure. In 1841 Wheatstone had stereo pairs made for him by both the calotype and the daguerreotype. But neither technique was well adapted to the purpose. To view each picture separately, they were held close to the eyes and looked at through two low-powered magnifiers. The calotype would not stand this magnification; the metallic glare of the daguerreotype made the images difficult to see.

Glass transparencies and paper prints were much more suitable. They could be handled easily, the instruments to view them were not cumbersome, and they could be produced in mass. During the fifties, sixties and seventies they were produced by the million. Cameras were designed with twin lenses, so that both photographs could be taken simultaneously. The negatives were small and thus easier to prepare than the "extra whole plate" (8 by 10 inches) which became a standard size for single views. Because the lenses were of short focal length, exposures could be more quickly made with the result that action photographs could, to a limited extent, be taken.

The focal length of a lens is a fixed characteristic which determines the point at which a sharp image will be formed of an extremely distant object. Imagine the light ray from a distant point as a lever, which is pivoted where it passes through the lens, and which continues until it forms an image. When the point at one end of the lever moves, its image at the other end moves; the shorter the arm of the lever behind the lens (a distance determined by the focal length), the less the image moves. Consequently, by the use of a short focal length lens the motion of the image of a moving object can be reduced on the plate to a degree so negligible that during the brief time the lens is open no appreciable blur will be produced.

The stereographs which exist are mainly records of events and places. We can see how Broadway looked when it was choked with horse cars and carriages. We can travel, as Oliver Wendell Holmes invited the readers of the *Atlantic Monthly*, over the world. We can visit the Holy Land; we can see European museums and historical buildings; the aspect of foreign cities; and we can go West into the American frontier country with the pioneers.

Besides Gardner, another war photographer, Captain Andrew Joseph Russell, documented the construction of the transcontinental railroad. Many of his vivid

HART: Meeting of the rails, Promontory Point, Utah, 1869. Collection Union Pacific Railroad

RUSSELL: Union Pacific Railroad west of Cheyenne, Wyoming, 1869. Collection Union Pacific Railroad. MOMA

views of the hurriedly constructed roadbed and scenery along the route were published by the explorer-scientist Ferdinand Vandiveer Hayden in *Sun Pictures of Rocky Mountain Scenery* (1870). Russell was present at the great moment on May 10, 1869, when the tracks of the Central Pacific Railroad reached those of the Union Pacific Railroad and the last spike was driven; his 10 by 13–inch glass negatives, now in the American Geographical Society, are the classic records of the event. The Mormon photographer Charles R. Savage and Alfred A. Hart of Sacramento, official photographer of the Central Pacific Railroad, were also on hand.

Photographers accompanied the government expeditions sent out to explore the territories. In *A Canyon Voyage*, F. S. Dellenbaugh described the photographic outfit as the terror of Major John Wesley Powell's exploration of the Grand Canyon in 1871:

The camera in its strong box was a heavy load to carry up the rocks, but it was nothing to the chemical and plate-holder box, which in turn was featherweight compared to the imitation hand organ which served

Above: O'SULLIVAN: Sand Dunes near Sand Springs, Nevada, 1867. GEH

Opposite page: O'SULLIVAN: Canyon de Chelley, Arizona, 1873. GEH

for a darkroom. This dark box was the special sorrow of the expedition, as it had to be dragged up the heights from 500 to 3000 feet.[9]

Men would travel miles over back-breaking terrain and come back empty handed. Two of the photographers, who had made a side trip to the Kanab Canyon did not get a single negative. "The silver bath had got out of order, and the horse bearing the camera fell off a cliff and landed on top of the camera, which had been tied on the outside of the pack, with a result that need not be described."[10]

John K. Hillers, who had joined the party as an oarsman, learned the hard technique of expeditionary photography in the field and, when both professionals

BISSON FRÈRES: The Alps: view of "The Garden" from Mont Blanc. From the album *Le Mont Blanc et ses glaciers; Souvenirs du voyage de LL Majestés L'Empereur et l'Impératrice,* Paris, 1860. MOMA GEH

quit, took over and for six years made spectacular 11 by 14 inch views of the canyon and hundreds of stereographs of vanishing Indian tribes.

T. H. O'Sullivan, one of the most daring of the war photographers, joined Clarence King's Geological Exploration of the Fortieth Parallel in 1867. Seventeen civilians and twenty cavalry troops left San Francisco for the Great Salt Lake via the Sierra Nevada. Two mules and a packer were assigned to O'Sullivan. At Virginia City, Nevada, he photographed hundreds of feet underground in the Comstock Lode mines by magnesium flare – dangerous and unpredictable anywhere, almost suicidal in mines where inflammable gas might be lurking. A later side trip took him into the desert sixty miles south of Carson Sink where, with the luxury of a darkroom in an ambulance drawn by four mules, he photographed the shifting sand dunes five hundred feet high.

In 1870 he was in Panama, photographing for Commander Thomas Oliver Selfridge's Darien Expedition. A self-portrait made there shows him lean, tough, mustachioed, standing beside his huge camera in a native village.

The following year, when he joined First Lt. George Montague Wheeler in the Engineer Corps' Geological & Geographical Surveys & Explorations West of the 100th Meridian, O'Sullivan was probably the most experienced expeditionary photographer in the country. He was to find high adventure and magnificent material for his camera in the Southwest. The expedition's first sortie was an ascent of the Colorado River. In camp thirty-five miles below the present site of Hoover Dam,

O'Sullivan made one of his finest views. In the foreground his boat, *Picture,* is drawn up to the bank, with the omnipresent black dark tent inside it. The waters of the Colorado appear deceptively smooth, due to the length of exposure. Behind rise the dark and menacing profiles of Black Canyon. As the party passed through the area now submerged by Lake Mead the going became increasingly tough. "… The boat party entered the jaws of the Grand Canyon, not knowing what was before them," Wheeler wrote. "Up to this time the rapids, though often very swift, had not been accompanied by heavy falls, and the estimate for the time to reach the mouth of the Diamond Creek [the rendezvous with the ground party] was based on our experience up to that time, which supposed due allowance for increasing difficulties."[11] Wheeler's papers were lost in an upset; at Camp 28, Starvation Camp, rations were so low that Wheeler guarded them personally, complaining to his diary that there were not enough to make even a decent pillow. After a month's trip the exhausted travelers reached Diamond Creek.

Some of O'Sullivan's most interesting photographs were made on the Survey's 1873 exploration of the area now known as the Canyon de Chelley National Monument in Arizona. The awe-inspiring scale of the Canyon is wonderfully sensed. One view was taken by brilliant, raking sunlight, which picks out every stratum of the Canyon wall. Two tiny figures pose on the famous White House ruin "in a niche 50 feet from the present Cañon bed," as the caption reads. Two other explorers stand among the lower ruins; one holds the rope by which the cliff was scaled.

Most photographers took several cameras into the field, partly as insurance against accidents and partly in order to make different sized negatives. Enlarging was infrequent and impractical. If large prints were required, large negatives had to be made, and as the expanse of western scenery demanded big pictures, field photographers were obliged to take big cameras. The limit was reached by William Henry Jackson who packed a 20 by 24 inch camera on a trip to the Rocky Mountains and the Southwest with Hayden's survey of 1875.

The technique was still the same old messy wet-plate process. The two-foot square glass plates could not be handled in a portable dark box: "for darkroom had a canvas tent lined with orange calico about six feet square at base with center pole," Jackson wrote in his diary. Nor could he use the conventional silver bath, a glass-lined box open at one end. "Used a flat wooden tray for bath."

Working with the oversize camera was exacting. His

FRITH: The Pyramids of Dahshur, Egypt, 1858. GEH

first exposure, of Lake San Cristobal, Colorado, cost him three days' work. Three times he climbed the mountain. On the first day the wind blew too strongly; on the second day the silver bath leaked; on the third day, "Everything worked lovely and secured a fine negative on first attempt."

Jackson recorded twelve of these huge negatives in the official government catalog: "These are the largest plates ever used in field photography in this country. They convey an impression of the real grandeur and the magnitude of mountain scenery that the smaller views cannot possibly impart."

The last of the frontier photographers, Jackson died in 1942 at the age of ninety-nine, a grand old man. He described his full life in his autobiography, *Time Exposure*. He joined Hayden's survey in 1870: in 1871 he made the first photographs of the Yellowstone area which Congress, largely on the evidence of these very pictures, set aside as the first National Park in the United States.

The documentation of the American West was matched by intrepid photographers all over the world. The brothers Louis Auguste and Auguste Rosalie Bisson, went from Paris to Switzerland with Napoleon III and the Empress Eugénie and produced a dazzling series of photographs of the Alps in 1860. Francis Frith went from London to Egypt and the Holy Land year after year; in 1858 he made a series of 16 by 20 inch plates in the desert under the most trying conditions. From India Felice Beato traveled to China, where he photographed the Mandarins signing the peace treaty with England in 1860, and then to Japan. Unlike most field photographers, Beato used albumen plates (p. 47); as late as 1886 he told the members of the London and Provincial Photographic Association that he preferred them to the gelatin plates he had used only a few months earlier as official photographer to the British expeditionary force sent to the relief of General Gordon in the Sudan.

In Australia there was great activity. When, for the second time, gold was discovered in New South Wales, Henry Beaufoy Merlin, proprietor of the American Australasian Photographic Company, went from Sydney to the gold fields, where he took several thousand negatives of the miners and the mining towns. His coverage was remarkably complete; he photographed with directness, sympathy and an eye for detail. Proprietors of business enterprises stand squarely facing

MERLIN: A Hill End home, Australia, 1872. Print from collodion negative in the Mitchell Library, Sydney, Australia

the camera in front of their buildings; women and children were photographed on the porches of their humble cottages. At the end of his life Merlin found a wealthy and enthusiastic patron: Bernhard Otto Holtermann, a German born settler who had made a fortune in the gold fields of Australia and determined to show the world, through photographs, the towns, the landscape and the resources of his adopted country. Unable to complete the assignment because of poor health, Merlin recommended his young assistant, Charles Bayliss. The crowning achievement of the team of patron and photographer was a negative of Sydney harbor 5 by 3½ feet in size – the largest wet-plate negative ever made. Holtermann had built a 74-foot tower. On top of it was a ten-foot camera with a 100-inch lens. Inside the camera Bayliss and Holtermann coated the glass plate, sensitized it, made the exposure, and carried out the processing. In 1876 Holtermann brought the mammoth negative to the Centennial Exhibition in Philadelphia, along with a thirty-foot-panorama of Sydney. En route he stopped in San Francisco and showed the negative to the members of the Photographic Society of the Pacific. In recognition of this spectacular work Holtermann was elected by acclaim a member of the society. The Holtermann Collection was recently discovered intact; the negatives of Merlin and Bayliss, so precious for their historical documentation of Australia, are now preserved in the Mitchell Library, Sydney.

Reading the journals of cameramen and other accounts of field photography in the mid-nineteenth century, we find that much of the cameraman's work was preparatory, prospecting for views. Perhaps this is the key to the excellence of these photographs. Perhaps the very despairs of the photographer worked, in the long run, for him. Casual, promiscuous snapshooting was impossible. Every exposure was an effort; every piece of glass carried by pack mule, boat or human brawn was precious. If a negative was a failure, the silver image was washed off and the glass used again. Only successes survived to be brought back for printing during the between-season layover.

JACKSON: Old Faithful geyser, Yellowstone National Park, 1872. GEH

ANTHONY: Broadway on a
rainy day, 1859. Stereograph.
GEH

FERRIER & SOULIER: The Rue
Royale, Paris, c. 1860.
Stereograph. GEH

In the earliest photographs action was not recorded. The almost universal praise of Daguerre's first work was tempered with the criticism that in depicting motion he was far less successful than in recording architecture. Indeed one critic went so far as to state that moving objects "can never be delineated without the aid of memory."[1]

The prediction was soon proved false. Fox Talbot in 1851 photographed by a sudden electric flash a page of *The Times* he had fastened to a rapidly revolving wheel; although he used albumen plates the illumination was sufficiently intense to give a well exposed negative. This was Talbot's last photographic experiment. He turned his attention to a photomechanical reproduction technique which he patented as *photoglyphic engraving* in 1852 and 1858. When he died in 1877 he was translating from the Assyrian, and the best obituary of the great inventor appeared in the *Transactions* of the Society for Biblical Archaeology.

Outdoors, under normal illumination, "instantaneous" photographs were occasionally taken in the fifties, but they were exceptional. In *A Manual of Photographic Manipulation* (1858) Lake Price said:

If there is one direction more than another in which we may look for greater artistic excellence and interest to be imparted to the photographic picture... it will be by the process being so much accelerated by optical and chemical improvements, that any dimension and class of picture may be taken *instantaneously*: nor need we despair of witnessing this result, when we see what progress a few past years have brought to this art.

The first photographs in which action was stopped with more or less regular assurance were stereoscopic views of city streets, peopled with minute figures of pedestrians. In 1859 George Washington Wilson photographed people walking on Princes Street, Edinburgh, and in the same year Edward Anthony made a remarkable series of instantaneous stereographs of traffic in New York, some of which were even taken on a rainy day. He sent samples to Thomas Sutton, the editor of the British magazine *Photographic Notes*, with a letter dated August 29, 1859, asking: "If you have any specimens of similar results obtained in Europe, we should be pleased to hear how they compare."[2] Sutton answered in his magazine: "...we can only say we know of no pictures, save two or three of Mr. Wilson's best, which could be put in comparison with those he has sent,"[3] and Wilson himself wrote: "Anthony's pictures are much quicker taken than mine, and I must get some sort of shutters to open and shut quickly."[4] Extremely detailed glass stereoscopic transparencies were made in 1860 in Paris by Claude-Marie Ferrier, A. Ferrier and Charles Soulier. When they were exhibited in Paris they were hailed by the *Photographic News* as "the most perfect things of the kind ever produced.... Not one of a thousand figures of all kinds, foot passengers and vehicles passing in all directions, shows the slightest sign of movement or imperfect definition. Figures standing in the shadows of porticos are all perfectly rendered, although the exposure was but the imperceptible fraction of a second."[5]

To Oliver Wendell Holmes these photographs proved invaluable in the study he was making of how man walks. As a physician he was deeply concerned with the problem of designing artificial limbs for those Civil War soldiers who had been maimed upon the battlefield. He tells, in *The Atlantic Monthly*, May, 1863, of basing his theory on

a new source, accessible only within the last few years and never, so far as we know, employed for its elucidation, namely the instantaneous photograph.... We have selected a number of instantaneous stereoscopic views of the streets and public places of Paris and New York, each of them showing numerous walking figures, among which some may be found in every stage of the complex act we are studying.

The article was illustrated with wood engravings drawn by Felix O. C. Darley directly from photographs. The Autocrat of the Breakfast Table found the attitudes in these pictures startlingly different from the conventions which had been used for centuries: he called attention to the length of stride and to the almost vertical position of the sole of the foot in one of the figures. Of another, showing a leg suspended in midair, he remarked: "No artist would have dared to draw a walking figure in attitudes like some of these."

Perhaps it was not so much dare as do, for the eye alone cannot detect attitudes which exist for mere fractions of a second. This inadequacy of human vision was even more convincingly demonstrated a decade

Drawings from instantaneous photographs to illustrate an article on human locomotion by Oliver Wendell Holmes in the *Atlantic Monthly Magazine*, 1863

later, when Muybridge, through his photographs, showed the world that nobody had accurately observed how a horse gallops.

Ex-Governor Leland Stanford of California owned a string of race horses and was especially proud of his trotter "Occident." According to the San Francisco *Alta* for April 7, 1873,

he wanted his friends abroad to participate with him in the contemplation of the trotter "in action," but did not exactly see how he was to accomplish it until a friend suggested that Mr. E. J. Muybridge be employed to photograph the animal while trotting. No sooner said than done. Mr. Muybridge was sent for and commissioned to execute the task, though the artist said he believed it impossible....

Muybridge, whose large photographs of Yosemite Valley, signed "Helios – the Flying Studio," were world famous, was born in Kingston-on-Thames, England, in 1830. He had taken the strange name Eadweard Muybridge in the belief that it was the Anglo-Saxon original of his real name, Edward James Muggeridge. In California he photographed the Pacific Coast for the government, accompanied the official expedition to Alaska when that territory was acquired from Russia in 1868, and became a specialist in industrial photography. In 1869 he invented one of the first shutters for a camera. His experience was to serve him in good stead.

The *Alta* reporter continued:

All the sheets in the neighborhood of the stable were procured to make a white ground to reflect the object, and "Occident" was after a while trained to go over the white cloth without flinching; then came the question how could an impression be transfixed of a body moving at the rate of thirty-eight feet to the second. The first experiment of opening and closing the camera on the first day left no result; the second day, with increased velocity in opening and closing, a shadow was

caught. On the third day, Mr. Muybridge, having studied the matter thoroughly, contrived to have two boards slip past each other by touching a spring, and in so doing to leave an eighth of an inch opening for the five-hundredth part of a second, as the horse passed, and by an arrangement of double lenses, crossed, secured a negative that shows "Occident" in full motion – a perfect likeness of the celebrated horse.

The experiments were interrupted when Muybridge was tried in 1874 for murdering his wife's lover; although he was acquitted, he left the country and the work for Stanford was dropped.

In 1877 Muybridge was able to resume work, with success enough to encourage him to send a photograph to the editor of the *Alta* with a letter dated August 2, 1877, explaining that it "was made while 'Occident' was trotting past me at the rate of 2.27, accurately timed... the exposure... being less than 1/1000 part of a second.... The picture has been retouched, as is customary at this time with all first-class photographic work, for the purpose of giving a better effect to the details. In every other respect the photograph is exactly as it was made in the camera."[6] The retouching was unfortunate, for the authenticity of the photograph was immediately questioned. So he began all over again, using a battery of cameras rather than a single one.

Beside the race track Muybridge ranged twelve cameras, each fitted with a shutter working at a speed he claimed to be "less than the two-thousandth part of a second." Strings attached to electric switches were stretched across the track; the horse, rushing past, breasted the strings and broke them, one after the other; the shutters were released by an electromagnetic control, and a series of negatives made. Though the photographs were hardly more than silhouettes, they clearly showed that the feet of the horse were all off the ground at one phase of the gallop – but, to the surprise of the world, only when the feet were bunched together under the belly. None of the horses photographed showed the "hobbyhorse attitude" – front legs stretched forward and hind legs backward – so traditional in painting. The photographs looked absurd.

They were widely published in America and Europe. The *Scientific American* printed eighteen drawings from Muybridge's photographs on the first page of its Oct. 19, 1878 issue. Six of them showed "Abe Edgerton" walking; the remaining twelve were of the same horse trotting. Readers were invited to paste the pictures on strips and to view them in the popular toy known as the *zoetrope*, a precursor of motion pictures. It was a topless drum, with slits in its side, mounted on a spindle so it could be twirled. Drawings showing

THE HORSE IN MOTION.

Illustrated by
MUYBRIDGE.   AUTOMATIC ELECTRO-PHOTOGRAPH.

"SALLIE GARDNER," owned by LELAND STANFORD; running at a 1.40 gait over the Palo Alto track, 19th June, 1878.
The negatives of these photographs were made at intervals of twenty-seven inches of distance, and about the twenty-fifth part of a second of time; they illustrate consecutive positions assumed in each twenty-seven inches of progress during a single stride of the mare. The vertical lines were twenty-seven inches apart; the horizontal lines represent elevations of four inches each. The exposure of each negative was less than the two-thousandth part of a second.

MUYBRIDGE: Galloping horse, 1878. GEH

successive phases of action placed inside the drum, and viewed through the slits were seen one after the other, so quickly that the images merged in the mind to produce the illusion of motion. The editor wrote: "By such means it would be possible to see not only the successive motions of a trotting or running horse, but also the actual motions of the body and legs in passing through the different phases of the stride."

In 1880, using a similar technique with a device he named the *zoogyroscope*, or *zoopraxiscope*, Muybridge projected his pictures on a screen at the California School of Fine Arts, San Francisco. Motion pictures were born.

Etienne Jules Marey, a French physiologist who had been specializing in the problem of locomotion, was inspired by Muybridge's work to invent a single camera which would take a series of exposures on a single plate. He clothed men in black, painted white lines along their arms and legs, and had them move against a black background while many exposures were made on the same plate. The result was a linear graph of the motion of arms and legs. He later devised a camera with a moving plate, so that each exposure was a separate picture.

The American painter Thomas Eakins wrote Muybridge in 1879, suggesting an improvement by superimposing scales of measurement over the image during printing. He owned a set of the 1878 photographs from which he made lantern slides, presumably for teaching. And he devised a camera similar to Marey's, with which he took action studies of nude athletes under strong top light to bring out the play of the muscles under stress. It is not unlikely that Eakins instigated the invitation extended to Muybridge by the Trustees of the University of Pennsylvania to continue his work under their auspices in Philadelphia. During his residence in Philadelphia from 1883 through 1885, Muybridge perfected his equipment: the shutters were controlled by a master electric switch driven by clockwork, so that exposures could be made at any desired interval; three cameras, each with thirteen lenses (one for viewing, twelve for taking), were used, to photograph from side, front and rear; and, most important, the newly perfected dry plate made it possible for him to secure well detailed images at short exposure times.

The results of Muybridge's labors were published in 1887 in the form of 781 collotype plates; they were sold

MUYBRIDGE: "Head-spring, a flying pigeon interfering, June 26, 1885." Plate 365, *Animal Locomotion*, 1887; print from original master negative. GEH

separately, or bound in eleven volumes with the title *Animal Locomotion*. In addition to horses, animals of all kinds were borrowed from the Philadelphia zoo for photographing. But the most significant work was the human figure. Male and female models, nude and draped, were photographed in all manner of activity – walking, running, laying bricks, climbing stairs, fencing, jumping. Muybridge even photographed one girl throwing a bucket of water over another girl's shoulders, and a mother spanking a child. His specific intention was to create an atlas for the use of artists, a visual dictionary of human and animal forms in action.

There were those who rejected the evidence so painstakingly gathered. Joseph Pennell, the American etcher, lithographer and illustrator, told the members of the London Camera Club that

if you photograph an object in motion, all feeling of motion is lost, and the object at once stands still. A most curious example of this occurred to a painter just after the first appearance in America of Mr. Muybridge's photographs of horses in action. This painter wished to show a drag coming along the road at a rapid trot. He drew and redrew, and photographed and rephotographed the horses until he had gotten their action apparently approximately right. Their legs had been studied and painted in the most marvellous manner. He then put on the drag. He drew every spoke in the wheels, and the whole affair looked as if it had been instantaneously petrified or arrested. There was no action in it. He then blurred the spokes, giving the drag the appearance of motion. The result was that it seemed to be on the point of running right over the horses, which were standing still.[7]

There is little doubt that Pennell was referring to *The Fairman Rogers Four-in-Hand* which Eakins painted in

1879, for it corresponds exactly to the description. The case of the "frozen" wheel continued to bother photographers themselves. The photographic scientist W. de W. Abney preferred the "fuzzy mass of wool-like matter radiating from the center,"[8] as drawn by John Leech, the *Punch* artist. He concluded that instantaneous photographs were untrue and artistically incorrect; the strange positions often assumed in them by men and animals could, he said, only be seen by the eye if the scene were illuminated by a flash of lightning, and he counseled photographers to represent only those phases of action which approach that of rest. H. P. Robinson stated that "it is the mission of the artistic photographer to represent what he sees and no more."[9] P. H. Emerson, artist-photographer and opponent of Robinson, found "nothing more inartistic than some positions of a galloping horse, such as are never seen by the eye, but yet exist in reality, and have been recorded by Mr. Muybridge."[10]

In these later experiments, Muybridge used the new gelatin dry plates. The universal demand for a more convenient technique than the wet-plate process led to many experiments. The first thought was to add a hygroscopic substance, such as honey, sugar, raspberry syrup, glycerine or even beer to the collodion in an effort to delay its drying and thus to postpone the crystallization of the excess silver nitrate on the surface. Then, in 1864, B. J. Sayce and W. B. Bolton showed how the silver bath could be eliminated by coating the glass plate with collodion mixed with ammonium and cadmium bromide and silver nitrate. Such plates could be used while dry; they could be manufactured, and the photographer needed no longer be his own plate maker. The Liverpool Dry Plate and Photographic

MAREY: Lunging fencer, 1885. Cinémathèque Française, Paris

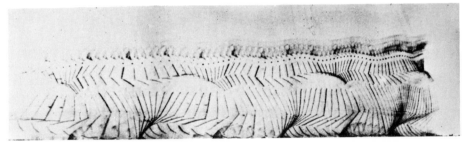

MAREY: Negative of man walking, clothed in black with white stripes, c. 1885. Cinémathèque Française, Paris

EAKINS: Double jump, 1885. The Franklin Institute, Philadelphia

Printing Company began to put these *collodio-bromide* dry plates on the market in 1867. But the convenience of being able to dispense with the wet-plate paraphernalia was gained at the expense of a pronounced loss of sensitivity. Sayce and Bolton noted that their first plate gave a perfect negative with an exposure of 30 seconds at a lens setting equivalent to *f*/24. The manufacturers stated that exposures with these dry plates averaged three times that of wet plates.

In 1871 the *British Journal of Photography* published a letter from a physician, Richard Leach Maddox, describing an emulsion made of gelatin, which the editor pronounced to be "the driest of the dry processes." Maddox soaked gelatin in water, added cadmium bromide in solution and then silver nitrate. Thus his technique was almost identical to that of Sayce and Bolton, with the substitution of gelatin for collodion. This emulsion was flowed on glass and allowed to dry. Maddox stated that he had been unable, because of the pressure of his medical practice, to perfect his experiment, and urged others to continue where he had been forced to stop. He later stated that he had been led to the use of gelatin not because he found the wet collodion process troublesome to manipulate, but because he could not stand the smell of ether in the hot glass house where he was doing photomicrographic work.

Over two years went by before Dr. Maddox's odorless process was refined to a workable technique. The first improvement was to wash the emulsion in its jelly state to remove the excess soluble salts, which tended to crystallize on the surface. Then in 1878 Charles Harper Bennett allowed the emulsion to ripen by holding it at 90° F. for several days before washing. With these plates he made successful negatives at snapshot speeds (approx. 1/25 second) which amazed the photographic world when they were shown at the South London Photographic Society. The editor of the *British Journal of Photography* wrote in 1879 that the year would "be looked back to in the future as one of the most noteworthy epochs in the history of photography." His prediction was exact.

In every camera club there was talk of gelatin:

Onward still, and onward still it runs its sticky way,
And Gelatine you're bound to use if you mean to
     make things pay.
Collodion – slow old fogey! – your palmy days
     have been,
You must give place in future to the
     plates of Gelatine.[11]

Manufacturers now began to make gelatin plates, and

MUYBRIDGE: Wrestler, 1885. Detail of plate 347, *Animal Locomotion*, 1887. Print from original master negative. GEH

Opposite page: Buffalo Bill, 1889. Stereograph by an unknown American photographer. Collection Guy L. Howe, M.D., Rochester, N. Y.

problems which had long plagued the photographer suddenly were solved. He was freed from the need of a darkroom at his elbow, for the plates could be processed at any reasonable time after exposure. He could give them to others to develop, and the industry of photo-finishing was born. Even more: the speed of the new process made the tripod no longer indispensable; the camera could be held in the hand.

A bewildering array of hand cameras appeared on the market in the 1880's. Many held several plates in a magazine, so that the photographer could take a dozen or more exposures without reloading. Some were disguised as paper parcels, luggage, watches, books; others were concealed in hats and behind neckties. Because with these cameras exposures could be made surreptitiously, they were called "detective cameras."

The most famous detective camera was invented and manufactured by George Eastman, a dry-plate maker in Rochester, New York. Introduced in 1888, it was named the *Kodak*, a word coined by Eastman to be short, pronounceable in any language, distinctive, and easily remembered. The original Kodak was a box camera, 3¼ by 3¾ by 6½ inches, with a fixed-focus lens of 57 mm focal length and aperture *f*/9, fitted with an ingenious barrel shutter. Eastman had already invented "American Film" – paper coated with gelatino-bromide emulsion on a substratum of plain gelatin. The new camera was loaded at the factory with a roll of this material sufficient for taking one hundred negatives, each 2½ inches in diameter. The cost of the Kodak was $25, which included the film and processing. After the owner had finished the roll, he sent the entire camera to the factory. The film was removed from the camera, cut into strips of twelve exposures and individually developed. The emulsion bearing the image was then stripped from the paper, pressed into contact with a sheet of clear gelatin, and dried. Prints were made from each negative and pasted on gilt-edged, chocolate mounts. These were returned to the owner with the camera which, at a cost of $10, was reloaded with a fresh roll of film. YOU PRESS THE BUTTON, WE DO THE REST brought the taking of photographs to the millions. George Eastman had done more than invent a camera; he invented a system and worked out machinery for producing standardized material in quantities sufficient to back up the system. In 1889 he further improved his system by substituting a clear plastic (nitrocellulose) for the paper base, thus eliminating the delicate stripping operation. Amateurs could easily process their own exposures.

The comparative ease with which photographs could now be taken led to new applications. A New York amateur, Alexander Black, was reveling in the freedom of the new hand camera. His painter friend, William Merritt Chase, was so impressed by the results that he urged Black to show lantern slides of them to the

FRED CHURCH: George Eastman with a Kodak on the S. S. Gallia, 1890. GEH

Snapshot made by an unknown amateur with a Kodak, c. 1890. GEH

Society of American Artists. As the pictures were thrown on the screen, the distinguished painters found one another's work mirrored in them. In his autobiography Black recollected that

a picture of New York bootblacks in action elicited a recognizing shout, "A perfect J. G. Brown!" A park scene brought "A Chase to the life!" "Ah, a Thayer!" was the comment on a tenement madonna.[12]

Following this success, Black lectured on photography in its relation to art to the students of the National Academy of Design, and then took his talk on the road, billed as "Ourselves as Others See Us."

In 1893 he had the idea of telling a story in photographs. He wrote a short comedy, *Miss Jerry*, about the adventures of a young lady reporter, which actors performed before his camera. The resulting 250 lantern slides he projected to audiences on a screen, while he read the dialogue. The part of Chauncey Depew, president of the New York Central Railroad, was played by himself. For his next production, *A Capital Courtship*, Black persuaded the President of the United States, Grover Cleveland, to be photographed in his White House office with the cast, signing a bill. These picture plays of Black's were forerunners in spirit, though not in technique, of the motion picture, as Black pointed out in 1895:

By carefully registering the backgrounds of the successive pictures in a scene the figures alone are made to appear to move, thus slowly producing the effect which Mr. Edison has wrought, in a different way, with his kinetoscope.... The range of the picture play gave it peculiar advantages, for not only could I pass from one fictitious scene to another, but I could introduce the backgrounds of real life.[13]

Edison's *Kinetoscope* was the first practical motion picture to win public acceptance as a form of entertainment. It relied for its success upon the perfection of flexible transparent roll film, which enabled a camera to be built that would take action photographs one after the other at a rate of about forty-eight per second. A positive film, made from the negative taken in this camera, was shown in the Kinetoscope. The film was driven by an electric motor between a light bulb and a whirling disk with a slot on its periphery. One person at a time peered through a magnifying eyepiece on the top of the Kinetoscope, and saw the pictures intermittently, one after the other, as the slot scanned the moving film. The pictures changed so quickly that the images merged in the mind to produce a convincing illusion of motion. A Kinetoscope Parlor, with ten machines, was opened in New York in April, 1894. In May, machines were shipped to Chicago, in June to

San Francisco, in September to Paris and London.

Popular as they were, the Kinetoscopes did not satisfy fully the public's demand. The pictures were too small, and had to be viewed individually. Inventors in Europe and America began, independently of one another, to devise projectors in which Edison's films, or ones like them, could be thrown on a screen, like a magic lantern show. The first projector to meet with instant success was the *Cinématographe* of the brothers Louis and Auguste Lumière. On December 28, 1895, they put on a program of subjects at the Grand Café, Paris, which resembled snapshots taken with hand cameras (a railroad train entering a station, workers leaving the Lumière factory at lunch time, a fishing boat entering a harbor). They also, in *The Sprinkler Sprinkled*, showed how a story could be told by motion pictures. A gardener is seen sprinkling the lawn. A small boy jumps on the hose. The gardener looks in the nozzle, puzzled that the stream of water suddenly stopped. The boy jumps off the hose, the gardener's face is doused with water, he throws down the hose, chases the kid, catches him, and spanks him.

By the end of 1896 films were being screened regularly in the principal cities of Europe and America with the *Vitascope*, the *American Biograph*, the *Theatrograph*, the *Phototachyscope*, the *Bioscop*, the *Kinetoscop*, and a host of other ingeniously designed projectors. The great twentieth-century medium of the motion picture was born, full fledged. So great has been its swift, astounding growth and its international importance that its history forms a field in itself; to report further upon it in these pages is not possible.

The perfection of gelatin emulsion not only led to the conquest, analysis and synthesis of action, but it brought about standardization of materials and the scientific investigation of the photographic process.

In 1876 Vero Charles Driffield, a scientist and amateur photographer, persuaded his friend and colleague, Ferdinand Hurter, to join him in his hobby. "But, to a mind accustomed like his to methods of scientific precision," Driffield wrote, "it became intolerable to practice an art which – at that time – was so entirely governed by rule-of-thumb, and of which the fundamental principles were so little understood."[14] They began a series of investigations. Their first aim was to devise a method of measuring the intensity of light, so that photographers could compute with accuracy the exposure time. When the first gelatin plates were marketed they found them so rapid in their reaction to light that the need for a method of calculating exposure became even greater. They studied the relationship between exposure, or the amount of light falling on the photographic plate, and density, a function which they defined as the amount of silver produced by development. With an apparatus made from an old sewing machine, and with a candle for standard illumination, they exposed plates to successively increasing amounts of light. The silver deposit they measured optically with a homemade photometer. They then plotted the measurements thus obtained on a graph. One would expect that as the amount of exposure was doubled, the density would double. This, however, is not the case; the relation varies. At first density lags behind exposure, soon equality is reached, and finally density proportionately increases. The resulting graph, with a concave foot, a straight line middle section, and a convex shoulder, they called the *characteristic curve*.

By plotting such curves, manufacturers were able to test their emulsions. Hurter and Driffield suggested that the "speed" of a plate (degree of sensitivity to light) could be measured geometrically from the characteristic curve.

In 1890 they announced the results of their researches in the *Journal* of the Society of Chemical Industry, for May 31. They opened their report with a statement which has become classic:

The production of a perfect picture by means of photography is an art; the production of a technically perfect negative is a science.[14]

The greatest value of their work to the practicing photographer was the simplification of the developing process. They showed that for every plate or film there is an optimum developing time, depending on the brightness ratio of the subject, the composition of the developer, and the temperature at which it is used. Negatives could be developed in total darkness by immersing them in the developing solution for a predetermined time. It was no longer needful to watch the gradual appearance of the image by red light. Thus plates sensitive to light of all colors, and which would be fogged by the red light of the darkroom, could be readily processed.

Wet plates and the first dry plates and film were overly sensitive to blue light and insensitive to red, orange and yellow. Thus blue sky was rendered white with an exposure sufficient to record a landscape. Red was indistinguishable from black, and portraitists advised sitters to avoid wearing red clothes. In 1873 Hermann Wilhelm Vogel, professor of photography at the Technische Hochschule, Berlin, discovered that by bathing the coated plate in a dye, it became sensitive to the colors absorbed by the dye. Thus by dyeing plates with coraline he was able to record yellow, which hitherto could not be photographed. He proved it with an experiment:

The picture of a blue ribbon on a yellow background was taken. With an ordinary iodide of silver plate I obtained a (positive) picture, representing a white ribbon on a black background. A coralline bromide of silver plate was tried next. It was natural that on such a plate the blue and yellow should be marked equally strong, and the result would have been nothing. I now placed in front of the objective a piece of yellow glass; through this plate all the yellow light could pass, but not so the blue; and I now obtained actually a strong impression of the yellow color... representing a dark ribbon on a light background.[15]

Plates made sensitive to all colors but red were called *orthochromatic* or *isochromatic*. Vogel's prediction that the sensitivity of photographic emulsions could be extended to all the visible rays was realized with the discovery of new dyes; these plates were named *panchromatic*. Using these plates in combination with a colored filter on the lens, photographers were given a new creative control. They could not only photograph clouds in the sky, but they could make the sky any desired tone of gray. At first "overcorrected" skies were not acceptable. As late as 1905 a landscape taken with the "deepest ray filter" showing fleecy white clouds against "a sky as seemingly black as that of midnight" was criticised as false and the amateur who sent it to *Camera Craft* magazine was advised to try to correct the distortion by printing. When commercial large-scale production of panchromatic plates was made possible in the 1930's, largely through the work of C. E. Kenneth Mees of the Eastman Kodak Company, the new emulsion soon came to be universally used.

The discovery of gelatin emulsion revolutionized techniques for making prints as well as negatives. It was no longer necessary to rely on sunlight for printing; exposures could be made by artificial light, and the latent image developed to a visible one. With this so-called "gaslight paper," enlarging at last became practical. In the wet-plate days, when photographers were limited to the relatively insensitive printing-out paper, the only light source bright enough to enlarge with was the sun. A cumbersome enlarger, the *solar camera*, had been invented by David A. Woodward in America in 1857. The exposures were hours long, and the camera, mounted on the roof, had to be turned with the sun. Quantity production was out of the question. Now artificial light – dependable and readily controlled – could be used in less cumbersome enlargers in the photographer's darkroom.

DEGAS: Self portrait with Zoë, c. 1895. Print courtesy The Metropolitan Museum of Art, New York

While these radical improvements in plate, film and paper manufacture were taking place, equally important improvements were being made in lenses.

In 1884 Otto Schott of the Schott Glass Works and Ernst Abbe of the Zeiss Optical Works, both in Jena, Germany, developed barium crown glasses which had a higher refractive index for a given dispersion than any glass previously available. For any lens to bring rays of different colors to the same focus, the positive elements must be of lower dispersive power than the negative elements, and in early days this meant that the refractive index of the positive elements had to be low, and that of the negative elements, high. This had two adverse effects: it gave a strongly inward-curving field and it made the surface of the positive elements strong and those of the negative elements relatively weak. As the lens on the whole is positive, this resulted in considerable amounts of aberration. With the introduction of barium crown glass, many new types of photographic lenses became possible. The first to be developed were cemented triplets of the Dagor type, in which the three glasses are common crown, light flint, and dense barium crown in that order.

These new *anastigmat* lenses were of greater relative aperture than the rapid rectilinear lenses which they quickly replaced. The first Zeiss Protar, for example, had a maximum aperture of $f/4.5$.

By the turn of the century, Daguerre's method of obtaining "the spontaneous reproduction of the images of nature received in the camera obscura" had become a highly refined technique. The camera was placed in the hands of everyone. With the division of the taking and processing operations, skill of hand was no longer needed to secure results. At this very time ways were found to reproduce photographs in books and magazines on the same press with type. The public became more photograph conscious than ever. Camera clubs sprang up throughout the world; magazines for amateurs appeared in great number; the taking of snapshots became a fad. It was said that President

VROMAN: Hopi Indian, Nawquistewa, Oraibi, 1901. Print by William Webb from original negative in Los Angeles County Museum

Grover Cleveland on a fishing trip with Joe Jefferson used his Kodak all day long but, alas, never once turned the key that wound the film. His disappointing experience was typical of the attitude that photography was an automatic process, an attitude inherent in the very genesis of photography (had not Talbot called it the Royal Road to Drawing?), but which, despite extraordinary technical advances, has never been accomplished. No matter how great the simplification of technique, the camera alone cannot produce pictures of creative significance without the will and the discerning eye of the man behind it.

Not all amateurs were casual. George Eastman in 1892 recognized two classes of photographers, outside of professionals:

The first are the true amateurs, who devote time enough to acquire skill in developing, printing, toning, &c., and their number is limited to those who have time to devote to it, inclination for experimenting, and such facilities as the dark-room, &c., required in practicing the art.

The second class are those who, lacking some, or all of the requisites of the "true amateur," desire personal pictures or memoranda of their everyday life, objects, places or people that interest them in travel &c. The number of this second class are limited only by those who have not the facility for making the pictures they want, and they bear a relation to the limited numbers of the true amateur of one thousand to one hundred.[16]

Many of these "true amateurs" produced outstanding photographs. They worked for their own satisfaction and did not regularly exhibit their pictures nor publish them to any extent; only recently have we discovered them. The novelist Emile Zola took hundreds of negatives of his family and his travels, which he developed and printed himself. He enjoyed his hobby and told a reporter in 1900: "In my opinion you cannot say you have thoroughly seen anything until you have got a photograph of it, revealing a lot of points which otherwise would be unnoticed, and which in most cases could not be distinguished."[17]

The painter Edgar Degas was an ardent amateur; he ordered panchromatic plates by the dozen in 1895 when they were still a novelty, and had enlargements made from his negatives so big they had to be sent to him rolled around a stick. Only a few of his photographs are known to us. They are mostly interiors, taken by artificial light. In pose and composition they are reminiscent of his painting, though there is no evidence that he made direct use of them as studies. Edouard Vuillard, too, was an amateur: a folding Kodak was a fixture in his house, and during social gatherings he liked to put the camera casually on a piece of furniture, point it at his guests, and ask them to hold still while he made short time exposures.

Adam Clark Vroman, a bookseller in Los Angeles, made between 1895 and 1904 a moving, sympathetic documentation of the Indians of the Southwest. His greatest difficulty was caused by casual snap shooters, who not only got in the way, but had made the Indians so camera conscious that only by befriending his models and winning their confidence could he take serious portraits of them.

There were other amateurs whose concern for photography went even deeper. They passionately believed it to be a fine art, deserving of recognition. With vigor and dedication they not only explored the esthetic potentials of the camera, but crusaded for their cause. As amateurs, they were not burdened with financial responsibilities, and could ignore limits self-imposed by professionals. They were free to experiment, and they had the imagination and will to break accepted rules. In Europe and America they banded together in clubs and societies, and through exhibitions and publications demonstrated their belief. Their style became universal; for a quarter of a century they dominated artistic photography.

VROMAN: Zuñi Pueblo, interior, 1897. Print by William Webb from original negative in the Los Angeles County Museum

ZOLA: The Eiffel Tower, Paris, 1900. Collection Kodak-Pathé, Vincennes, France

EMERSON: Gathering Water Lilies, 1886. Platinum print. MOMA GEH
"The first case in which Dr. Emerson invited public attention and criticism was the issue in May, 1886, of the autogravure 'Gathering Water Lillies,' the first of its class from a negative from nature ever published separately as a work of art... In breadth and technique it is magnificent." – *International Annual of Anthony's Photographic Bulletin*, 1888.

Art-photography, as championed by Rejlander and Robinson in the late fifties, was languishing in England when the dry-plate revolution took place. Robinson himself was still the leader – subscribers still looked forward to his annual photographs – but the walls of exhibition galleries were crowded from floor to ceiling with the same kind of anecdotal genre scenes, sentimental landscapes, and weak portraits that characterized academic painting of the most unimaginative sort.

Against the artificiality of these stiffly posed studio scenes and patchwork prints made up of pieces of different negatives, Peter Henry Emerson protested with a vehemence which shook the photographic world. His weapons were his own photographs, lectures, articles and books. In March, 1886, he spoke to the Camera Club in London on "Photography, a Pictorial Art." Sweeping aside John Ruskin as a "spasmodic elegant of art literature," because he denied any connection between science and art, and dismissing Robinson's book as "the quintessence of literary fallacies and art anachronisms," Emerson laid before his audience a theory of art based on scientific principles. He held that the artist's task was the imitation of the effects of nature on the eye, and pointed to Greek sculpture, Leonardo da Vinci's *Last Supper*, and the recent paintings of the "naturalistic" school of Constable, Corot and the Barbizon group as the peaks of artistic production of all times. Trained as a physician, he was greatly impressed by Hermann von Helmholtz' *Physiological Optics*, which he quoted as the ultimate authority on correctness of representation.

Emerson came to the conclusion that photography was "superior to etching, woodcutting and charcoal drawing" in the accuracy of its perspective rendition, and that it was second to painting only because it lacked color and, he believed, the ability to reproduce exact tonal relationships.

In the same year he published in a limited edition *Life and Landscape on the Norfolk Broads*, a collection of forty actual prints mounted to form a handsome folio volume. These photographs had all been made in East Anglia, and presented a record of the strange amphibian life of the marsh dwellers. The publication was followed by similar volumes with letterpress describing the manners and customs of the peasants, and photogravures made directly from his negatives. These books were ethnological studies, of which the photographs were an integral part. Each picture had been made on the spot, often with great difficulty, always with direct honesty. Free from sentimentality and artificiality, they were diametrically opposed to the art-photographs of Robinson and his followers.

Having established himself as a photographer, Emerson proceeded to explain his esthetic and technical approach in a textbook, *Naturalistic Photography* (1889). It was not illustrated: students were referred to the plates of *Pictures of East Anglian Life*, a handsome folio volume containing thirty-two photogravures. To camera clubs all over Britain he gave copies of a special edition, containing a variant plate and, pasted to the inside of the front cover, a page of notes on the photographs. *Naturalistic Photography*, called "a bombshell dropped in a tea party,"[1] is a curious mixture of truth and fallacy. In it Emerson expanded his warped history of art and again propounded the Helmholtzian theory of vision. His practical advice was often sound, however, and the book can still be read with profit; he had a respect for the medium and understood both the limitations and the capabilities of photography.

The equipment which Emerson recommended was the simplest – a view camera, preferably of whole plate size (6½ by 8½ inches), a sturdy tripod, and a lens of relatively long focal length – at least twice the plate's longest side. He had no use for hand cameras. He condemned enlarging. He saw no relation between size and artistic quality: "An artistic quarter plate [3¼ by 4¼ inches] is worth a hundred commonplace pictures forty by thirty inches in size." The student was advised to develop his negatives on the very day they were taken "whilst yet the mental impression of what you are trying for is fresh." He rejected retouching as "the process by which a good, bad, or indifferent photograph is converted into a bad drawing or painting.... The technique of photography is perfect, no such botchy aids are necessary." For printing he advised two processes, the platinotype and photogravure.

Platinum is a more stable metal than silver; its first use in photography was to make prints which would

EMERSON: Pond in winter, 1888. Platinum print. GEH

be permanent. The technique was invented in England by William Willis in 1873. When his Platinotype Company put ready-sensitized paper on the market in 1880, the new printing process became extremely popular. To Emerson the permanence of this method of printing, although important, was secondary to its esthetic quality. He liked the delicacy and soft grays it could yield. "For low-toned effects, and for grey-day landscapes, the platinotype process is unequalled," he wrote. And he criticized the Platinotype Company for insisting upon making brilliant prints: "...It is to be hoped they will soon have their eyes opened to this fact, and cease to encourage the false notion that good, ergo plucky, sparkling, snappy negatives are those required for the use of the paper." He further stated:

Every photographer who has the good and advancement of photography at heart, should feel indebted to Mr. Willis for placing within his powers a process by which he is able to produce work comparable, on artistic grounds, with any other black and white process. ... No artist could rest content to practice photography alone as an art, so long as such inartistic printing processes as the pre-platinotype processes were in vogue. If the photogravure process and the platinotype process were to become lost arts, we, for our part, would never take another photograph.

Photogravure is a means of producing the photographic image in printer's ink. It is based upon Fox Talbot's invention of 1852 (p. 175). First a glass transparency is made from the negative. A copper plate is then dusted with grains of bitumen, and heated so that the powder is fixed to the surface. A carbon print, exposed beneath the transparency, is transferred to the plate, which is then bathed in warm water. The unex-

posed gelatin of the carbon print is thus washed away, leaving the image in relief. The plate is then etched with ferric chloride, which bites into the copper in proportion to the highlights and shadows of the gelatin relief. The result is an etched plate which, when inked, yields prints on paper. Emerson saw it as a direct printing technique, allied to the traditional art process of etching. The photogravure plates of his albums were made directly from his negatives and under his supervision.

This much of Emerson's advice was sound: it was an approach to photography based on tradition, and it formed the tenets of what was to be called "straight photography." Emerson's theory of focusing, however, raised debate. He reasoned that our field of vision is not entirely uniform. The central area is clearly defined, while the marginal areas are more or less blurred. To reproduce human vision with the camera, he advised the photographer to put the camera's lens slightly out of focus. But he warned,

it must be distinctly understood that so-called "fuzziness" must not be carried to the length of *destroying the structure* of any object, otherwise it becomes noticeable, and by attracting the eye detracts from the harmony, and is then just as harmful as excessive sharpness would be....

Nothing in nature has a hard outline, but everything is seen against something else, and its outlines fade gently into that something else, often so subtly that you cannot quite distinguish where one ends and the other begins. In this mingled decision and indecision, this lost and found, lies all the charm and mystery of nature.

British photographic magazines were full of stormy letters pro and con this theory.[2] "Naturalistic focus, then, according to Emerson, means no focus at all, a blur, a smudge, a fog, a daub, a thing for the gods to weep over and photographers to shun," wrote "Justice." "It is not in man, even in f.64 man," George Davison replied, choosing the technical designation of one of the smallest lens apertures to imply concern with overall sharpness in the negative, "to overlook the unnaturalness of joinings in photographic pictures, and the too visible drawing-room drapery air about attractive ladies playing at haymaking and fishwives." Robinson thundered: "Healthy human eyes never saw any part of a scene out of focus," and hinted that the Naturalists were indebted to his teaching for their knowledge of composition. Emerson retorted, "I have yet to learn that any one statement or photograph of Mr. H. P. Robinson has ever had the slightest effect upon me except as a warning of what not to do."

Many of Emerson's followers ignored his qualifying advice, and "soft focus" photographs began to appear in quantity.

Then, in January, 1891, Emerson courageously and dramatically renounced what he had so passionately advocated. He declared that "a great painter," whom he did not identify, had shown him the fallacy of confusing art and nature, and the experiments of Hurter and Driffield had convinced him that control of the image was less than he had expounded. Photography was not art.

In a black-bordered pamphlet, *The Death of Naturalistic Photography*, he explained that

the limitations of photography are so great that, though the results may and sometimes do give a certain aesthetic pleasure, the medium must always rank the lowest of all the arts... for the individuality of the artist is cramped, in short, it can scarcely show itself. Control of the picture is possible to a *slight* degree, by varied focusing, by varying the exposure (but this is working in the dark), by development, I doubt (I agree with Hurter and Driffield, after three-and-half months of careful study of the subject), and lastly, by a certain choice in printing methods.

But the all-vital powers of selection and rejection are fatally limited, bound in by fixed and narrow barriers. No differential analysis can be made, no subduing of parts, save by dodging – no emphasis – save by dodging, and that is not pure photography, impure photography is merely a confession of limitations.... I thought once (Hurter and Driffield have taught me differently) that true values could be *altered at will* by *development*. They cannot; therefore, to talk of getting values in any subject whatever as you wish and of getting them true to nature, is to talk nonsense.

...In short, I throw my lot in with those who say that photography is a very limited art. I deeply regret that I have come to this conclusion.

But Emerson could not recall the fresh spirit he had brought to photography in a period when it was verging on academicism. He did not give up photography. Whether or not the delicate photogravures in his *Marsh Leaves* of 1895 are "art" seems to us of little importance: among them are fine photographs. His bold renunciation was more a matter of semantics than of esthetics, for to Emerson "art" and "painting" appear to have been synonymous. In 1898 he published a third and revised edition of *Naturalistic Photography*, which was substantially the same as the first two editions, except for the final chapter, which instead of "Photography, a Pictorial Art," became "Photography – Not Art."

The acceptance of photography as an art became a burning issue. With evangelical passion passive defense gave way to active campaigning; the battle was on,

simultaneously, in Europe and America. The first skirmish was by the Vienna Camera Club: in 1891 they held an exhibition exclusively of photographs judged as works of arts. The project was hailed by the *American Amateur Photographer*:

If we had in America a dignified "Photographic Salon," with a competent jury, in which the only prizes should be the distinction of being admitted to the walls of the "Salon," we believe that our art would be greatly advanced. "Art for art's sake" should be the inspiring word for every camera lover.[3]

This pattern was followed almost literally by The Linked Ring, a society formed in London in 1892 by Robinson, George Davison (Emerson's one-time champion), Lionel Clark, H. Hay Cameron (Mrs. J. M. Cameron's son), and Alfred Maskell, who were dissatisfied that the annual exhibitions of the Photographic Society made no distinction in hanging between photographs taken with artistic intent and those for more utilitarian purposes. The Linked Ring had, as its express object

the complete emancipation of pictorial photography, properly so called, from the retarding and nanizing bondage of that which was purely scientific or technical, with which its identity had been confused too long; its development as an independent art; and its advancement along such lines as to them seemed the proper track of progress into what, as the perspective of logical possibilities opened itself to their mental visions, appeared to be its promised land.[4]

Their first annual exhibition, held in the fall of 1893, they called "The Photographic Salon." They stated that the name "was suggested through its application by the French to certain fine-art exhibitions of a distinctive and high-class character." Critics were irked by the group's self-conscious assertion that the work exhibited was "The New Photography"; they were shocked by the dogmatic statement, printed in the catalogue of the 1895 Salon, that "on the pictorial side, chemistry, optics and mechanism no longer predominate; they have become subservient and of secondary importance, very little knowledge of them indeed is in any way necessary."[5]

We can best reconstruct these rival photographic exhibitions from the annual issues of *Photograms of the Year*,[6] a record of pictorial photography published since 1895. The editors not only reviewed the exhibitions in detail, but illustrated many of the contributions. The difference between the two seems less to us than it must have in the nineties. In presentation the Salon took the lead; the pictures, instead of being packed frame to frame from floor to ceiling, were asymmetri-

No. 1.—"A GOOD JOKE."　　　　　By *Alfred Stieglitz, Berlin.*

STIEGLITZ: " A Good Joke," 1887. Prize-winning picture reproduced in *The Amateur Photographer*, July 11, 1888. Yale University, Alfred Stieglitz Collection. MOMA

Opposite page:
STIEGLITZ: Paula, 1889.
MOMA GEH

cally arranged more or less on eye level, vases of flowers were placed above them on a narrow shelf, designs in pastels were drawn on the wall surface and "here and there elsewhere, even on the frames." The "haphazard" arrangement was grudgingly admitted to be effective, for "each picture arrests your attention, and for this reason the Salon deserves praise for a bold experiment that offers a pleasant change to those who are wearied with many galleries."[7]

The character of camera clubs elsewhere began to change. The *Bulletin* of the Photo-Club de Paris, for years a modest news sheet with technical data and accounts of photo excursions to picturesque corners of France, published a series of articles, "La Photographie moderniste," by H. Colard. In the July, 1893 issue there was announced the "First Exhibition of Photographic Art." The rules of entry emphasized, in bold-face type, that "only work which, beyond excellent technique, presents real artistic character... will be accepted." The jury was made up of four painters, a sculptor, an engraver, an art critic, and the National Inspector of Fine Arts, as well as two amateur photographers. The exhibition was held from January 10–30, 1894; the Photo-Club announced proudly that it was "the standard bearer of photographic art... through propaganda by exhibition."[8] The first five exhibitions

were accompanied by handsome de luxe catalogues of folio size with tissued photogravures.

In Germany artistic photography was launched by Alfred Lichtwark, art historian and the dynamic director of the Kunsthalle in Hamburg. In 1893, with admirable tact, he enlisted the support of both professionals and amateurs in organizing an "International Exhibition of Amateur Photography" in the museum. The public was astounded to find over seven thousand photographs on display in the painting galleries of an art museum. "To them it seemed like holding a natural history congress in a church," Lichtwark recollected.[9] As if in justification, he said that the purpose of the exhibition was to revive the dying art of portrait painting. The stilted, studio portraits of professional photographers, with their painted backgrounds, fake columns, and imitation furniture, were not shown. Lichtwark felt that the only good portraiture in any medium was being done by amateur photographers, who had economic freedom and time to experiment, and he persuaded the professionals, for their own good, to study and emulate their work. For the first time Germans saw the new art photography movement; they learned how to frame photographs, and how to use the new printing papers which were replacing albumen. From the Hamburg museum's

STIEGLITZ: The Terminal, 1893. From the original lantern slide. GEH

exhibition came a great stimulus: "With fiery ardour amateurs and very soon professionals rushed out on the newly opened road," Lichtwark wrote.[10] The Hamburg exhibition became a yearly event; in the 1899 exhibition Lichtwark showed for the first time in Germany calotypes by D. O. Hill.

At these international exhibitions a most frequent and honored American exhibitor was Alfred Stieglitz; of the twenty-five photographs accepted by the Vienna Salon of 1891 from the 350 submitted by Americans, five were by him. While a student in Berlin, Stieglitz won his first recognition from Emerson, who awarded him the first prize – two guineas and a silver medal – in a contest held by the British *Amateur Photographer* in 1887. It was the first of a hundred and fifty medals which he was to win. Emerson wrote Stieglitz that of the thousands of photographs he had seen, the only truly spontaneous one was his *A Good Joke*, a genre picture of a group of Italian children clustered around a fountain, each one laughing heartily. While the picture lacked intensity, it had been taken directly and

honestly, without straining for effect; it was not forced into an obvious compositional pattern. Emerson's choice had been prophetic, for Stieglitz carried on the fight for the recognition of photography as an independent art from the point where Emerson renounced it.

Stieglitz had gone to Germany from New York in 1881, when he was seventeen years old, to study mechanical engineering. In a Berlin shop window he saw a camera, which he at once bought. It seemed, he later recollected, to have been waiting for him by predestination, and he soon found himself more interested in photography than in engineering. He had the advantage of studying under H. W. Vogel, the famous photochemist who had invented orthochromatic emulsion, and he acquired a brilliant technique. While most of the pictures made in his student days were genre scenes that recall the popular paintings of the day, some showed a new vision. *Paula* of 1889 remains a brilliant photograph: a young German girl is writing a letter in a room filled with sunlight broken into bands of light and dark by a Venetian blind. It was a technical problem to resolve the harsh contrasts; it was an esthetic problem to see in the subject a picture of lasting quality.

When Stieglitz returned to America in 1890 to live, he found amateur photography flourishing. There were many camera clubs and photographic societies, but none of them seemed to have the passionate belief in the art of photography which was spreading throughout Europe. He joined the Society of Amateur Photographers, became editor of *The American Amateur Photographer*, and through his photographs and writing, through his publication of others' work, through lectures and demonstrations, he showed Americans esthetic potentials of photography which they had not yet realized.

He now began to push technique beyond the accepted limits. The hand camera had been universally regarded in artistic circles as unworthy of the "serious worker." Stieglitz saw in it a challenge. Borrowing from a friend a 4 by 5-inch detective camera, he waited three hours on Fifth Avenue in a blinding snowstorm on February 22, 1893,[11] to photograph a horse-drawn coach; the next day he photographed the steaming horses of the Harlem streetcar at the downtown terminal. When he developed them, fellow club members called these negatives, made in such poor light, worthless. Yet from these negatives Stieglitz made excellent lantern slides.

He considered that a good lantern slide, properly projected, was one of the finest ways to look at a photograph. Here again, he was breaking down prejudices, because magic lantern slides had generally been used for entertainment or for illustrating lectures. Emerson had dismissed them as "toys" having no place in art. Stieglitz worked out ingenious techniques for controlling the contrast and the tone of the lantern slide by chemical means, and for expanding the range of values by the use of a mask, or as he called it, "compensating cover glass." In 1896 he twice gave demonstration exhibitions of his slides to the Society of Amateur Photographers, showing pictures made in Europe and America. The Society's *Journal* remarked:

Mr. Stieglitz' pictures are examples of pure photographic processes – no retouching or hand drawing having been done on any of the negatives, even in the case of the large portrait heads – and wherever any softening of the detail or forms of the figures has been necessary, it has been obtained by the simple and legitimate expedient of additional exposure.[12]

By this time Stieglitz had an international reputation. The editor of *Photograms of '97*, in noticing his contributions to the London exhibition, fairly ran out of words:

Mr. Stieglitz is so astoundingly clever that it leaves a critic with nothing to say. He pushes the limits of his craft a shade further every year, yet always in orthodox ways, and gains his sensation by legitimate effects. One wishes that he were a Briton, to add to the list of brilliant workers home-born.

But Stieglitz was an American, and he wanted to see American pictorial photographers equal the British, who were winning prizes right and left. He pleaded with his countrymen: "We Americans cannot afford to stand still; we have the best of material among us, hidden in many cases; let us bring it out... let's start afresh with an Annual Photographic Salon to be run upon the strictest lines."[13]

The Society of Amateur Photographers and the New York Camera Club merged in 1896 to become The Camera Club. Stieglitz was elected its vice-president. As chairman of its publications committee he transformed the Club's journal into the handsome periodical *Camera Notes*, containing superb reproductions of photographs by members and non-members, articles, and critical reviews of exhibitions.

The first attempt to hold a salon in America was a compromise. In 1896 the Camera Club of the Capitol Bicycle Club of Washington announced a two-part

DEMACHY: Cigarette Girl—A Poster Design. Photogravure from a gum bichromate print in *Camera Notes*, July, 1902

KÄSEBIER: "Blessed Art Thou Among Women." Platinum print, c. 1900. MOMA

In 1898 the Philadelphia Photographic Society announced an exhibition which would be limited strictly to "such pictures produced by photography as may give distinct evidence of individual artistic feeling and execution."[15] It was held in the galleries of the Pennsylvania Academy of The Fine Arts; two painters and an illustrator had consented to serve with two photographers on the jury; and it seemed that a definite step forward had been made in the recognition of photography as an art.

Salons became yearly fixtures, and brought recognition to many younger American photographers. Clarence H. White of Newark, Ohio, Edward Steichen of Milwaukee and Alvin Langdon Coburn of Boston first became known through them. The style of these Americans was characterized by soft focus, deep shadows relieved with brilliant highlights and strong, linear composition. The influence of Whistler and Japanese prints lay heavily upon them. They liked to fasten their photographs on mounts of softly colored textured paper which were in turn fastened to one or more additional mounts of harmonizing or contrasting colors and of increasing size. Prints so mounted were often signed with a monogram, and they were almost invariably exhibited in large frames.

In 1900 F. Holland Day brought an exhibition of the "New American School" to London. He and Steichen, with the help of Coburn, arranged the photographs in the Royal Photographic Society's building. Most of the more prominent American photographers, with the exception of Stieglitz, were represented. The exhibition demonstrated a new trend in photography, and was a sensation.

Some of the photographs exhibited at these various salons were actually mistaken by visitors for reproductions of paintings, to the pleasure of the more extreme pictorialists and to the scorn of those who believed in pure photography. Emerson explained this tendency as a reaction:

There was a time when the great bubble of sharpness enveloped the photographic world, but that has burst, and the explosion thereof seems to have upset the sanity of some, who have been carried away in the explosion, and lost all reason and sense, all tone and texture, those vital and great qualities of photography.[16]

He denounced in particular the newly rediscovered gum bichromate process, a technique based on the property of gum mixed with potassium bichromate to change its degree of solubility in water upon exposure to light. The more strongly the light acts upon it, the less easily can it be dissolved. Pigments may be applied

"Washington Salon and Photographic Art Exhibition." Class A, the Salon, was to consist of "such pictures only as possess special merit from an artistic point.... The class will include work which may be termed 'impressionist' if produced intelligently and with definite art aim." It was to be judged by artists. Class B, limited to amateurs, were "photographs of merit, though not of sufficient artistic excellence to be admitted to the Salon."[14] This group was to be judged by photographers. The exhibition so impressed the Director of the United States National Museum that fifty photographs from the exhibition were purchased for $300 for its permanent collection – the first recorded museum purchase of photographs as works of art.

Stieglitz, who did not participate, regretted the compromise, the slack standards (only 80 photographs were rejected, 485 were hung), and the awarding of prizes; it was not the Salon he proposed.

to paper with bichromated gum as a medium. After exposure to light beneath a negative the print is "developed" by washing it in warm water. Areas can be locally treated by applying hot water with a brush, or directing a stream of water on the print. Weak areas can be reinforced by recoating the print with light-sensitized pigment and again exposing it beneath the negative. The process can be carried on with pigments of different color on the same support. The temptation of this easily controlled technique is to imitate charcoal or chalk drawings by using rough paper, black or red pigments, and by freely washing away unwanted details. Criticizing a gum-print by Davison as devoid of photographic quality, Emerson said,

If pure photography is not good enough or "high" enough for such as he, by all means let him become an artist and leave us alone and not try and foist "fakes" upon us.[17]

But what was "pure photography"? Stieglitz and his friend Joseph T. Keiley had invented what they called the glycerine process, which permitted local development of platinotypes; they said it was a "purely photographic process" because handwork in the sense of retouching played no part in it. The matter could not be settled by accepting this or rejecting that technique; what mattered was the photographer's intent, his taste and his vision.

As Stieglitz expressed it: "The result is the only fair basis for judgment. It is justifiable to use any means upon a negative or paper to attain the desired end." He went on to point out that "some of the most maligned prints generally considered 'faked' are in fact nothing more than 'straight photography' from beginning to end."[18]

He was speaking at the opening of "An Exhibition of American Pictorial Photography Arranged by the 'Photo-Secession'" at the National Arts Club, New York, in 1902. It was a carefully selected show, hung with taste and a sense of intimacy unusual in photographic exhibitions. Art critics were positive about it: some found it a revealing demonstration of hitherto unsuspected esthetic possibilites of the camera, others condemned it as a pretentious display of imitation paintings and wondered if the aim of the photographers was "to hold as 'twere a smoked glass up to nature."[19]

"What is the Photo-Secession?" the chairman of the exhibition committee of the National Arts Club had asked Stieglitz. "Yours truly for the present, and there'll be others when the show opens," Stieglitz answered. "In Europe, in Germany and in Austria, there have been splits in the art circles and the moderns call

CLARENCE H. WHITE: The Orchard, 1902. Platinum print. MOMA GEH

STEICHEN: The Frost-Covered Pool, 1899. Platinum print. MOMA "The picture, if picture you can call it, consisted of a mass of light gray ground, with four or five vertical streaks of gray upon it.... Among artists in oil and water colors the impressionist leaves out of his picture much, if not all, of the finer detail, because he assumes—whether rightly or wrongly it is for you to decide —that the public can supply this detail much better than he can portray it.... What is true of the oil or water color is equally true of the photograph." *The Photo-Era*, May, 1900

tion; Photo-Secession Loan Collections went from New York all over the world. The official organ of the group was the handsome new quarterly, *Camera Work*.

Stieglitz' determination to win for pictorial photography recognition as a fine art had not been shared by all the members of the Camera Club. Many had been slighted by Stieglitz in his eagerness to reproduce in *Camera Notes* the best, no matter by whom. The members felt that the periodical, with its emphasis upon pictorial photography, was not representative of the interests of the club, and Stieglitz found himself forced to resign the editorship. At the urging of his friends he planned a new magazine, *Camera Work*; to avoid confusion and compromise he took upon himself the entire responsibility of editing and publishing it, choosing as co-workers friends in the Photo-Secession. The associate editors were Joseph T. Keiley, Dallett Fuguet and John Francis Strauss, whose names had appeared in similar capacity on the masthead of *Camera Notes*. The first number was devoted to Gertrude Käsebier, the second to Steichen.

Steichen, while working as an artist for a lithographic firm in Milwaukee, first exhibited photographs at the Second Philadelphia Salon of 1899; the photographs which he submitted to the Chicago Photographic Salon of 1900 attracted the attention of Stieglitz and Clarence H. White, two of the five judges. They became friends and co-workers. Two years later his first one-man show was held in Paris; it brought him international recognition. In Paris, where he settled to paint and to photograph, he met Auguste Rodin, and made a series of highly romantic photographs of the great Frenchman and his sculptures. The prints were reproduced in *Camera Work* with critical articles. Charles H. Caffin hailed Steichen as a photographer who was also a painter. To the Photo-Secessionists this fact was the strongest proof that photography was a potential fine-art medium. In addition to the Rodin series, there were also reproduced many of Steichen's portraits. In their direct spontaneity and in their dramatic posing and lighting they foretold the outstanding work which Steichen was to do in this difficult field. His best known portrait, of John Pierpont Morgan, was taken in 1903, while making photographic studies for the use of the painter Fedor Encke. The painting lies forgotten; Steichen's portrait remains a most striking interpretation of the financier. By accident or by design, a highlight on the arm of the chair suggests a gleaming blade.

What impresses one most, going through the fifty numbers of *Camera Work* published between 1902 and 1917, are the illustrations. The choice was varied,

themselves Secessionists, so Photo-Secession really hitches up with the art world."[20]

The society which grew out of this exhibition was informal in nature. Stieglitz was director of the Council, which was made up of the twelve founders: John G. Bullock, William B. Dyer, Frank Eugene, Dallett Fuguet, Gertrude Käsebier, Joseph T. Keiley, Robert S. Redfield, Eva Watson Schütze, Edward Steichen, Edmund Stirling, John Francis Strauss and Clarence H. White. Membership was divided into Fellows and Associates. Its stated aim was threefold:

To advance photography as applied to pictorial expression;
To draw together those Americans practicing or otherwise interested in art;
To hold from time to time, at varying places, exhibitions not necessarily limited to the productions of the Photo-Secession or to American work.[21]

The group exhibited only as a body and upon invita-

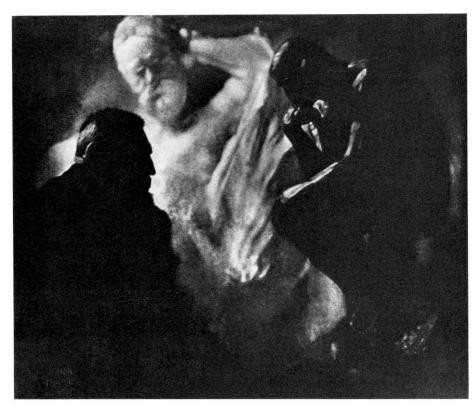

STEICHEN: Rodin—Le Penseur, 1902. Mr. and Mrs. Hans Hammarskiöld, Stockholm, Sweden

ranging from bold gum prints by Steichen to delicate architectural platinotypes by the Englishman Frederick Evans, from the quasi-etchings of Frank Eugene to luminous, often high-key, prints of Clarence H. White, from the poster-like multiple gum prints of the Viennese trio of Heinrich Kühn, Hans Watzek and Hugo Henneberg to the unmanipulated platinum prints of Stieglitz himself. Every reproduction was of the highest possible quality, printed on the finest paper and tipped in by hand in each copy of each issue. It was more than once remarked that the reproductions in *Camera Work* were often better presentations of a photographer's work than his own prints.

The variety of visualization and technique in the work reproduced makes the common ambition of the contributing photographers all the more apparent. They were determined to win artistic recognition. Every step of the struggle was recorded, and the pages of *Camera Work* were open to all critics and to all who spoke with sincerity. Arguments broke out over the artistic legitimacy of some of the work, in which a large part of the effect was often due to skill of hand.

In 1905 the Little Galleries of the Photo-Secession was opened at 291 Fifth Avenue, where exhibitions were to be arranged not only of photographs, but also of "such other art production...as the Council...will

from time to time secure."[22] On the walls of "291," as the Little Galleries came to be called, the American public began to see work of the most daring and progressive modern painters and sculptors. Many of the artists whose work was shown had never before exhibited in America. There were drawings by Rodin, watercolors by Cézanne, sculpture by Matisse, abstractions by Picasso, Brancusi, Braque and Picabia. From the start paintings by Americans were shown with those of European origin: by John Marin, Marsden Hartley, Max Weber, Arthur Dove and, later, by Georgia O'Keeffe. *Camera Work* published for the record and *in extenso* all newspaper criticisms. Stieglitz said that the Little Galleries was "a laboratory, an experimental station, and must not be looked upon as an Art Gallery, in the ordinary sense of that term."[23] In this broadening of the scope of the Photo-Secession's activities, Steichen was of the greatest help. Stieglitz acknowledged his debt to him in *Camera Work* No. 42–43, the seventh issue of the periodical to contain reproductions of Steichen's work:

It was he who originally brought "291" into touch with Rodin, the recognized master, and with Matisse, at the time that he was regarded as "The Wildman." It has been Steichen also who, living in Paris, has constantly been on the watch for talent among young

STEICHEN: John Pierpont Morgan, 1903. MOMA

Americans there, and, as for example, in the case of Marin, has introduced them to the spirit of "291."[24]

In 1910 the Photo-Secession was invited to arrange an international exhibition of pictorial photography at the Albright Art Gallery in Buffalo. Complete control of the presentation was demanded and secured: Stieglitz, with the aid of his friends Paul Haviland, Clarence White and the painter Max Weber, transformed the Museum. They covered the exhibition walls with olive and blue cloth, and hung over six hundred photographs. Each photographer invited was represented by enough prints to enable his artistic development to be traced.

It was gratifying to the Photo-Secessionists to be able to show photographs with such dignity in an art museum; it was even more gratifying that the museum purchased fifteen prints from the exhibition for its collection and planned to set aside a room for their permanent display, for it was a vindication of their belief that photography had the right to recognition as a fine art. *Camera Work* No. 33 contains criticisms of the exhibition by various writers. They unanimously praised the exhibition as the most impressive they had ever seen. Its retrospective emphasis was so apparent that one critic asked if the show was the *nunc dimittis* of the Photo-Secession. Another, Sadakichi Hartmann, noted that "the pictorial army is divided in two camps," one favoring "painter-like subjects and treatment" and the other, in which Stieglitz was numbered, made up of those "who flock around the standards of true *photographic themes and textures*." He went on to observe that "the camp of the former... becomes more and more deserted, the old flag hangs limp and the fires burn low...."

The year of the Buffalo exhibition marked a turning point. The Linked Ring had dissolved. *Camera Work* itself threw more and more emphasis upon modern painting. To those who complained that *Camera Work* had less and less photographic content, Stieglitz wrote: "Photography should take its place in open review with other mediums in order that its possibilities and limitations might be more fully judged."[25] Charles H. Caffin pointed out that

after claiming for photography an equality of opportunity with painting, Stieglitz turns about and with devilishly remorseless logic shows the critics, who have grown disposed to accept this view of photography, that they are again wrong. As long as painting was satisfied, as it had been for half a century, to represent the appearances of things, photography could emulate it. Now, however, that it is seeking to render a vision of things not as they are palpable to the eye, but as they impress the imagination, Mr. Stieglitz

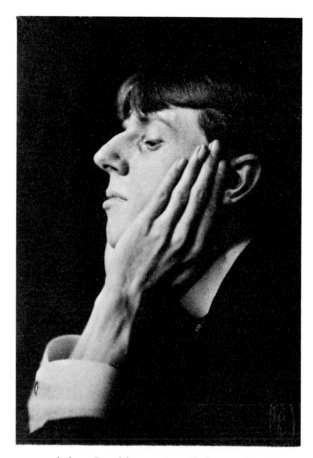

EVANS: Aubrey Beardsley, c. 1894. Platinum print. GEH

proves what he has known all along, that photography is powerless to continue its rivalry with painting.[26]

When the Association of American Painters and Sculptors decided to hold a great international exhibition of contemporary painting and sculpture in the Armory of the 69th Regiment in New York in 1913, the organizing committee consulted Stieglitz. He did not actively participate, but he wrote a challenging article in the *New York American*[27] titled "A Clinic for Revitalizing Art," urging the public to see the show. And he put on the walls of "291" the first one-man exhibition of his own work in fourteen years. To him this was a demonstration of what photography was and painting was not; and the Armory Show was a demonstration of what painting was and photography was not.

That same year, 1913, he was judge at a photographic contest sponsored by Wanamaker's department store in New York. He stated in the catalogue:

Photographers must learn not to be ashamed to have their photographs look like photographs. A smudge in "gum" has less value from an esthetic point of view that an ordinary tintype.[28]

EVANS: The Sea of Steps—Wells Cathedral, England, 1903. GEH
"By use of a 19 in. Zeiss anastigmat on a 10 by 8 in. plate, I succeeded in getting a negative that has content-
ed me more than I thought possible.... The beautiful curve of the steps on the right is for all the world like
the surge of a great wave that will presently break and subside into smaller ones like those at the top of the
picture. It is one of the most imaginative lines it has been my good fortune to try and depict, this superb
mounting of the steps ...." — F. H. Evans in *Photography*, July 18, 1903.

In 1912 an exhibition was held at the Montross Galleries in New York of photographs by Alvin Langdon Coburn, Gertrude Käsebier, Clarence H. White and twenty-seven other less well known photographers. The *New York Times* noted:

Nearly all of the work shown is what is called by the knowing "straight photography"; not photography, that is, which has been supplemented by manipulation. The advocates of pure or "straight" photography feel that by manipulating a print you lose the purity of tone which belongs especially to the photographic medium in trying to get effects that can be more satisfactorily obtained with the painter's brush.[1]

The esthetic use of the functional properties of the photographic technique, the appreciation of both the camera's potentials and its limitations, and the divorce of photography from the canons guiding the esthetic principles of the other visual arts, was becoming recognized by critic and artist alike. Alfred Stieglitz had consistently applied this principle. Although he had frequently championed photographers whose prints often resembled paintings and drawings, and although he occasionally made gum prints himself and experimented with other manipulative processes, he preferred all his life to stick closely to the basic properties of camera, lens and emulsion. Charles H. Caffin said in 1901 that Stieglitz was

by conviction and instinct an exponent of the "straight photograph," working chiefly in the open air, with rapid exposures, leaving his models to pose themselves, and relying for results upon means strictly photographic. He is to be counted among the Impressionists; fully conceiving his picture before he attempts to take it, seeking for effects of vivid actuality and reducing the final record to its simplest terms of expression.[2]

In 1907 he photographed *The Steerage*, a picture which in later years he considered his finest. He related that while he was promenading the first-class decks of the S. S. *Kaiser Wilhelm II* on an eastbound voyage to Europe, he saw:

A round straw hat, the funnel leaning left, the stairway leaning right, the white drawbridge with its railings made of circular chains, white suspenders crossing on the back of a man in the steerage below, round shapes of iron machinery, a mast cutting into the sky, making a triangular shape... I saw a picture of shapes and underlying that the feeling I had about life.[3]

Hurriedly he rushed to his cabin for his Graflex, hoping that the figures would not move in the meanwhile. He found all as he had left it, made the exposure, developed the negative in Paris, and brought it back in the plateholder. The composition was bold: some of his friends told him that the picture was split in two. He liked to tell that Picasso had praised it; the father of Cubism was at that time painting his *Les Demoiselles d'Avignon*, the canvas which was to mark a turning point in the style of the century.

Only a few of the photographs which Stieglitz made during the first two decades of the century were published in *Camera Work*. Some of the more outstanding were taken in New York: ferryboats, the liner *Mauretania*, buildings rising sheer from the waterfront. He was making many portraits, and they formed a pictorial biography of the participants of the activities of "291." Konrad Cramer has described sitting for him:

His equipment was extremely simple, almost primitive. He used an 8 × 10 view camera, its sagging bellows held up by pieces of string and adhesive tape. The lens was a Steinheil, no shutter. The portraits were made in the smaller of the two rooms at "291" beneath a small skylight. He used Hammer plates with about three-second exposures.

During the exposure, Stieglitz manipulated a large white reflector to balance the overhead light. He made about nine such exposures and we then retired to the washroom which doubled as a darkroom. The plates were developed singly in a tray. From the two best negatives he made four platinum contact prints, exposing the frame on the fire escape. He would tend his prints with more care than a cook does her biscuits. The finished print finally received a coat of wax for added gloss and brilliance.[4]

In 1921 Stieglitz, who had not shown his photographs publicly since the war, arranged an exhibition of both old and new work in the Anderson Galleries, New York. Every one of the photographs was startlingly direct, and the effect upon the public was electric. John A. Tennant, publisher of *Photo-Miniature*, reviewed the exhibition:

Never was there such a hubbub about a one-man show. What sort of photographs were these prints, which caused so much commotion? Just plain, straightforward photographs. But such photographs! Different from the photographs usually seen at the exhibi-

STIEGLITZ: The Steerage, 1907. Photogravure in *291*, No. 7–8, 1915. MOMA

tions? Yes. How different? There's the rub. If you could see them for yourself, you would at once appreciate their difference. One might venture the comparison that in the average exhibition print we have beauty, design, or tonal scheme deliberately set forth, with the subject as motive or material merely, the subject as the photographer saw it or felt it, an interpretation, a phase; whereas, in the Stieglitz prints, you have the subject itself, in its own substance or personality, as revealed by the natural play of light and shade about it, without disguise or attempt at interpretation, simply set forth with perfect technique – and so on, multiplying words. There were portraits, some of them of men whom I knew fairly well. Sometimes it was a single print, at other times several prints side by side, giving different aspects of the subject but grouped as "one Portrait." Well, they were just portraits of those men, compellingly intimate, betrayals (if I may so use the word) of personality, satisfying in likeness, convincing in characterization, instinct with the illusion of life. They gave one the impression of being in the presence of the men whom they portrayed. They offered no hint of the photographer or his mannerisms, showed no effort at interpretation or artificiality of effect; there were no tricks of lens or lighting. I cannot describe them better or more completely than as plain straightforward photographs.... They made me want to forget all the photographs I had seen before, and I have been impatient in the face of all photographs I have seen since, so perfect were these prints in their technique, so satisfying in those subtler qualities which constitute what we commonly call "works of art."[5]

In the catalog Stieglitz wrote that the exhibition was "the sharp focusing of an idea... My teachers have been life – work – continuous experiment.... Every print I make, even from one negative, is a new experience, a new problem.... Photography is my passion. The search for Truth my obsession."

Those who knew Stieglitz knew the force of his personality, and they attributed his success in portraiture to a kind of hypnotic power. To answer this challenge, Stieglitz began to photograph clouds.

I wanted to photograph clouds to find out what I had learned in forty years about photography. Through clouds to put down my philosophy of life – to show that my photographs were not due to subject matter – nor to special privileges, clouds were there for everyone – no tax on them yet – free.[6]

He produced hundreds of these pictures of sun and clouds, mostly made with a 4 by 5-inch Graflex camera. He processed them by means within the reach of any amateur, printing by contact on commercial Azo paper. He called these pictures "equivalents," and he put them in series with other pictures of expressive, often evocative, content and handling – a meadow glis-

STIEGLITZ: Konrad Cramer, 1912. Platinum print. GEH

tening with raindrops, a woman's hands pressed palm to palm between her knees. He found them to be equivalents to his thoughts, to his hopes and aspirations, to his despairs and fears. Viewed objectively, many of these rich prints with deep blacks and shimmering grays and incandescent whites delight us for their sheer beauty of form. They are photographic abstractions, for in them form is abstracted from its illustrative significance. Yet paradoxically the spectator is not for an instant left unaware of what has been photographed. With the shock of recognition he realizes almost at once that the form which delights his eye is significant, and he marvels that such beauty can be discovered in what is commonplace. For this is the power of the camera: it can seize upon the familiar and endow it with new meanings, with special significance, with the imprint of a personality.

Among the last photographs which Stieglitz made (poor health forced him to abandon using the camera around 1937) were pictures of New York taken from high windows, and the meadows and trees around the old family house at Lake George where he spent his

STIEGLITZ: Equivalent, 1930. GEH

summers. He continued all the while to champion modern art: at An American Place, his New York gallery, the series of exhibitions of paintings continued, with occasional photographic shows up to his death in 1946. Stieglitz was always there, and from him many a young man or woman found counsel and direction.

In the last two issues of *Camera Work*, dated 1916 and 1917, Stieglitz reproduced photographs by a newcomer, Paul Strand. They included a forceful series of people taken unawares in the streets with a Graflex camera, and pictures in which form and design were emphasized – a semi-abstraction of bowls, a downward view from a viaduct, an architectural scene dominated by the vertical accents of a white picket fence. As Stieglitz said, the work was "brutally direct, pure and devoid of trickery." It was in striking contrast to much of the work which had been produced by the Photo-Secession. It was prophetic of the re-orientation in photographic esthetics and of the return to the traditions of straight photography which was to gain force in the years after the war.

The photographer's problem [Strand wrote in 1917] is to see clearly the limitations and at the same time the potential qualities of his medium, for it is precisely here that honesty no less than intensity of vision is the prerequisite of a living expression. This means a real respect for the thing in front of him expressed in terms of chiaroscuro...through a range of almost infinite tonal values which lie beyond the skill of human hand. The fullest realization of this is accomplished without tricks of process or manipulation through the use of straight photographic methods.[7]

Strand was among the first to discover the photographic beauty of precision machines. He made a series of extreme close-ups of his Akeley motion picture camera (he was earning his living making films) and of power lathes. On a trip to Maine he discovered the beauty of large-scale details of driftwood, cobwebs, plants and other natural objects. In 1923, lecturing to the students of the Clarence H. White School of Photography, he made a strong plea for the revival of craftsmanship and told them of the need to free photography from the domination of painting, and to recognize that the camera had its own esthetic.

Strand's negatives are seen with intensity and with sureness; his work has a quality rarely found in photography, a quality which can only be described as lyrical. He has photographed people and landscapes in the Southwest, Mexico, the Gaspé, New England, France, Italy, the Hebrides, Egypt, Yugoslavia and Morocco – seeking always the feeling of the place, the land, and the people living on the land. He has done a series of

STIEGLITZ: Grape Leaves and House, Lake George, 1934. GEH

STIEGLITZ: Georgia O'Keeffe, 1922. Palladium print. GEH

books, beginning with *Time in New England* (1950), edited by Nancy Newhall, who chose New England writings from the seventeenth century to the present to put with the photographs. Words and pictures reinforce and illuminate one another with synergistic effect. For *La France de profil* (1952) Strand found a collaborator in Claude Roy, who used a somewhat similar editing technique. The Italian scenarist Cesare Zavattini wrote the text for *Un Paese* (1955) to accompany photographs taken in his native village of Luzzara. Strand's *Tir A'Mhurain, Outer Hebrides* (1962), with a commentary by Basil Davidson, explores an island north of Scotland.

Strand is a brilliant printer. Until it went off the market in 1937, he preferred platinum paper. It will be remembered that this paper was prized by Emerson for its ability to yield soft results emphasizing middle tones at the expense of shadows and highlights. Strand used it to make brilliant, long-scale prints. Not content with the quality of Japine platinum paper, which had a smooth, semi-mat surface, he persuaded the manufacturers, the Platinotype Company of London, to produce double coated paper, after demonstrating to them the improved results which paper so prepared by himself could produce. For years he made all of his prints by contact, and they were consequently the size of the negative, 8 by 10 inches or less. Recently he has found that with precision equipment he can make enlargements which will retain the quality which he demands, and consequently has made more use than before of a hand-held reflex camera. He lives in the village of Orgeval, outside of Paris.

In 1914 Charles Sheeler began to discover with his camera the beauty of indigenous American architecture, photographing with honest directness the texture of white painted and weathered wood, and the beautifully proportioned rectangular forms of Pennsylvania barns. First and foremost a painter, Sheeler had a keen appreciation of the photograph as a distinct medium. He told his biographer, Constance Rourke,

I have come to value photography more and more for those things which it alone can accomplish, rather than to discredit it for the things which can only be achieved through another medium. In painting I have had a continued interest in natural forms and have sought the best use of them for the enhancement of design. In photography I have strived to enhance my technical equipment for the best statement of the immediate facts.[8]

Charles Sheeler's contribution to photography has been his sensitive interpretation of the form and texture of man's work in precise, clean photographs of African Negro masks (1918), the industrial achitecture

STRAND: Portrait, New York, 1915. Photogravure in *Camera Work* No. 49–50, 1917. MOMA GEH

STRAND: The White Fence, 1916. Photogravure in *Camera Work*, No. 49–50, 1917. MOMA GEH

Opposite page: STRAND: Rock, Port Lorne, Nova Scotia, 1919

STRAND: Town Hall, New England, 1946

STRAND: The Family, Luzzara, Italy, 1953. MOMA GEH

SHEELER: Bucks County barn, 1916. MOMA GEH

of the Ford plant at River Rouge (1927), the Cathedral of Chartres, seen in a series of details (1929) and in the photographs of ancient sculpture which he did for the Metropolitan Museum of Art (1942–45).

Edward Steichen, placed in charge of aerial photography of the American Air Service during the second Battle of the Marne, was faced with the problem of securing photographs with a maximum of detail, definition and brilliance. He found such beauty in these straight photographs that in 1920 he repudiated his gum prints, abandoned painting, and set out to master pure photographic processes almost as if he were a beginner, setting himself such extreme problems as the rendition of the brilliant contrasts of a white teacup on black velvet. Armed with this mastery of technique, and with his brilliant sense of design and ability to grasp in an image the personality of a sitter, he began to raise magazine illustration to a creative level (see chapter 13).

Around 1920 Edward Weston, a Californian photographer who had been honored by election to the London Salon (successor to the Linked Ring) began a critical re-examination of his work which, up to that time, had been soft in focus, but always done with a sense of light and form. He experimented with semi-abstractions: *R. S. – A Portrait* was a bold, unconventional placing of the upper half of the model's head at the very bottom of a composition of triangles and diagonals. A detail of a nude – circle of breast and diagonal of arm – was equally abstract. In Ohio he discovered the beauty of industrial constructions. His work was taking two trends: abstraction and realism. In 1924, while working in Mexico, he recognized this duality, and chose to emphasize the latter. "The camera must be used for recording life [he wrote in his *Daybook*] for rendering the very substance and quintessence of

Opposite page: SHEELER: Stair well, 1914. GEH

EDWARD WESTON: Palma Cuernavaca II, 1925. Platinum print. GEH

Opposite page top: EDWARD WESTON: Cloud, Mexico, 1926. Platinum print. GEH

Opposite page bottom: EDWARD WESTON: Nude, 1925. Platinum print. GEH

the thing itself... I shall let no chance pass to record interesting abstractions, but I feel definite in my belief that the approach to photography is through realism."[10] His technique and esthetic became one: "Unless I pull a technically fine print from a technically fine negative, the emotional or intellectual value of the photograph is for me almost negated." He simplified his working method, preferring contact prints to enlargements, glossy bromide paper to the softer platinotype. He replaced his expensive soft focus lens with an inexpensive sharply cutting rapid rectilinear. "The shutter stops down to 256,"* he noted. "This should satisfy my craving for more depth of focus."

The most important part of Edward Weston's approach was his insistence that the photographer should previsualize the final print before making the exposure. The classic 8 by 10-inch view camera which had become his favorite instrument enabled him to see and study the image in its full size upon the ground glass. He respected this image so highly that cropping or trimming the final print he considered an admission of failure to see in a creative way.

Weston developed this approach to the point of virtuosity. He used the 8 by 10 camera, developed his negatives with finger-blackening pyro, printed by contact on glossy paper. He rejected enlarging because he felt that there was inevitably some loss of the precision of image, that quality of definition which he so highly prized. He demanded clarity of form, he wanted every area of his picture clear-cut, with the substances and textures of things appreciable to the point of illusion. The fact that the camera can see more than the unaided eye he long regarded as one of the great miracles of photography. In a Weston landscape, everything is sharp from the immediate foreground to the extreme distance: looking at the same scene in nature our eyes take in one detail after another. Constantly roving, jumping from spot to spot, they scan the panorama and send to the brain a series of reports from which a composite image is mentally created. In the photographs the details are so compressed and reduced that the scanning process requires far less muscular effort on the part of the beholder, who unconsciously feels a physiological release. In 1909 Willi Warstat, in his *Allgemeine Ästhetik der Photographie*, a book which is perhaps the earliest systematic examination of photographic esthetics from the standpoint of modern psychological and physiological theories of vision, succinctly analyzed this aspect of the mechanics of seeing. He found that

* The lens, now in the George Eastman House Collection, the gift of Brett Weston, is marked in the Uniform System. The *f*-number is 64.

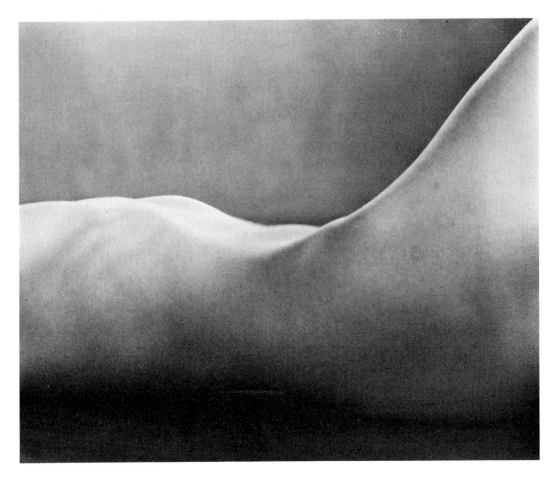

EDWARD WESTON: Artichoke, halved, 1930. MOMA GEH

EDWARD WESTON: White dunes, Oceano, California, 1936. MOMA GEH

EDWARD WESTON: Nude, 1936. MOMA GEH

the compression of all-over detail was something to be avoided by the photographer in his "battle with realism." Weston had no quarrel with realism. His vision led him to a straight, often brutally direct, approach which made use of the phenomenon with powerful effects. It must be noted, however, that the rendering of detail alone was not his criterion; it was governed by his taste, imagination, and feeling for form.

In 1937 Edward Weston was awarded a John Simon Guggenheim Memorial Foundation Fellowship – the first photographer to be so honored. His style expanded, the variety of subject matter increased, and a rich human quality pervaded his later work. His last photographs, intricately organized and of great force, were made on his beloved Point Lobos on the California coast not far from his home in Carmel in 1948. Tragically he was stricken with Parkinson's disease, and could no longer photograph. Through the generosity of friends he was able to supervise the printing by his sons of a thousand of the negatives he considered his best. He died in Carmel on New Year's Day, 1958.

In 1932 a number of younger photographers, greatly impressed by Weston and his work, formed a society to which they gave the name "Group f.64," choosing that technical term because they set their lenses at small apertures to achieve detailed images. The charter members – Ansel Adams, Imogen Cunningham, John Paul Edwards, Sonia Noskowiak, Henry Swift, Willard Van Dyke, and Edward Weston – formulated an esthetic based on the straight approach. It was a reaction against pictorial photography, which had become so conservative that it had been defined in *The Encyclopaedia Britannica* in 1929 as "photography applied to the production of pictures in the accepted artistic tradition." There was no room in the salons for independent photographers who had no desire to follow an accepted artistic tradition, but felt a compulsion to break out upon new paths. They held their own exhibitions: the M. H. de Young Memorial Museum in San Francisco threw open its doors to them for the inaugural show in 1932. For several years the informal group was the most progressive photographic society in the country. Even after they disbanded, their influence persisted; and "f.64" came to be a convenient label for straight

EDWARD WESTON: Point Lobos, California, 1946. MOMA GEH

ADAMS: Picket fence, 1936

photography, applied to photographers who had nothing to do with the original group.

Ansel Adams, in his photography, his writing and his teaching, has brilliantly demonstrated the capabilities of straight photography as a medium of expression. He was trained as a musician, and began to photograph as an avocation under the strong influence of pictorialism. In 1930 he met Paul Strand, whose negatives so impressed him that he realized the validity of the straight approach and began to devote all of his time to photography. His new work received international recognition when the London *Studio* published in 1935 his *Making a Photograph*, an instruction manual distinguished for its illustrations, which are such faithful reproductions that they have more than once been mistaken for actual photographic prints. When the book appeared it seemed as if the substance of weathered stone, glass and flesh had never been so brilliantly rendered. His work was shown by Stieglitz at An American Place in 1936; it had sensitivity and direct, honest integrity that were rare. Conservationist, mountaineer, lover of the wilderness, he has long specialized in the interpretation of the natural scene. His spectacular photographs have appeared in many books produced under his direct supervision. Like Strand, and in the tradition of Emerson, Stieglitz and Coburn, he has learned the complexities of photomechanical reproduction. He produces prints specifically for the engraver's camera and checks proofs on the printing press itself, so that the results will be as close to his original concept as possible. *This Is the American Earth* (1960) is a magnificent poem of the land and man's relation to it, with photographs by Adams and others, edited and written by Nancy Newhall.

Adams uses all kinds of cameras and constantly experiments with new techniques. He has worked out a highly ingenious and practical rationale for determining exposure and development, which gives the photographer precise control over his materials, based upon the scientific investigations of Hurter & Driffield and the subsequent work of C. E. K. Mees, H. P. Rockwell, and John Davenport. Adams first teaches the photographer to master the characteristics of the photographic emulsion by determining – not by laboratory test, but with the photographer's own working equipment – the interrelation of the three principal variables: subject luminance (i.e, brightness), exposure and development, so that he can obtain upon his negative any one tone which he has visualized, and will know exactly the tones that other subject luminances will create. The infinite gradations of light and shade found

in nature he groups in ten zones. Zone O is black; IX, white. Between these extremes are eight tones of gray, zone V being the "middle" tint – not by objective measurement, but by subjective judgment – and next to it, marked VI, the value which conveys to the photographer the feeling of the tone of average, well-lighted skin. By the use of a photoelectric exposure meter he measures the luminances of the various parts of the scene which he is photographing. These measurements are correlated with exposure and development procedures, so that the photographer can visualize the entire gamut of values which will appear in the final print. The control is comparable to that which a musician has over his instrument. Guesswork is eliminated, and the photographer can concentrate upon esthetic problems, secure in the knowledge that his results will not only be of technical excellence, but will embody his subjective interpretation of the scene.

On the Continent the functional spirit of the 1920's found its expression more in the design potentialities of the photographic medium, and in the ability of the camera to isolate form so it can be appreciated abstractly, without relation to its function. There were exceptions. Albert Renger-Patzsch's book *Die Welt ist schön* – "The World is Beautiful" – was hailed on its appearance in 1928 as the photographic counterpart of the New Objectivity ("Neue Sachlichkeit") movement in painting. What the critics overlooked was the significance of the title, for Renger-Patzsch, unlike the studio-bound painters of the time, looked at the world and found it beautiful. He took his camera everywhere at a time when European artists in all media were avoiding any contact with nature, and creating their own world. Like Strand, Sheeler, Weston and Adams, he was exploring and interpreting the exterior world. He died in Wamel Dorf, near Essen, Germany, in 1966. His most recent book was a series of photographs of forests.

ADAMS: Mono Lake, California, 1947. GEH

ADAMS: Mount Williamson—Clearing Storm, 1944. MOMA GEH

ATGET: Lampshade peddler, Paris, c. 1910. GEH (Man Ray Coll.)

The growing appreciation of straight photography brought about the recognition in the late twenties of photographers of the older generation whose work had been overlooked by the pictorialists. Jean Eugène Auguste Atget was virtually unknown when he died in 1927. He never showed in a salon. Not a single one of the hundreds of photographs which he had taken since 1898 of his beloved Paris had been reproduced in a photographic magazine. Painters had found his street scenes helpful documents, and the Surrealist artists, ever sensitive to the melancholy that a good photograph can so powerfully evoke, reproduced a few of his pictures in 1926 in their magazine *La Révolution surréaliste*. When, a year later, Atget died, Berenice Abbott, the American photographer, rescued his negatives from oblivion, became custodian of them, printed them, arranged exhibitions and published his work; it is to her that we owe the rich heritage of Atget.

Of his early life we know but little. From his friend André Calmettes, Berenice Abbott learned that he was born near Bordeaux in 1856, early lost his parents, was reared by an uncle, and went to sea. He was an actor when Calmettes first met him in Paris, but not a particularly successful one, and he decided, after considering painting, to take up photography. "He already had the ambition of creating a collection of everything artistic and picturesque in and about Paris," Calmettes wrote. *Photographe d'art*, photographer of works of art, he called himself, and he hand lettered a sign "Documents pour artistes" for the door of his fifth-floor apartment-darkroom at 31 rue Campagne Première. A great deal of his work was photographing the historic buildings of Paris in detail. He made a series of photographs of iron grill work, another of the fountains of Paris. He photographed the statues in the park at Versailles, and statues on the medieval churches in Paris. These he sold to the Parisian museums. But he did not limit himself to works of art and historic monuments: he photographed the face of Paris in all its aspects: shop fronts and carriages of all sorts, the little people who earn their living peddling umbrellas or lampshades, delivering bread or wheeling pushcarts. He photographed inside palaces, bourgeois homes and ragpickers' hovels. He photographed trees and flowers and fallen autumn leaves. Each of these categories is a series, each comprising hundreds of photographs. For Atget was in truth, as Calmettes wrote, a collector. He was, too, a picture maker, *un imagier*, in the words of his friend.

His technique was of the simplest: a view camera – always used on a tripod – for plates 18 by 24 centimeters ($7\frac{1}{8}$ by $9\frac{3}{8}$ inches) in size. His lens was a rapid rectilinear, used well stopped down. Its focal length is not known – it was discarded after his death – but it must have been fairly short, for so many of his pictures show steep perspective and the tops of many of the negatives show bare glass where the image fell off. He printed the glass plates by daylight on glossy surfaced printing-out paper, toning them with gold chloride. Atget's technical approach was, therefore, that of the nineteenth century and, looking at his prints, it is often hard to believe that he did most of his work after 1900. He seldom made an exposure which could be called a snapshot: moving objects are often blurred, and when he photographed people it is obvious that he asked them to pose. In an Atget photograph every detail stands forth with a clarity which is remarkable.

Among the thousands of photographs which Atget took, there are those which reach beyond the record and approach the lyric. For he had a remarkable vision.

ATGET: Uniforms, Les Halles, Paris, c. 1910. GEH (Man Ray Coll.)

ATGET: Shop window: Tailor dummies, c. 1910. GEH (Man Ray Coll.)

THOMSON: The Temperance Sweep. Woodburytype in *Street Life in London*, by J. Thomson and Adolphe Smith, London, 1877. MOMA GEH

THOMSON: Covent Garden Flower Women. Woodburytype in *Street Life in London*, by J. Thomson and Adolphe Smith, London, 1877. MOMA GEH

He could find human quality where no human being appears. His interiors lead one to feel that the people whose home he is photographing have just stepped behind the camera while he focuses and makes his exposure and will return the moment the lens is closed. Out-of-doors he worked early in the morning to avoid being disturbed by the curious, and his pictures have the atmosphere of early light. His work has no reference to any graphic medium other than photography. The example of his work inspired many younger photographers and greatly influenced the development of documentary photography.

The quality of authenticity implicit in the sharply-focused, unretouched straight photograph often gives it special value as evidence or proof. Such a photograph can be, according to dictionary definition, "documentary," for Webster defines the noun "document" as "an original or official paper relied upon as the basis, proof, or support of anything else; – in its most extend-

ed sense, including any writing, book, or other instrument conveying information."

In 1889 a plea was made in the *British Journal of Photography*[1] for the formation of a great archive of photographs "containing a record as complete as it can be made... of the present state of the world" and it was pointed out that such photographs "will be most valuable documents a century hence." *McClure's Magazine* published in 1893–94 a series of photographic portraits under the title "Human Documents." And Henri Matisse, the painter, wrote Alfred Stieglitz in 1908: "Photography can provide the most precious documents existing."[2]

The documentary photographer seeks to do more than convey information through his photographs: his aim is to persuade and to convince. The United States Congress was persuaded to set apart the Yellowstone region as a national park by the convincing evidence of William H. Jackson's photographs which had been

RIIS: Baxter Street Alley in Mulberry Bend, New York, 1888. Print by Alexander Alland from original negative in the Museum of the City of New York. MOMA GEH
"At 59 Baxter street is ... an alley in from the sidewalk with tenements on either side crowding so close as to almost shut out the light of day. On the one side they are brick and on the other wood, but there is little difference in their ricketiness and squalor. This is also an Italian colony and the bags of rags and bones and paper shown are gathered by these people, despite the laws and ordinances and the 3,000 police."—— Jacob A. Riis in New York *Sun*, Feb. 12, 1888.

presented to its members by Ferdinand V. Hayden as documents; they made credible the reports of natural wonders which until then had been dismissed as the tall tales of travelers. Public conscience was awakened to injustices by the power of the camera's evidence: in 1862 the editor of the English *Art Journal* found a series of photographs of Manchester to "have an especial, though painful, interest just now, from the fact that they were views of the great manufacturing districts, where terrible destitution prevails."[3]

Wood engravings from daguerreotypes taken by Richard Beard were used to document the three-volume *London Labour and London Poor* (1851–1864), a pioneer sociological study by Henry Mayhew, John Binny, and others. The engravings were crude, and lacked the conviction which the original daguerreotypes must have had. Inspired by this work, John Thomson and Adolphe Smith wrote and illustrated a similar book, *Street Life in London* (1877), illustrated with thirty-six photographs of London poor, probably taken by Thomson, who had photographed extensively in the Far East. The photographs were reproduced in facsimile by the woodburytype process (Chapter 13), and carried great impact and sense of authenticity. In their preface Thomson and Smith stated that they had brought to bear

the precision of photography in illustration of our subject. The unquestionable accuracy of this testimony will enable us to present true types of the London Poor and shield us from the accusation of either underrating or exaggerating individual peculiarities of appearance.

A decade later Jacob A. Riis, through photographs as well as his writing, not only showed Americans how the other half lived, but persuaded them to take action which led to the betterment of the living conditions of the New York poor.

For seven years Riis, who arrived in New York from Denmark in 1870, suffered the lot of every immigrant. He took what jobs he could find. He came to know from personal experience the tenements, the police-station lodging houses, the all-night two-cent restaurants. When he came to be a police reporter his work took him back to those wretched quarters of the city, for they were the seed beds of crime. Horrified, he began the crusade which led to the condemnation of Mulberry Bend, to housing reforms, and to the building of the neighborhood house which bears his name.

He reported what he saw not only in words, but also in pictures. In 1888 the *Sun* published twelve drawings from his photographs with an article headlined "Flashes from the Slums" and told how

RIIS: Italian mother and her baby in Jersey St., New York, 1888. Print by Alexander Alland from original negative in the Museum of the City of New York. MOMA GEH

a mysterious party has lately been startling the town o'nights. Somnolent policemen on the street, denizens of the dives in their dens, tramps and bummers in their so-called lodgings, and all the people of the wild and wonderful variety of New York night life have in their turn marvelled at and been frightened by the phenomenon. What they saw was three or four figures in the gloom, a ghostly tripod, some weird and uncanny movements, the blinding flash, and then they heard the patter of retreating footsteps and the mysterious visitors were gone before they could collect their scattered thoughts and try to find out what it was all about.[4]

The intruders were two amateur photographers, Henry G. Piffard and Richard Hoe Lawrence (members, be it noted, of that Society of Amateur Photographers of New York which later consolidated with the Camera Club), Dr. John T. Nagle of the Health Board, and Riis. The purpose of their trip, Riis stated, was to make a collection of views for lantern slides to show "as no mere description could, the misery and vice that he had noticed in his ten years of experience... and suggest the direction in which good might be done."[5]

In the 1880's facsimile reproduction techniques had not reached the point at which photographs could be printed in newspapers, and the column-wide drawings accompanying the article were not convincing. When Riis's famous book *How the Other Half Lives* was published in 1890, seventeen of the illustrations were halftones, but of poor quality, lacking detail and sharpness. The remaining nineteen photographs were shown in drawings made from them: some of them are signed "Kenyon Cox, 1889, after photograph."

HINE: Carolina Cotton Mill, 1908. MOMA GEH

The result was that the photographic work of Jacob Riis was overlooked until, in 1947, Alexander Alland, himself a photographer, made excellent enlargements from the original 4 by 5-inch glass negatives which the Museum of the City of New York, through his efforts, had acquired. The exhibition held by the Museum, and the subsequent publication of some of the best of the prints in *U. S. Camera 1948*, revealed Riis as a photographer of importance.

The photographs are direct and penetrating, as raw as the sordid scenes which they so often represent. Riis chose unerringly the camera stand which would most effectively tell the story. Not all of his photographs were made at night, nor did he always use the flash-and-run technique. There are glimpses in *How the Other Half Lives* of his experiences:

Yet even from Hell's Kitchen had I not long before been driven forth with my camera by a band of angry women, who pelted me with brickbats and stones on my retreat, shouting at me never to come back.... The children know generally what they want and they go

for it by the shortest cut. I found that out, whether I had flowers to give or pictures to take.... Their determination to be "took" the moment the camera hove into sight, in the most striking pose they could hastily devise, was always the most formidable bar to success I met.

Riis was one of the first in America to use *Blitzlichtpulver* – flashlight powder – invented in Germany in 1887 by Adolf Miethe and Johannes Gaedicke. This innovation was a highly explosive mixture of powdered magnesium, potassium chlorate and antimony sulphide. Because it burned instantaneously – in a flash – it was an improvement over the magnesium flare, with its several seconds duration, which O'Sullivan had used in the Comstock Lode mines. Yet it was dangerous and difficult to control. Riis succeeded in its use; the blinding flash reveals with pitiless detail the sordid interiors, but deals almost tenderly with the faces of those whose lot it was to live within them.

He was always sympathetic to people, whether he was photographing street Arabs stealing in the street

HINE: Italian family seeking lost baggage, Ellis Island, 1905. MOMA GEH

TINA MODOTTI: Mother and child from Tehuantepec, Oaxaca, Mexico, c. 1929. MOMA

from a handcart, or the inhabitants of the alley known as Bandits' Roost peering unselfconsciously at the camera from doorways and stoops and windows. The importance of these photographs lies in their power not only to inform us, but to move us. They are at once interpretations and records; although they are no longer topical, they contain qualities which will last as long as man is concerned with his brother.

This is true, too, of the work of Lewis W. Hine, who began to photograph in 1905. A sociologist, trained at Chicago, Columbia and New York Universities, he found the camera a powerful tool for research. His training enabled him to comprehend instantly, and without effort, the background and its social implications; unbothered by unnecessary details, his sympathies were concentrated on the individual before him; throughout his pictures this harmony can be felt. When, with his 5 by 7-inch camera and open flash, he photographed children working in factories, he showed them at the machines, introducing a sense of scale which enabled the reader to grasp the fact that the workers were in-

deed small children. His work was widely published; indeed, the word "photo story" was first used to describe his work, which was always of equal importance with the writer's and in no sense an "illustration" to it. His revelation of the exploitation of children led to the passing of child labor laws. In the years before the First World War Hine took his camera to Ellis Island, to record the immigrants who were then arriving by the tens of thousands. He followed them into the unsavory tenements which became their homes, penetrated into the miserable sweatshops where they found work, and photographed their children playing among the ash-cans and the sprawling human derelicts in the slums of New York and Washington. Hine realized, as Riis did before him, that his photographs were subjective and, for that very reason, were powerful and readily grasped criticisms of the impact of an economic system on the lives of underprivileged and exploited classes. He described his work as "photo-interpretations." They were published as "human documents." Hine by no means limited his photography to negative criticism, but brought out the positive human qualities wherever he found them. In 1918 he photographed American Red Cross relief in the Middle European countries; years later he concentrated on American workmen, and a collection of photographs of them was published in 1932 as *Men at Work*.

Perhaps the best photographs in the book were chosen from the hundreds he took of the construction of the Empire State Building in New York. Day by day, floor by floor, he followed the steelwork upwards. With the workmen he toasted sandwiches over the forges that heated the rivets; he walked the girders at dizzying heights, carrying over his shoulder his 5 by 7-inch view camera complete with tripod or, more rarely, a 4 by 5-inch Graflex. When he and the workmen reached the pinnacle of the world's tallest building, he had them swing him out over the city from a crane, so that he might photograph in mid-air the moment they had all been striving for – the driving of the final rivet at the very top of the skyscraper. These spectacular pictures are not melodramatic; they were not taken for sensation; they are a straightforward record of a job that happened to be dangerous. Among the photographs there is not one of Hine himself perched high above the city. His interest was entirely absorbed by the workmen and their job.

On his death in 1940, Hine's negatives were preserved by the Photo League, a society of photographers who had received much counsel from him and who had frequently exhibited his photographs. On the dissolu-

LANGE: Migrant mother, Nipomo, California, 1936. MOMA GEH
"Camped on the edge of a pea field where the crop had failed in a freeze. The tires had just been sold from the car to buy food. She was 32 years old with seven children." — Dorothea Lange, field notes.

EVANS: Interior detail, West Virginia coal miner's house, 1935.
Library of Congress, Washington, D.C.

tion of the society, the negatives were deposited at the George Eastman House, Rochester, N. Y.

When the darkness of the depression fell upon the world in the 1930's, many artists at once reacted to it. In the field of painting, the return to realism became more pronounced; following the lead of the Mexican muralists, painters began to instruct the public through their work. A group of independent moving-picture makers had already begun to make films which, in contrast to the typical Hollywood productions, were rooted in real problems, real situations, in which the participants themselves were the actors. John Grierson, spokesman for a British group, recollects that they felt that the moving picture

in the recording and the interpretation of fact was a new instrument of public influence which might increase experience and bring the new world of our citizenship into the imagination. It promised us the power of making drama from our daily lives and poetry from our problems.[6]

They called this type of film *documentary*.

As social photographers they shied away from the word "artistic," and the voluminous literature of the movement is full of insistence that documentary film is *not* art. "Beauty is one of the greatest dangers to documentary," wrote the producer Paul Rotha in his *Documentary Film*.[7] He came to the astonishing conclusion that photography – the very life blood and essence of the moving picture – was of secondary importance, and that, if too good, might prove detrimental. "Photographic excellence in documentary must never be permitted to become a virtue in itself." Yet Grierson said, "documentary was from the beginning... an 'anti-aesthetic' movement ...what confuses the history is that we had always the good sense to use the aesthetes. We did so because we liked them and because we needed them. It was, paradoxically, with the first-rate aesthetic help of people like Robert Flaherty and Alberto Cavalcanti... that we mastered the techniques necessary for our unaesthetic purposes."[8]

Documentary is, therefore, an approach which makes use of the artistic faculties to give "vivification to fact" – to use Walt Whitman's definition of the place of poetry in the modern world.

At the same time that film makers began to talk about "documentary," here and there photographers were independently using their cameras in a similar way. Walker Evans had returned to America from Paris with a heightened perception of the American spirit. A number of his photographs published in the magazine *Hound and Horn* for 1930 show a tendency to-

Opposite page: EVANS: Maine pump, 1933. MOMA

BOURKE-WHITE: Hamilton, Alabama. From *You Have Seen Their Faces*, by Erskine Caldwell and Margaret Bourke-White, New York, 1937

ward abstraction somewhat Continental in feeling: *Wash Day*, for example, is a pattern of laden clothesline against the sky. In this year he began a series of photographs of the homespun and then little appreciated architecture of the Victorian period. In contrast to these sharply focused four-square architectural studies he also did pictures of people in the streets, catching them unawares in characteristic and revealing attitudes.

Like so many citizens, Evans felt the consequences of the depression sharply; with a sense of responsibility to his fellow men he used the camera to awaken the public to the plight of the unemployed. *South Street 1932* shows men sleeping on the sill of a waterfront façade. It is a fine photograph. Its sensitive rendition of texture and form reinforces by its beauty the sociological comment to which the photographic image lends authenticity.

In San Francisco Dorothea Lange, a member of Group *f*.64, had for years a successful portrait studio. During the depression she saw the breadlines of the homeless and unemployed and wondered if she could photograph them so that others would feel as she did. She met Paul Taylor, a professor of economics, who gave her work to do; on a trip with him she began to see how the photographer could complement the work of the economist. The State of California was her first employer, and she documented the problems of the migratory workers.

In 1935 the Federal Government turned to photographers for help in fighting the depression, for those in Washington found that the evidence of the camera could be a great tool for education. Photographers were hired at a fair salary, given the best equipment, and sent to stricken areas to report conditions. The Department of Agriculture, under Rexford G. Tugwell, formed an historical section of the Resettlement Administration (later known as the Farm Security Administration); Roy E. Stryker, who had been a colleague of Tugwell's at Columbia University, was put in charge. The first to be hired was Arthur Rothstein, now Director of Photography for *Look* magazine, in July, 1935. There followed others, notably Walker Evans and Dorothea Lange.

Evans continued his dual interest in American form and in the American face, the architectural and the portrait. He traveled to the South and documented the conditions of the land, the sharecroppers themselves, their houses, their belongings, the way they worked, their crops, their schools, and churches and stores. Much of what he photographed was necessarily squalid, but the interpretation was always dignified. Glenway Wescott pointed out that

ROTHSTEIN: Father and son walking in the face of a dust storm, Cimaron County, Oklahoma, 1936. MOMA GEH

SANDER: *Peasant Couple*, 1931. MOMA

others have photographed squalid scenes wonderfully; but it has been a wonder dispersed, hit-or-miss in a thousand rotogravure sections, etc. Here is a lot of it, all hanging together: fantastic martyred furniture, lampshades and pictures, rags, hats. Usually Mr. Evans has dismissed the dweller from his dwelling, but we can deduce him. Thus one sometimes sees, in wild grass, the indentations where a rabbit has been lying, hungering, quaking. Countrymen of ours like rabbits.... For me this is better propaganda than it would be if it were not aesthetically enjoyable. It is because I enjoy looking that I go on looking until the pity and the shame are impressed upon me, unforgettably. And on the superb, absurd old houses... there has fallen – along with the neglect and decay – an illumination of pearl, shadows of sable, accentuations as orderly as in music. Look at them. I find that I do not tire of them. Look at the old mansion upon which the rottenness of the wood appears like the marks of a sort of kiss.[9]

Dorothea Lange specialized in the problem of the migratory workers, and documented the long trek across the country of the people tractored off their land. Pare Lorentz noted in *U. S. Camera 1941*[10] that

if there are transient camps, and better working conditions, and a permanent agency seeking to help migratory workers, Lange, with her still pictures that have been reproduced in thousands of newspapers, and in magazines and Sunday supplements, and Steinbeck, with two novels, a play, and a motion picture have done more for these tragic nomads than all the politicians of the country.

Steinbeck's novel, *The Grapes of Wrath*, and the motion picture made from it, grew from an assignment from *Life* magazine. In the issue dated February 19, 1940, the editors published six pairs of photographs taken in 1938 by Horace Bristol "when he and author Steinbeck toured the Oakie camps in search of material for a picture book and a story for *Life*. The picture book was dropped to make way for a best-selling novel called *Grapes of Wrath*. Never before had the facts behind a great work of fiction been so carefully researched by the newscamera."

The scope of the FSA photographic project included all phases of rural America. The small town is such an integral part of our agricultural fabric that it could not be overlooked. Sherwood Anderson found enough material in the thousands of photographs in the FSA files to make a picture book, *Home Town*, showing the positive side of typical American community life.

During the course of its seven years, until its entire resources were, during the war, turned over to the Office of War Information, the FSA photographic project employed, in addition to Rothstein, Evans and Lange, Ben Shahn, Russell Lee, John Vachon, Theodor Jung, Paul Carter, Marion Post Wolcott, Jack Delano,

Carl Mydans, John Collier, Jr., and Arthur Siegel. The work which is now deposited in the Library of Congress is remarkably cohesive and yet individual. Each photographer contributed to the project: working together, sharing common problems, they helped one another. The scope of the documentation and its general aim were controlled and guided by Stryker, who briefed the photographers on the sociological background of their assignments, stimulated their imagination and encouraged their curiosity. Not a photographer himself, Stryker wisely left all questions of equipment, technique and style of visualization to the individual photographers. Stryker has pointed out:

Documentary is an approach, not a technic; an affirmation, not a negation.... The documentary attitude is not a denial of the plastic elements which must remain essential criteria in any work. It merely gives these elements limitation and direction. Thus composition becomes emphasis, and line sharpness, focus, filtering, mood – all those components included in the dreamy vagueness "quality" – are made to serve an end: to speak, as eloquently as possible, of the thing to be said in the language of pictures.... The question is not what to picture nor what camera to use. Every phase of our time and our surroundings has vital significance and any camera in good repair is an adequate instrument. The job is to know enough about the subject matter to find its significance in itself and in relation to its surroundings, its time, and its function.[11]

The documentary approach was eagerly pursued elsewhere. Margaret Bourke-White, who had made an enviable reputation as a photographer of industry and as an associate editor of *Fortune* and *Life* magazines, produced with Erskine Caldwell a photographic survey of the South in *You Have Seen Their Faces* (1937). Eleven pages of *Life* for May 10, 1937 were devoted to her photographs of Muncie, Indiana, the city which had been chosen by Robert and Helen Lynd for their sociological study, *Middletown*, published in 1927. Bourke-White's photographic essay was presented as "an important American document"; it showed the aspect of the city from the ground and from the air, the homes of the rich and the poor; it was an unusually graphic cross section of an American town.

New York found its interpreter in Berenice Abbott, who in 1929 decided to give up her Paris studio, where she had produced many striking portraits of artists and writers, and return to America. Impressed by the complex and ever-varied life of New York, she began the task of interpreting not alone the outward

ABBOTT: Exchange Place, New York, 1933. MOMA

aspect of the metropolis, but its very spirit. At first she worked alone, then under the auspices of the Art Project of the Works Progress Administration. The negatives which she made, and a master set of prints from them, are now in the Museum of the City of New York; they are historical source material, for many of the landmarks which she photographed no longer exist. A selection of her work was published in book form with the appropriate title *Changing New York* in 1939. She writes:

To make the portrait of a city is a life work and no one portrait suffices, because the city is always changing. Everything in the city is properly part of its story – its physical body of brick, stone, steel, glass, wood, its lifeblood of living, breathing men and women. Streets, vistas, panoramas, bird's eye views and worm's eye views, the noble and the shameful, high life and low life, tragedy, comedy, squalor, wealth, the mighty towers of skyscrapers, the ignoble façades of slums, people at work, people at home, people at play....[12]

In her instruction manual, *A Guide to Better Photography*, she advises the photographer to use as large a camera as possible, so that the records will be fully detailed and rich in information. Such photographs can be read; they are not mere illustrations, but actual source material.

Fox Talbot observed in *The Pencil of Nature* that

it frequently happens, moreover – and this is one of the charms of photography – that the operator himself discovers on examination, perhaps long afterwards, that he had depicted many things he had no notion of at the time. Sometimes inscriptions and dates are found upon the buildings, or printed placards more irrelevant, are discovered upon their walls....

It is significant that, time after time, the documentary photographer includes in his image printed words and wall scrawls. More than one photographer, in the bitterness of the thirties, chose to contrast billboard slogans with the contrary evidence of the camera. A sign, photographed as an object, carries more impact than the literal transcription of the words it bears. Signs alone have furnished subject matter: Todd Webb, returning to America from overseas service, made a moving series of documents of those temporary and homespun "Welcome Home GI Joe" signs which flourished in New York in 1945.

However revealing or beautiful a documentary photograph may be, it cannot stand upon its image alone. Paradoxically, before a photograph can be accepted as a document, it must itself be documented – placed in time and space. This may be effectively done by context, by including the familiar with the unfamiliar, either in one image or in paired images. A series of

photographs, presented in succession on exhibition walls or on the pages of a book, may be greater than the sum of the parts. Thus in *American Photographs*, published by The Museum of Modern Art at the time of his exhibition, Walker Evans arranged his photographs in two separate series, and relied upon the sequence of images to show, in the first part, "the physiognomy of a nation," and in the second part, "the continuous fact of an indigenous American expression," to quote from Lincoln Kirstein's text. Each photograph was numbered, and factual titles were supplied at the end of each section. In a collaborative work with the writer James Agee, *Let Us Now Praise Famous Men* (1941), Evans grouped thirty-one photographs in the front of the book, in front of the title page itself. They were presented without a single word of explanation. They were, Agee wrote, "...not illustrative. They, and the text, are coequal, mutually independent, and fully collaborative."

In contrast to the austerity of this technique, Dorothea Lange and Paul Taylor in *An American Exodus* (1939) presented a close relation between the image and the word by printing with the photographs excerpts from conversation heard or overheard at the time of photographing – an approach in itself fully documentary in spirit. Yet another device was used in *Land of the Free* (1938), a collection of documentary photographs, mostly from the FSA files, to which Archibald MacLeish supplied a "sound track" in the form of a poem. He explained that

The original purpose had been to write some sort of text to which these photographs might serve as commentary. But so great was the power and stubborn inward livingness of these vivid American documents that the result was a reversal of that plan.

In all of these, and in many other publications of similar nature, the chief characteristic is that the photographs assert their independence. They are not illustrations. They carry the message together with the text.

"Documentary," in the sense in which we have described it, has been accepted as the definition of a style. Since World War II the movement has lost impetus, and most of the photographers active in it have turned to photojournalism and the publication of books. Substitutes have been suggested for the word documentary: historical, factual, realistic. While each of these qualities is contained within documentary, none of them conveys the deep respect for fact and the desire to create active interpretations of the world in which we live that mark documentary photography at its best apart from bald camera records.

MORGAN: Martha Graham in "Letter to the World," 1944. GEH

JACQUES HENRI LARTIGUE: Grand Prix of the Automobile Club of France, 1912. MOMA

The use of small cameras to produce big pictures was first suggested as a convenience. In 1840 John W. Draper reported that he was making enlarged copies of daguerreotypes

with a view of ascertaining the possibility of diminishing the bulk of the traveler's Daguerreotype apparatus, on the principle of copying views on very minute plates, with a very minute camera, and then magnifying them subsequently to any required size, by means of a stationary apparatus.[1]

With the perfection of the collodion process, this system was put to use. Thomas Skaife devised a miniature camera with an $f/2.2$ lens in 1858 for plates one inch square. They were enlarged by hand: the negative was projected to the desired size, and the image was traced. In 1865 Charles Piazzi Smyth, Astronomer Royal for Scotland, made an expedition to Egypt to study the alleged mathematical and astronomical symbolism of the Great Pyramid. Unable to afford the initial expense and upkeep of a standard size camera, he devised a miniature one. For plates he used 1 by 3-inch microscope slides, a square inch of which he sensitized and developed in the camera itself. In a pamphlet, *A Poor Man's Photography at the Great Pyramid* (1870), he claimed that enlargements from his negatives showed as much detail as contact prints from whole plates. He had planned to illustrate his three-volume book, *Life and Work at the Great Pyramid* with his photographs, and made sixty positive transparencies for the purpose, but the cost of reproducing them was so great that he abandoned the plan and gave them away.

Piazzi Smyth argued that his system had the advantage not only of portability, but also of flexibility:

with his little box of very little negatives brought home modestly in his waistcoat pocket [the impecunious photographer] sits him down at a table, having a compound achromatic microscope before him... and then... wanders at will, truly the monarch of all he surveys, over the various parts of each picture; recalls the circumstances under which it was taken; discovers characteristic detail which he never dreamed of before; and then – each picture you will remember having been taken *square* – he decides whether a positive copy should be shaped as a long, i.e. horizontal, rectangle, or as a tall, i.e. vertical, rectangle; whether it should include from side to side of the negative plate or stop short of its extreme parts, in order to secure a better balance of light and shade, or a more harmonious composition of light and angles; whether he should give preponderance to the sky or to the foreground; or whether some special scientific purpose may not be better served by extracting one little subject alone out of the whole scene, and making a very highly magnified picture of that one item by itself.

With all these notes taken at the microscope, the poor man then inserts his little negative into a copying and magnifying camera, and proceeds to realize all these various positive pictures, hitherto only sketched out in art or scientific idea, and makes them on any size that he can afford.[2]

With the advent of hand cameras and dry plates at the close of the century, and with the perfection of enlargers and rapid printing paper, Piazzi Smyth's system of choosing a portion of the negative for the final print became regular practice. Stieglitz in 1896 wrote that his hand camera negatives were "all made for the express purpose of enlargement, and it is but rarely that I use more than part of the original 'shot.'"[3] Instruction manuals and camera magazines became full of a new kind of criticism; beginners were shown how their prints could be improved by cropping or trimming, and they were advised to try masking their proofs with L-shaped cardboards. Except for isolated experiments like Piazzi Smyth's, the entire image formed by the camera had previously been so rigidly respected that daguerreotypes, tintypes, cartes-de-visite and stereographs were all made in standard sizes.

The portable hand camera thus brought about a change in working methods. The photographers' output was increased, and oftentimes the recorded camera image was merely a starting point for the final composition. The hand camera also increased the scope of photography, for with it many subjects generally considered beyond the limits of photography were now brought within grasp.

At the turn of the century, technical innovations broadened the camera's field of operation still further. Lenses were designed which produced images far more brilliant than before, and small, compact precision cameras fitted with high speed shutters were made, on which the powerful lenses could be used. The small negatives were intended for enlarging.

Jules Carpentier, who built the Cinématographe for the Lumières, designed a precision camera in 1892 which he named the *Photo-Jumelle*, because it looked like a pair of binoculars (*jumelle* in French). It had two identical lenses. One formed an image on the 2¼ by 1½-inch dry plate; the other formed an image on a ground glass which the photographer could see through a red filter when he held the little camera to his eye. The Photo-Jumelle was built to exacting specifications. Carpentier demanded a tolerance of ±0.001 in., a degree of precision unheard of in the camera industry of the day. The camera was loaded with twelve plates which were changed by pulling out and pushing in a brass rod. A sliding, spring-operated shutter worked at a speed of 1/60 second. The lens was set at fixed focus; Carpentier stated that photographers were incapable of focusing accurately enough to permit sharp enlargements to be made. A fixed-focus enlarger was sold as an accessory: he boasted that with it "the original negatives are easily increased to ½-plate size [6½ × 4¼ in.] – a matter of considerable moment to operators making views for practical purposes."[4]

The Photo-Jumelle was so popular that it was widely imitated, and became a classic camera type. Jumelles were fitted with lenses of larger diameter than Carpentier's modest *f*/11 doublet, and focal plane shutters with adjustable speeds replaced his simple guillotine. Guido Sigriste in 1899 brought out an elegant single-lens jumelle with optical finder fitted with a precision focal plane shutter which operated at a speed of 1/2,500 sec.[5] With it Sigriste took remarkable action photographs of horses and racing automobiles.

SALOMON: Visit of German statesmen to Rome, 1931: Mussolini, Heinrich Brüning, Grandi, Julius Curtius. MOMA GEH

A focal plane shutter is a curtain with a slit in it which moves across the plate or film during exposure. If the subject photographed is in rapid motion, what the negative records will be a distortion: a revolving wheel becomes an ellipse because the image has moved during the time taken for the slit to scan the plate. If furthermore the camera is swung during exposure, the image is still further distorted – sometimes with a remarkable impression of swift motion.

Although by the use of specially sensitized panchromatic emulsions snapshots were occasionally taken of stage performances and by street lights as early as 1902, the potentials of what has come to be called "existing light" or, more popularly and less accurately, "available light," photography first became apparent in 1924 when the Ernemann-Werke A. G. in Dresden put on the market the *Ernostar* lens. Its diameter was at first half of its focal length, and marked accordingly *f*/2; later it was increased to *f*/1.8. Lenses of such large diameter are practical only in short focal lengths, for it is a rule of optics that, at the same *f*-number, the greater the focal length, the shorter will be its depth of field, i.e., the zone between the nearest and farthest points that are in sharp focus. The Ernostar had a focal length of 4 inches and it was fitted to a camera called the *Ermanox* or *Ernox*, which used glass plates or cut film 4.5 by 6 cm (about 1¾ by 2¼ inches). The manufacturer boasted that

this extremely fast lens opens a new era in photography, and makes accessible hitherto unknown fields with instantaneous or brief time exposures without flashlight: night pictures, interiors by artificial light, theater pictures during performance, children's pictures, scientific records, etc.[6]

Learning of this seemingly miraculous camera, Erich Salomon began in 1928 to use it to photograph famous people in Berlin. At first, when he asked permission to photograph at indoor functions, he was refused, for officials could not believe that a blinding flash would not interrupt the formalities, leaving a dense pall of acrid smoke to hang over the dignitaries. Salomon convinced them by taking pictures unawares and showing them the results. Soon he gained the confidence of prominent statesmen and began to photograph in the very rooms where they foregathered. He took diplomats attentive and suave at eleven at night and then at one in the morning, slumped in their chairs, exhausted and haggard. Aristide Briand is reported to have said, "There are just three things necessary for a League of Nations conference: a few Foreign Secretaries, a table and Salomon."[7] When an English editor saw these pic-

BRASSAÏ: "Bijou," Paris, c. 1933. MOMA GEH

BRANDT: Coal Searcher, England, 1937. GEH

tures, so utterly different in revelation from the usual posed studio portraits, he called them "candid photographs," a phrase which stuck with the public.

The camera most suited for Salomon's approach, and which came to be dubbed the "candid camera," was the *Leica*. With its many imitators it had the advantage over the Ermanox that thirty-six negatives, each approximately 1 by 1½-inches in size, could be taken on a single loading of inexpensive 35mm moving-picture film. It was the invention of Oskar Barnack, who was constructing microscopes at the optical works of E. Leitz in Wetzlar, Germany. Just before the First World War he devised for his own use a camera to take single pictures on standard motion-picture film. He was apparently unaware that two somewhat similar 35mm cameras had been put on the market in America in 1914: the *Tourist Multiple* of Herbert & Huesgen and the *Simplex Multi-Exposure* of the Multi-Speed Shutter Co. But it was just as well that Barnack did not know that these cameras existed, for neither of them met with public favor.

After World War I the Leitz company saw that Barnack's little camera had potentials. The design was improved, and the first Leica was introduced in 1924. It was fitted with a collapsible lens of 50mm focal length, and the relatively moderate aperture of $f/3.5$.

The first improvement was to make the lens removable and to offer the photographer a choice of other lenses of varying focal lengths which could be readily interchanged. In 1932 Ikon Zeiss AG brought out a similar camera, the *Contax*; it was fitted with a built-in rangefinder, coupled with the focusing mechanism in such a way that the photographer, by simply moving the lens until a double image of the subject became one, could be assured that the negative would be as sharp as possible. Soon lenses of apertures as large as $f/1.5$ were offered for both cameras.

The 35mm camera has its drawbacks. It cannot produce a picture so detailed as the larger camera. Only in the hands of a photographer who knows how to create a framework of dominant form can it carry its message, and then it is usually best in close-ups or in subjects large in scale, where the loss of detail is of no consequence. Many of the fields first explored by the 35mm miniature camera have since been explored by somewhat larger cameras, of which the *Rolleiflex* is typical. First put on the market by Franke & Heidecke in 1929, it takes twelve negatives 2¼ inches square on roll film. It has two lenses: one forms an image on a ground glass on the top of the camera, the other forms an identical image on the film. The photographer by observing the ground glass image can see exactly what

KERTÉSZ: Blind beggar, Hungary, 1927. MOMA

Roosevelt's office and showed them a president at work, not consciously posing.

The miniature camera not only proved to be of great use to photojournalists, but it opened up new esthetic possibilities. The ease with which the camera could be handled freed the photographer to seek unusual view points and to record segments of the flow of life.

André Kertesz as early as 1915 was taking sensitive, unposed photographs of people amid their surroundings. In Paris, where he came from Hungary in 1926, his vision became more architectural, and he learned to capture the fleeting, never-to-be-repeated instant. From him Brassaï learned the technique which he used so eloquently in photographing Paris by night, by whatever light he could find. Brassaï pioneered in the discovery of form in the most unlikely aspects of the city: wall scrawls (graffiti), time-worn masonry, weathered boardings. He photographs people unobtrusively yet directly, with human warmth. His massive documentation of fellow artists at work – he is himself a sculptor and draftsman – is most impressive. In a spirit of fantasy, not without surrealist overtones, Bill Brandt began to photograph the English at home; his book by that title (1936) and his *London by Night* (1938) are counterparts to Brassaï's *Paris de Nuit* (1933). With perception and imagination he photographed the homes of British authors and scenes evocative of their literary contributions; recently he has concentrated on a highly individual approach to the nude.

When miniature camera work by the French photographer Henri Cartier-Bresson was first shown at the Julien Levy Gallery in New York in 1933, it was called awkwardly enough, "antigraphic photography."[8] The impression arose that the photographs had been taken almost automatically and that they owed their strange and provocative beauty to chance; they were described as "equivocal, ambivalent, anti-plastic, accidental." For Cartier-Bresson showed the unreality of reality: the rhythm of children playing in ruins, a child lost to the world as trance-like he catches a ball; a bicyclist streaking by iron grill work. It was hard to believe they were deliberate records of previsioned images. Yet that was precisely how he photographed.

Cartier-Bresson was able to seize the split second when the subject stood revealed in its most significant aspect and most evocative form. He found the miniature camera ideal for he could bring it into action almost at once, as "an extension of the eye." Far from relying upon accident he composed through the finder, invariably using the full negative area. In his earlier work – he bought his first Leica in 1933 – there is an

he is taking. While snapshots cannot be taken with this type of camera under quite such extreme light conditions as with the smaller 35mm camera with its larger aperture lens, still it is possible to work rapidly and with mobility in situations normally closed to more bulky, less flexible cameras.

Amateurs were fascinated by the convenience of these miniature cameras. They vied with one another, not in making pictures, but in technical performance. At the height of the "minicam" enthusiasm, amateurs brazenly forced their way anywhere that offguard pictures could be taken. Promiscuous snapshooting while the play went on became such a nuisance that theatres were forced to prohibit unauthorized picture-taking by the audience.

Professional work was, however, being done with the miniature camera: Alfred Eisenstaedt covered the Ethiopian War; Peter Stackpole made pictures of the construction of the Golden Gate Bridge in San Francisco as the workmen saw it, from vantage points hardly accessible to the cameraman with standard equipment; Kip Ross covered day in day out regular newspaper assignments; Thomas McAvoy took the readers of *Time* magazine into President Franklin D.

CARTIER-BRESSON: Children playing in ruins, Spain, 1933. MOMA GEH

emphasis on form, and a delight in capturing aspects of the ordinary unseen in time and space by the ordinary eye. His interest in people became stronger. Not infrequently he produced studies amounting to caricature as, for example, the pictures of the Coronation Parade of George VI in London in 1938, where he showed not the glittering pageantry, but the bystanders. He has the remarkable ability to capture those peak instants when the ever-moving image formed by his lens has attained a timeless harmony of form, expression and content. There have been few photographs of religious emotion more intense than Cartier-Bresson's picture of homage being paid to Cardinal Pacelli, or of more stimulating form than his picture of children playing in ruins.

The development of powerful yet portable light sources has given the photographer the opportunity to create his own lighting effects anywhere and to record the most rapid action.

With flash powder the photographer had little control over the quality of the lighting; it was hardly more than a way of creating enough illumination to take snapshots in dark places. In 1925 Paul Vierkötter

patented a radically new method of producing a flash: the inflammable mixture was put inside a glass bulb, from which the air had been evacuated. When weak electric current was passed through the mixture it ignited at once, giving forth, for the fraction of a second, brilliant light. J. Ostermeier perfected this flash bulb in 1929 by stuffing it with aluminum foil, and it was put on the market in Germany as *Vacu-Blitz*. It was introduced in England as *Sashalite* and in America as *The Photoflash Lamp* in 1930. The noiseless and smokeless flash bulb was immediately adopted by news photographers; its earliest use in America is said to have been photographing President Hoover signing the Unemployment Relief Bill. At first the "open flash" method was used: with the camera on a tripod, the shutter was opened, the flash bulb set off, and the shutter was closed. Later the release of the shutter was mechanically synchronized with the discharge of electric current and the camera could be held in hand. For convenience, the flash gun (battery case, flash bulb and reflector) was fastened to the side of the camera.

With this equipment pictures could be taken anywhere. But the results were, for the most part, gro-

CARTIER-BRESSON: Cardinal Pacelli (later Pope Pius XII) at Montmartre, Paris, 1938. GEH

tesque, because the harsh front light flattened faces, cast unpleasant shadows, and fell off so abruptly that backgrounds were unrelieved black. This unreal lighting of the flash from the camera can be used effectively; in many instances the New York news photographer Weegee has made comments which reach into the field of social caricature. It is obvious, however, that photographs so lighted are far removed from naturalistic indoor pictures made with a wide-aperture lens on a miniature camera, in which we seem to be magically transported into the very presence of people and to be an onlooker of their activities together with the photographer. A further mechanical development made it possible to ignite several flash bulbs, placed at distant points from the camera and connected to it by extension wires. With this "multiple synchroflash" technique the lighting can be arranged either for dramatic effect, or to simulate existing light sources; people can be photographed with it instantaneously, amid their normal surroundings, relaxed or in action. One of the first to make use of this technique was Margaret Bourke-White of *Life*, who wrote in 1937:

I am deeply impressed with the possibilities of flash bulbs distributed through the room instead of using one attached to the camera in the usual way. I work mine with extension cords from a synchronizer attached directly to the shutter but always use two sources of light and sometimes three or four or even six distributed around the room. The flashlight gives a soft, very fine quality of light. The beauty of it, of course, is that you can watch your subjects until they show just the expressions or movements you wish and then release your flash. I feel, too, that it is very useful in dark places like night clubs and restaurants. Frequently I have set up a camera with remote control in the corner of a room, seated myself at a table some little distance, and released the flash, possibly an hour later, when everybody had forgotten about the camera.[9]

Brilliant use of artificial lighting, and particularly of the synchroflash technique, has been made by Barbara Morgan in her photographs of the dance. She lights dancers specifically for the purpose of photographing them; they perform for her camera; instead of mere records of action, she gives us interpretations. Light is her medium:

I am grateful for man-made light and the creative free-

dom it gives…. With synchroflash and speedlamps I can illuminate *what I want and no more. At will* I can create zones of importance by dominant and subordinate lighting. I can impart sculptural volume or flat rendering to the same object. By controlling direction and intensity I can launch light as a dynamic partner of dance action, propelling, restraining, and qualifying. Light is the shape and play of my thought… my reason for being a photographer.[10]

Too often dance photographs are nothing more than technical accomplishments, in which action is stopped, and the performers are left awkwardly in space. In Barbara Morgan's photographs every shape has meaning. Sometimes "freezing" of action is demanded; at other times a slightly blurred image helps to convey the emotion. Often both renderings are needed simultaneously, to show part of the action arrested and part in flow. Experience has enabled her to visualize what the lens will record during the fraction of a second it is open. She sees the dance not as a spectator, nor as a performer, but as a photographer. She has brought her sense of light and form to many other fields besides the dance, always bringing out the human qualities with warmth and acute sympathy.

When action is to be "frozen," so that each lock of hair and every thread of whirling costume is to be rendered with breathless sharpness, the so-called stroboscopic lamp is used, which gives brilliant light for as short a time as one microsecond (i.e. $1/1,000,000$ sec.).

In 1931 Harold Edgerton of the Massachusetts Institute of Technology designed an electronic lamp: current built up in a condenser to a high voltage was allowed to discharge in a gas-filled tube. The resulting flash was of great intensity, yet of extremely brief duration, and could be repeated at will. He built it to examine rapidly moving machine parts, by the long familiar stroboscopic method: a light flashing at exactly the rate that a regularly moving object revolves or oscillates will illuminate the same phase of the motion at each flash, and the object will appear to stand still.

Edgerton's light was so brilliant that photographs could be taken with it, and it was of such brief duration that the splash of a drop of milk, a bullet in flight, the beating of a hummingbird's wing could be recorded on film with a single flash. This use of the new light had many applications. Even with subjects comparatively motionless, more detail was secured because imperceptible movements of the camera and subject were eliminated. The flash was so brilliant that color film, of comparatively low photosensitivity, could be exposed instantaneously.

Recently battery-operated electronic flash units have

CARTIER-BRESSON: Abruzzi, Italy, 1953. GEH

been perfected which are so small that they can be fastened onto the camera. News photographers are replacing their flash bulbs with these powerful lights because they can be used over and over again.

When repeated flashes are made in true stroboscopic fashion with the Edgerton lamp while the lens of the camera is open, a series of images is recorded on the film. This refinement of Marey's chronophotography spreads out in space phases of action normally invisible. Thus the rush of a tennis player's body, arm and racket is recorded in consecutive images which enable us to analyze each part of the stroke. Gjon Mili has used this multi-exposure technique to picture, in an imaginative way, the flow of motion – the cycle of drumsticks, a pas de ballet. The camera has gone beyond seeing and has brought us a world of form normally not seen.

COBURN: The Octopus, New York, 1912. MOMA GEH

In 1913 Alvin Langdon Coburn, a member of the Photo-Secession, included in his one-man show at the Goupil Gallery, London, a series of five photographs under the title *New York from its Pinnacles*. They were all views looking down, and the distorted perspective emphasized the abstract pattern of streets and squares and buildings. In the catalogue he pointed out that one of them was

almost as fantastic in its perspective as a Cubist fantasy; but why should not the camera artist break away from the worn-out conventions, that even in its comparatively short existence have begun to cramp and restrict his medium, and claim the freedom of expression which any art must have to be alive?

Four years later Coburn produced completely nonobjective photographs. These *Vortographs* were deliberate abstractions:

There was at that time a notion that the camera could not be "abstract," and I was out to disprove this. The Vortographs were made with three mirrors clamped together in a triangle, into which the lens of the camera was projected, and through which various objects (bits of crystal and wood on a table with a glass top) were photographed. I greatly enjoyed making the Vortographs, for the patterns amazed and fascinated me.[1]

Christian Schad, a member of the Zurich Dada group of modern artists, in 1918 produced abstractions photographically without a camera. He laid cutout paper and flat objects on light-sensitive paper which, upon exposure to light, recorded designs that closely resemble those cubist *collages* made of pieces of newspaper and bric-a-brac stuck onto canvas.

Around 1921 Man Ray (an American painter in Paris) and László Moholy-Nagy (a Hungarian painter in Berlin) began to make, quite independently, their somewhat similar *rayographs* and *photograms*. They placed three-dimensional objects on the light-sensitive paper; thus not only were contours recorded and, in the case of translucent objects, texture as well, but also cast shadows. The photogram technique has been enriched by modulating the light which is allowed to fall on the object-strewn paper. A moving beam of light may be used, or the projected image of textured objects. Sometimes the paper is first covered with glass on which an abstract design has been painted, or to which texture

has been applied. Often several exposures are made, each with different objects.

Technically, the photogram is a revival of Talbot's photogenic drawing. Esthetically, however, it is entirely different. Talbot sought to exploit the representational characteristics of the medium. He related in *The Athenaeum* in 1839:

Upon one occasion, having made an image of a piece of lace of an elaborate pattern, I showed it to some persons at the distance of a few feet, with the inquiry, whether it was a good representation? when the reply was, "That they were not so easily to be deceived, for that it was evidently no picture, but the piece of lace itself."[2]

Moholy-Nagy, on the other hand, found that the photogram

opens up perspectives of a hitherto wholly unknown morphosis governed by optical laws peculiar to itself. It is the most completely dematerialized medium which the new vision commands.[3]

The photogram is visually so closely related to abstract painting that it may be considered a branch of that artistic discipline. It was devised by painters; the most significant results have been achieved by them; Moholy-Nagy discovered the technique through painting, and a more recent photogram maker, Gyorgy Kepes, speaks of his products as "photo-drawings." It is a synthetic rather than an analytic process, a tributary of the main stream of photography in which the camera has been the indispensable instrument, second in importance only to the photographer's eye. One can only agree with Sir Kenneth Clark's observation: "Whether or not one is in sympathy with the style of negation, one must surely concede that the attempt to make the camera, with all its powers of subtle record, aspire to the condition of a blueprint was singularly ill judged."[4]

The phenomenon of edge reversal, known to scientists as the Sabattier effect, was used as a plastic control, particularly by Man Ray. When a sensitive emulsion that has been developed, but not fixed, is exposed to naked light and developed again, the image shows a reversal of tones wherever there is a sharp edge. A print from such a negative has its contours rimmed with black lines. The phenomenon is somewhat similar

COBURN: Vortograph, 1917. GEH

SCHAD: Schadograph, 1918. MOMA

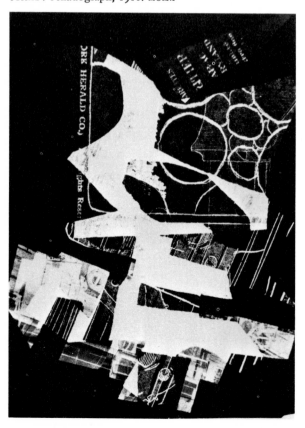

to tone reversal caused by gross overexposure – noticeable especially in platinum prints – which photographers called "solarization." Although scientifically inaccurate, the term has received general acceptance in artistic circles.

Man Ray also made negative prints, processed both normally and with edge reversal. He diffused the image by deliberately increasing the size of the silver grains. These controls are adaptations of the photographic process. Other physical methods of distorting the camera's natural image have been devised. Texture is introduced in the gelatin emulsion of the negative by subjecting it to rapid temperature changes, producing reticulation, or a net-like structure in the normally transparent film. Or the gelatin is melted, so that the image it bears droops and sags. A pseudo bas-relief appears when a negative and transparent positive are printed together slightly out of register. The film is deliberately double exposed. These methods have all been used singly or in combination by experimentalists who are impatient with the camera's normal image.

Most of these techniques for distorting the camera image, or eliminating the camera image entirely, were long known. Louis Ducos du Hauron, who made the first successful color photographs, devised a method of making distorted images by using crossed slits instead of a lens, a device he patented in 1888. "Transformisme en photographie," he called this invention, and he predicted its use not only for making caricatures, but for the positive correction and emphasis of the features in portraiture. And he declared that photographs of the natural scene taken through the crossed slits would "create visions of another world."

But there was little serious interest in images which varied from the classical rules of perspective, and his technique was published in amateur magazines as "trick photography" – along with anamorphic images, exaggerated perspective, "worm's-eye" and "bird's-eye" views, double exposures, composite prints, photomontages. A whole book of them was published in 1896 under the title *Photographic Amusements*.[5]

The vision which led to the acceptance of these aberrations as esthetic controls is quite separate from the vision of those who seek to interpret with the camera the world of nature and of man. Viewing photograms and solarized prints and distorted negatives, we are constantly reminded, not of photographs, but of paintings. Indeed Louis Aragon has said, "one completely unfamiliar with the painters alluded to would not be able to appraise fully the results."[6] James Thrall Soby – the critic, historian and collector of modern painting –

pointed out in *U. S. Camera Magazine*,[7] that in his experience abstract photographs did not wear well when hung as pictures.

The non-objective photographs – the rayographs, the odd angle shots, the composite prints – have one by one been taken from their frames and filed away against the day when they may have some minor value as commentary on the aspirations of certain artists in the 1920's.

Although both Man Ray and Moholy-Nagy, as painters, looked upon photography as a means rather than an end, neither were unappreciative of the direct camera image. Man Ray produced photographic portraits of uncompromising directness, and he was the first to recognize the esthetic value of Atget's photographs. Moholy-Nagy took quantities of photographs wherever he traveled; he even produced a picture book on Eton College and documentary films on Marseilles, the biology of the lobster, and the London Zoo. What separates him, however, from the straight photographer is that he discovered beauty *after* the photograph had been taken, and it did not matter to him who made the photograph or why it had been made. Once, looking at a photograph which he had taken years previously from a bridge tower at Marseilles, his attention was held as if it were a new thing and the work of another. "What a wonderful form!" he said, pointing to a coiled-up rope. "I never saw it before." It was this attitude of approaching photographs in the quest of form that led him to appreciate scientific photographs for their quite often accidental beauty. In them he found the "new vision" of the world.

Certain it is that scientists by means of photography have made visible the unseen, laid bare the structure of the microcosmos, and penetrated the worlds which lie beyond seeing. While the precise scientific significance of these factual photographs may escape us as laymen, our imagination is gripped by their strange and often provocative beauty.

Already in 1839 Fox Talbot had shown the value of his process to record the image of the microscope:

The objects which the microscope unfolds to our view, curious and wonderful as they are, are often singularly complicated. The eye, indeed, may comprehend the whole which is presented to it in the field of view, but the powers of the pencil fail to express these minutiae of nature in their innumerable details.[8]

His experiments were limited to low magnifications, but he clearly foresaw the time when the microscope would become a camera. The form of the microcosmos has been laid open to all, permanently and beautifully. Complex crystalline structures which defy description

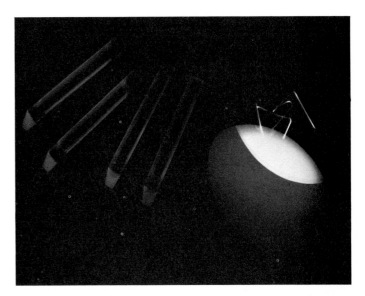

MOHOLY-NAGY: Photogram, c. 1925. University Art Museum, University of New Mexico, Albuquerque

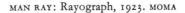

MAN RAY: Rayograph, 1923. MOMA

MAN RAY: Sleeping woman, 1929. MOMA GEH

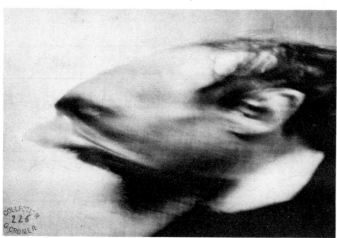

DUCOS DU HAURON: Self-portrait, 1888. GEH

BRUGUIERE: Light abstraction, c. 1925. GEH

MOHOLY-NAGY: Spring, Berlin, 1928. GEH
"A bird's-eye view of trees which form a unity with the pattern of the street. The lines running in many directions, placed each behind the other, form a rich spatial net work."
—Written by Moholy-Nagy on the back of the photograph.

LICK OBSERVATORY, UNIVERSITY OF CALIFORNIA: Spiral Nebula in the Constellation of Canes Venatici, 1960. Photographed with 120-inch reflecting telescope

are precisely recorded, and we can enjoy the beauty of their forms. With the electron microscope magnifications of unheard-of power are regularly attained: so evanescent a substance as smoke is seen to be an architecture of bold geometry.

The photographic emulsion reacts to rays which are invisible. In 1895 Wilhelm Conrad Roentgen discovered X-rays, and the world was startled to see photographs of living skeletons. The truth of the first radiographs was doubted: a photograph of the bones of the hand with one finger encircled by a ring was said to be considerably retouched if not actually a drawing. When the technique was still a novelty, readily verifiable and easily identified objects were X-rayed for the wonder of it, and many of these still lifes of a phantom necklace inside a locked jewel box, with every screw delineated through the wood, possess a strange and quite accidental beauty. Although the greatest use of X-ray photography is in medicine, industry finds it of value in the examination of cast parts for invisible imperfections.

The modern astronomer no longer watches the heavens, but studies a photographic plate. The telescope has become a camera, fitted with precision mechanism to guide it so that the images of moving heavenly bodies will remain immovable upon the photographic plate for hours. During these long exposures light so weak that it cannot be seen by the eye accumulates a silver deposit on the sensitive emulsion. Harlow Shapley, Director of the Harvard Observatory, has noted:

On one plate in the Harvard collection of stellar photographs more than a thousand external galaxies have been discovered, measured, and catalogued; each is probably a richer stellar system encompassing more space than that occupied by all the naked-eye stars.... Whether galaxies or planets, stars or meteors, they all yield up their secrets through the agency of the photographic plate.[9]

The land's surface seen from great heights often presents patterns of great beauty. The aerial camera allows us to isolate a section of the earth's surface for contemplation. Our eyes alone are not of sufficient optical acumen to give us at once the over-all dominant pattern and wealth of enclosed detail. Most aerial photographs are dull enough records. But when the ground possesses a rich pattern, we can often select from photographs taken purely for scientific purposes some which will appeal strongly to our esthetic imagination. Many of the aerial reconnaissance photographs are of intrinsic beauty. They were taken by pilots high above enemy territory flying straight and level on a predetermined course while three automatic cameras made exposures at intervals of a few seconds. The dozens of photo-

ADOLPHE BERTSCH: The phosphorescent apparatus of a glow worm. Photomicrograph, original magnification 100 diameters, Kodak Museum, Harrow, England

An X-ray photograph taken in 1896. From *Wilson's Photographic Magazine*, May, 1896

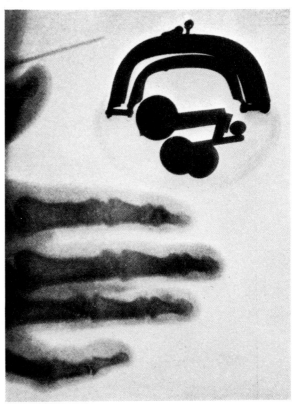

RADIO CORPORATION OF AMERICA LABORATORIES: Zinc oxide smoke, magnified 31,488 times with an electron microscope

ROYAL AIR FORCE: Germans plowing up an airfield at Ghindel, Libya, to render it unusable to occupying forces, 1942. Imperial War Museum, London

WILLIAM A. GARNETT: Nude Dune, Death Valley. 1954

U. S. AIR FORCE: Mud flats at low tide near St. Brieuc, France, 1944

BRAGAGLIA: Fotodynamic portrait, 1911. Courtesy Signorina Antonella Vigliani Bragaglia, Centro Studi Bragaglia, Rome, and Dr. Piero Racanicchi

EDGERTON: Swirls and eddies of a tennis stroke, 1939. Courtesy Massachusetts Institute of Technology Cambridge, Mass. MOMA

graphs taken on each flight overlap to form a topographical record of many miles of the earth's surface. Each single print, therefore, is not an independent picture, but merely one unit of a series from which interpreters could extract military information. The pictorial quality which we see is a by-product.

The "new vision" is thus the revelation of what the unaided eye cannot see but which has ever existed; as more powerful tools for observation are built, more worlds of form are revealed. They seem new only because we have not seen them before: the forms themselves are basic, and not the product of man's imagination and invention. Scientific photographs taken throughout the past hundred years are basically similar; it is our acceptance of them as *esthetic* revelations which is new. If Bertsch's photomicrograph of a glow worm seems to us a challenging abstraction, it is because painters have taught us to appreciate new forms. Such a picture could hardly have been accepted by artists when it was presented in 1857 as a scientific investigation. The similarity of certain scientific photographs to modern paintings has often been remarked. It is no coincidence, for our vision has been conditioned by scientific discoveries; painters of the modern movement were the first to be moved and stimulated by these revelations of the physicists. The new vision disclosed by the laboratory has, in general, been assimilated rather than imitated. Marcel Duchamp has stated that when he was painting his famous *Nude Descending a Staircase* in 1912, art circles in Paris were stimulated by stroboscopic and multiple-exposure high-speed photographs. The futurist painters were greatly influenced by this type of photography. Antonio Giulio Bragaglia worked out his *Fotodinamismo Futurista* in 1911 by making time exposures of moving objects which proved the futurist doctrine of the destruction of form by motion and showed how the continuity of action could be made static in a dynamic graphic record. He photographed his friend Giacomo Balla beside his famous painting, *Dynamism of a Dog on a Leash (Leash in Motion)*: during the series of exposures Balla moved, to produce on the plate the effect he had painted.

Among the documents which Le Corbusier presented in his manifesto on decorative art (1925) are scientific photographs and drawings. He pointed out that the illustrations in popular scientific magazines

take the cosmic phenomenon to pieces under our eyes; amazing, revealing and shocking photos, or moving diagrams, graphs, and figures. We are attacking the mystery of nature scientifically.... It has become our folklore.[10]

EDGERTON: Wire struck by bullet. Photographed in 1962 by stroboscopic light. Duration of each exposure, one-third of one-millionth of a second. Courtesy Polaroid Corp., Cambridge, Mass.

SMITH: The Thread Maker. From *Life*, April 9, 1951. MOMA GEH

The camera and the printing press were linked from the very birth of photography. Daguerreotypes themselves were made into printing plates. A satirical lithograph of 1839 by Théodore Maurisset, captioned *Daguerréotypomanie*, shows Alfred Donné at work with camera, aqua fortis bottle and etcher's press, while camera fans pass beneath him in procession bearing the banner, "Down with Aquatint!" Donné made the metal daguerreotype plates printable by etching out the clear silver areas and building up the highlights by the newly discovered electrotype process; they could then hold ink and be printed like an etching or copper-plate engraving. The technique was improved by Hippolyte Louis Fizeau, who borrowed from the aquatint engraver the trick of breaking up middle tones into minute divisions of black and white dots by sprinkling the plate with powdered resin. For the album *Excursions Daguérriennes*, which N. P. Lerebours began to publish in 1840, he contributed two of these primitive photogravures: a distant view of the Hôtel de Ville in Paris, showing the Seine and the quais, and a detail of the Gothic carving on the Cathedral of Notre-Dame.

The negative-positive process brought more successful photomechanical reproduction techniques. Fox Talbot himself patented in 1852 and again in 1858 *photoglyphic engraving*, which produced printable steel plates. To reproduce the middle tones, Talbot broke those areas up into minute divisions of black and white either with grains of resin, or by double exposing the negative with a screen of fine-mesh muslin.

Experiments were also made in the production of photographic images which could be printed by the lithographic process.

Another method of reproducing the photographic image in facsimile with ink was the *woodburytype*, invented in 1866 by Walter Bentley Woodbury. He printed negatives on gelatin, made light-sensitive with potassium bichromate. The exposed film, when "developed" in hot water like a gum print, becomes a relief map of light and shade: the highlights are valleys and the shadows are hills. A mold of these contours is made by forcing a block of lead against the gelatin under great pressure. The lead plate is then filled with a jelly-like ink, paper pressed against it, and a perfect facsimile of the photograph is obtained, with variations of tone reproduced by proportionate variations in the thickness of the deposit. No finer process for reproducing photographs than the now unfortunately obsolete woodburytype has ever been devised.

But all of these methods – photogravure, photoglyphic engraving, photolithography, woodburytype and dozens of variants of them, had a common disadvantage. They could not be printed on an ordinary press together with type. Although these methods made possible the reproduction of photographs in great quantity, the reproductions themselves had to be published exactly as photographic prints had been published: pasted down on blank pages of books, bound into them as separate plates, or mounted on cards.

Type is in relief. The ink is applied to the raised portions. To print photographs in the same press with type, a method was needed by which the highlights would be depressed and the shadows would remain upon the surface of the block.

The goal was attained with the invention of the halftone plate in the 1880's.

This important invention was perfected at precisely the time that the technical revolution in photography was taking place. Dry plates, flexible film, anastigmat lenses and hand cameras made it possible to produce negatives more quickly, more easily, and of a greater variety of subjects than ever before. The halftone enabled these photographs to be reproduced economically and in limitless quantity in books, magazines and newspapers. The consequent demand for photographs became so great that specialization became common: photographers began to produce pictures for the printed pages of magazines and newspapers.

The pattern had already been set. News photographs were taken as early as 1842, and the great illustrated weeklies began to use them from time to time as models for their wood engravings. Copies of *The Illustrated London News* and its counterparts, such as *L'Illustration* (Paris), the *Illustrierte Zeitung* (Leipzig) and *Gleason's Pictorial Drawing-Room Companion* (Boston), of the 1850's not infrequently contained portraits of celebrities and pictures of railroad wrecks and collapsed or burnt-out buildings which bear the credit "From a Daguerre-

BARNARD: Burning mills at Oswego, N. Y., 1853. Daguerreotype. GEH

otype." The use increased with wet plates. Fenton's Crimean War pictures were reproduced in *The Illustrated London News*, and *Il Fotografo* (Milan). Many of the Civil War photographs appeared in *Harper's Weekly*, the *New York Illustrated News*, and *Frank Leslie's Illustrated Newspaper*.

But wood engravers were not draftsmen. They were skilled technicians, who faithfully followed with their burins the drawing which the artist had made on the block, cutting away the wood between the lines. To make a wood engraving of a photograph, a drawing of it had first to be prepared. So long as it was necessary to go through this intermediate step, relatively few illustrations were cut from photographs, and although artist-correspondents could make a living specializing

in the pictorial reporting of news, it was hardly possible for a photographer to do so.

The entire economy of news photography was changed with the introduction of the halftone process, by which a facsimile relief block was made mechanically. The first use of the process in a daily newspaper appears to have been in the *New York Daily Graphic* for March 4, 1880. In this issue of the newspaper samples were given of all the various ways of reproducing pictures. Special attention was drawn to a facsimile, made by Stephen Henry Horgan, of a photograph by Henry J. Newton showing "Shantytown," the squatters' camp which then disgraced uptown New York. The editors said,

We have dealt heretofore with pictures made with

drawings or engravings. Here we have one direct from nature.... We are still experimenting with it, and feel confident that our experiments will in the long run result in success, and that pictures will eventually be regularly printed in our pages direct from photographs without the intervention of drawing.

Yet it was years before prejudice could be overcome. While Stephen Horgan was art editor of the *New York Herald* in 1893, he suggested to its owner, James Gordon Bennett, that halftones could be printed in the paper. Bennett consulted his pressman who told him that the idea was impossible and preposterous. Horgan was fired. He had more success at the *Tribune*, and in 1897 halftones were first printed on speed presses.

By the turn of the century the public began to expect to see news of the day in photographs. Cameramen began to specialize in fast, on the spot, coverage of news events, and agencies were set up for the distribution of pictures. But to send photographs by special messenger, fast mail, or ocean liner proved too slow. William Gamble, editor of *Penrose's Pictorial Annual* wrote in 1898:

Editors and publishers are fully conscious of the public craving for illustrations, but it is difficult to meet it because the methods of producing them are too slow to compete with the word-pictures, which can be flashed over the telegraph wires, written out, set up in type, and printed off long before an artist has made a sketch to illustrate the same fact.

But suppose it were possible to transmit the picture over the wires with the same facility as we now transmit the words, and suppose that the same electric current rendered a transcript of the picture in a form suited for immediately using or converting into a printing surface, what a revolution it would effect in the methods of giving news to the public.[1]

The prediction was inspired by the experiments of N. S. Amstutz of Cleveland, Ohio, who in 1895 described a highly ingenious and remarkably prophetic technique for producing at a distant point an engraving of a photograph, ready for the printing press. "Photo-telegraphy," or "wire transmission," was not put to practical use, however, until 1907, when a regular service was inaugurated by the French weekly *L'Illustration* and *The London Daily Mirror*. The technique used was the invention of Alfred Korn, a professor at the University of Munich. It depended on the property of selenium to vary its electric conductivity according to the light falling upon it. A positive transparency on a drum was spirally scanned by a light beam focused on a selenium cell. The light varied in brightness according to the density of the area of the photograph scanned, and thus more or less current was sent to the

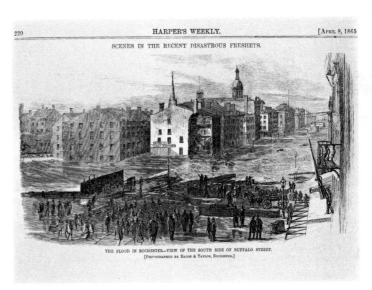

Top: FRANKLIN W. BACON & JOHN WILSON TAYLOR: Flood in Rochester, N. Y. 1865. GEH

Above: Wood engraving from photograph, Flood in Rochester. *Harper's Weekly*, April 8, 1865

ARNOLD GENTHE: San Francisco fire, 1906. Print by Ansel Adams from original negative in the California Palace of the Legion of Honor, San Francisco. MOMA GEH

distant receiver. There photographic paper on a drum revolving at the same speed as the transmitter was gradually exposed to a light beam which varied in brightness exactly according to the current received.

Coincidentally with Korn, the French scientist Edouard Bélin invented a somewhat similar system, which he demonstrated to the Société Française de Photographie by transmitting and receiving in the society's lecture room a photograph over the 1067-mile closed circuit Paris-Lyons-Bordeaux-Paris. Phototelegraphy took a great step forward with the introduction of the vacuum tube, and in 1925 the American Telephone and Telegraph Company opened a commercial service between New York, Chicago and San Francisco. Today wire transmission is routine; there are two services in the United States, the Associated Press and United Press International, each serving over 1200 newspapers, and each transmitting upwards of 100 pictures per day. Similar networks cover Europe, Latin America, Australia and the Orient.

Obviously all news is not photogenic. Diplomats seated around the table may be reshaping the world, but it is the exceptional photographer who can make the reader feel the drama underlying such a conference. The immediate drama of accidents, the exaggerated emotions brought out on faces under the tension of disaster or crime, the violent split-second action of sports can be imparted vividly by the camera. The photographer needs not so much artifice, subtlety of light and shade and sense of composition as boldness, strong nerves, and a mastery of his camera so complete that handling it is an automatic reflex.

Although the technique of the news photographer does not differ from that of any other cameraman, the special demands made on his skill, daring and ingenuity in getting unusual pictures, and the need of turning out a print with all possible speed, make his work a special branch.

Sensing the exact instant to release the shutter becomes instinctive. A second's hesitation, and a picture scoop may be missed. When Warnecke of the *New York World* went on a routine assignment to photograph Mayor William J. Gaynor of New York as he was about to sail to Europe on a vacation in 1910, he arrived after the other cameramen. Hurriedly he asked the Mayor for a last minute pose. Just then an assassin

WARNECKE: Shooting of Mayor William J. Gaynor of New York, 1910. Courtesy *New York World-Telegram*. MOMA

SAM SHERE: Explosion of the *Hindenburg*, Lakehurst, N. J., 1937. Courtesy International News Service. MOMA

fired two shots of a revolver at the Mayor. Warnecke, in the midst of the confusion, remained cool, and photographed that sickening moment when the victim staggered into the arms of his companion.

Chance often gives news photographers their opportunity, yet great news photographs are not accidentally made. Twenty-two photographers, representing New York and Philadelphia newspapers, were gathered at Lakehurst, N. J., on May 6, 1937, for a routine assignment: the dirigible *Hindenburg* was due, and although it was the airship's eleventh transatlantic crossing, the event was still considered newsworthy. At dusk the great silver giant sailed majestically in from the Atlantic, and the cameramen were preparing to compose "art shots" for the feature editors, when suddenly flames shot out from the hull. In forty-seven seconds the great dirigible lay on the ground, a mass of twisted flaming wreckage. In those forty-seven seconds, every one of those photographers produced pictures

that are still memorable. Jack Snyder of the Philadelphia *Record* said,

I've been carrying my camera around for sixteen years, but I never got an opportunity for really good pictures before. I waited for hours for the Hindenburg in a pouring driving rain, as I wanted to get a close-up. I thought, "I'll get close to the mooring mast to see her tied up." Then I heard a crackling over my head, a sort of roaring crackle, and then W-H-A-A-M. There was a terrible flame and the heat singed my hair.[2]

He rushed for shelter, but not before he had clicked his shutter. Another photographer worked so fast that he threw the film holders on the ground at his feet after exposing only one of the two films which each contained, for fear that in his excitement he might make a double exposure. A messenger collected the holders; they were flown to New York. The metropolitan newspapers, all of them, told the story of the tragedy not in words but in pictures, which were often enlarged half a page in size. The *New York World-Telegram* carried twenty-one photographs; the *New York Post* had seven pages of pictures, the *Daily Mirror*, nine. Never had a disaster been so covered by photography.

The press photographer thinks in terms of a single picture or a group of single pictures. He specializes in "spot news," and seldom has opportunity to plan a sequence of pictures which will build up a total effect greater than the sum of the parts. This approach to photography has been stimulated by magazines.

Picture stories are not, of course, new. The pictorial press of the forties used picture essays: the first number of *The Illustrated London News* took its readers to Queen Victoria's masked ball in eight pictures; the following week it traced the overland route from India to England, and showed a series of pictures of Horace Walpole's Strawberry Hill mansion.

The rapidity with which pictures could be taken with a camera made it possible for several views to be taken of a single incident. O'Sullivan took three photographs of a Civil War staff meeting near Massapomax Church, Virginia, on May 21, 1864, alike except for the position of General Grant: by viewing the three in succession we almost have the illusion of motion. In a similar 1-2-3 fashion, Alexander Gardner photographed the hanging of the Lincoln conspirators. Full use of chronological sequences in magazines, however, awaited halftone techniques as rapid as photography.

On the occasion of the one-hundredth birthday of the French scientist Michel-Eugène Chevreul in 1886, Nadar's son Paul took a series of exposures of him in conversation with his secretary and with Nadar père, which were published as a "photo-interview" in *Le Journal illustré* for September 5, 1886. A stenographer noted the very words which Chevreul spoke at each exposure, and these were printed as captions. A second photo-interview was made two years later of General Georges Boulanger; some of the pictures were circular. They had been taken with one of the first Kodak cameras.

The first magazine deliberately planned to exploit this type of photography appears to be the *Illustrated American*. In its first issue, dated February 22, 1890, the publisher stated that "its special aim will be to develop the possibilities, as yet almost unexplored, of the camera and the various processes that reproduce the work of the camera." The first number carried six photographs of the U. S. Navy, twenty-one of the Westminster Kennel Club Bench Show, eight of the Chicago Post Office, fifteen of a production of *As You Like It*, six of historical sites in Bordentown, New Jersey, fourteen to illustrate "A Trip to Brazil," and five showing the latest millinery. Of a layout of twelve photographs

HECTOR RONDIN: Aid from the Padre: Father Luis Manuel Padilla, Venezuela Navy Chaplain, holds up a government soldier in Puerto Cabello Street after the soldier was wounded during a two day revolt early in the week of June 3, 1962, by Communist-backed rebels. Associated Press Photo. Winner of Pulitzer Prize, 1963

«...Regardez bien ceci : je vais faire tourner ce disque rouge et blanc, et vous aurez la sensation d'un vert uniforme ....»

"...Now look carefully at this: I am going to spin this red and white disk, and you will have the sensation of... green...."

«...Je me rencontrai avec Monsieur Hersent, le peintre académicien, en 1840, dans la cour de l'Institut, en sortant de la séance dans laquelle Arago &c...et je lui dis que le jaune à côté du bleu donne de l'orangé, et que le bleu à côté du jaune passe au violet...»

"...I met Monsieur Hersent, the academic painter, in 1840, in the court of the Institute... and I told him that yellow beside blue gives an orange color, and that blue beside yellow becomes violet...."

«...Monsieur Hersent que notre dissertation avait un peu animé, me répondit : —Tout autre que monsieur Chevreul me disait cela, je dirais qu'il en a menti! Mais monsieur Chevreul me le disant, je veux le voir pour le croire.....»Je l'invitai aussitôt à venir à mon laboratoire des Gobelins où je lui donnerais la preuve...»

"...Monsieur Hersent, not a little upset...replied: 'If anybody but Chevreul had told me that, I would say he was lying! But Monsieur Chevreul having said so, I want to see it to believe it.' So I invited him to come to my laboratory in the Gobelins where I would prove it to him."

«...Il est mort vingt ans après, sans être jamais venu me voir aux Gobelins, comme je l'en avais prié......»

"...He died twenty years later, *without ever having come to see me at the Gobelins,* as I had begged him to do...."

PAUL NADAR: Photographic interview with Michel-Eugène Chevreul, at the time of the 100th birthday of the scientist and discoverer of the laws of the simultaneous contrast of colors, 1886. From an album of twenty-one signed photographs, with handwritten captions of the stenographic report. GEH. A number of these photographs were reproduced in sequence in *Le Journal illustré,* Sept. 5, 1886, with slightly different captions.

of the Chicago Public Library in a subsequent issue the editors pointed out: "These are no fancy sketches; they are the actual life of the place reproduced upon paper, and they tell more than words could of the immense usefulness of the institution."

But the *Illustrated American* found that it could not rely upon photographs alone. Month by month more and more words appeared in its pages, until it had lost its original character.

The same tendency can be observed in other picture magazines. The *Mid-Week Pictorial*, founded in 1914 by *The New York Times* as an outlet for the flood of war photographs which were arriving from Europe, was at first so dominantly photographic that the letterpress was limited to captions of one or, at the most, two lines. By 1915 the captions had become deeper, and there was a good amount of writing; before the war was over, feature articles had become numerous and drawings appeared frequently; emphasis on pictures had given way to the illustration of literary essays.

The idea of a purely photographic magazine was revived in 1934 by Henry Luce, publisher of *Time* and *Fortune*. A new magazine was envisaged as the "Show Book of the World." Its purpose was stated in a prospectus:

To see life, to see the world; to eyewitness great events; to watch the faces of the poor and the gestures of the proud; to see strange things – machines, armies, multitudes, shadows in the jungle and on the moon; to see man's work – his paintings, towers, and discoveries; to see things a thousand miles away, things hidden behind walls and within rooms, things dangerous to come to; the women that men love and many children; to see and to take pleasure in seeing; to see and be amazed; to see and be instructed.

To accomplish this ideal, the editors proposed to replace the "haphazard" taking and publishing of pictures with the "mind-guided camera," and to "harness the main stream of optical consciousness of our time." The first issue of the new magazine, which was called *Life*, appeared on November 23, 1936. The cover was an industrial photograph by Margaret Bourke-White of the construction of a great dam near Fort Peck, Montana, in the style for which, as a photographer for *Fortune*, she was noted. The opening picture story, however, focused not on the construction, but on the life of the builders of the dam and their families in temporary cities in the desert. It was not what the editors had assigned, and they wrote, by way of introduction:

What the Editors expected – for use in some later issue – were construction pictures as only Bourke-White can take them. What the Editors got was a human document of frontier life which, to them at least, was a revelation.

Three other photographers were on the original

WEEGEE: The Critic, 1943.
MOMA

EISENSTAEDT: Bertrand Russell. From *Life*, Jan. 14, 1952.GEH
HALSMAN: Dr. Robert Oppenheimer, 1958. Courtesy *Saturday Evening Post*

staff: Alfred Eisenstaedt, who had come from Germany, Peter Stackpole, a former member of Group *f*.64, and Thomas D. McAvoy. *Life* published two types of pictures: spot news photographs, supplied for the most part by news agencies, and feature stories, written and photographed on assignment by staff members.

Independently, and at the same time, the somewhat similar picture magazine *Look* was founded by Gardner Cowles and his brother John Cowles. The first issue was datelined January, 1937. It relied more upon feature stories than covering the news.

What distinguished *Life* and *Look* from earlier picture magazines was not so much the number of photographs they published but the theory of the "mind-guided camera." The typical picture essay is the co-operative work of editors and staff photographers. A story is decided upon, background research done, and a shooting script prepared to give the photographer as complete an understanding as possible of the type of pictures needed, their mood, and their purpose. Many more photographs are taken than will be used, for it is hardly possible to previsualize what the photographer will find when he starts work. From the stack of prints delivered by the laboratory, the editors – usually without consulting the photographer – choose those they consider will best tell the story. A layout is planned, with blocks to be filled with words by writers.

This approach lends itself to forceful statements and to clear exposition. Unfortunately it also tends to overemphasize the caption. John R. Whiting, in his *Photography is a Language*, made an illuminating experiment: he reprinted, in sequence and without the accompanying photographs, the captions of a typical *Life* picture essay. The result was a somewhat telegraphic, but completely coherent and readily grasped personality story to which the photographs were embellishments. Indeed, as Whiting states, "It is very often the caption you remember when you think you are telling someone about a picture in a magazine."[3]

In an effort to retain the informal quality of the miniature camera and the detail of the larger camera, the picture editors of the new magazines at first encouraged the use of flash bulbs as illumination indoors. But *Picture Post*, founded in London in 1938, and originally edited by Stefan Lorant, formerly of the Munich *Illustrierte Zeitung*, encouraged the use of the miniature camera without supplemental lighting. Although the results did not compare in clarity and definition to most photographs published in *Life* and *Look*, the "candid" approach gave spontaneity and directness. Even though they were not infrequently posed, the

DE MEYER: A wedding dress, modeled by Helen Lee Worthing, 1920. Courtesy Condé-Nast Publications, Inc.

STEICHEN: Lillian Gish as Ophelia, 1936. For *Vanity Fair*. MOMA

STEICHEN: Greta Garbo, 1928. For *Vanity Fair*. MOMA

pictures consistently appeared "natural." The *Picture Post* photographers, notably Kurt Hutton, Bert Hardy and Felix H. Man, went anywhere – in the King's castle, to political meetings, to pubs, railroad stations, operating rooms, to bring back vivid pictures. Unfortunately the magazine met with financial reverses, and in 1957 discontinued publication. During its lifetime it had a great influence on other illustrated magazines, which began to accept "available light" photographs. An ex-*Picture Post* photographer, Leonard McCombe, joined *Life's* staff in 1946; his contract contained a clause described by Ray Mackland, *Life's* picture editor, as "unique in the history of photography": McCombe was absolutely forbidden to use flash.

Remarkable photographs have occasionally been made on magazine assignments. W. Eugene Smith, while a *Life* photographer, produced a series of photographs of life in a Spanish village which will be remembered long after the picture essay is forgotten. Seventeen pictures were published in the issue of April 9, 1951. *Life's* editors regretted that so few had been selected, and put out, for promotional purposes, a portfolio of full-page reproductions of eight of the pictures not used. They were presented without text, for their own sake and not the visual elements of a pictorial essay. Smith photographed the very atmosphere of the village and the very personality of its people. Yet the photographs, however particular, are universal, for he photographed the culture of the Mediterranean. It has been said that *The Thread Maker* is "at once a village woman at work and an image haunting and eternal as a drawing by Michelangelo of one of the Three Fates."[4]

Alfred Eisenstaedt, a most experienced and versatile magazine photographer, produced a series of fine portraits of English notables which *Life* published in its January 14, 1952, issue. Unlike studio photographers, Eisenstaedt did not set up a battery of flood lights and spotlights and a bulky 8 by 10 tripod camera with an impressive focusing cloth. He did not apply make-up to models to mask Nature's deficiencies. Describing his experiences, he wrote "My approach was not that of a photographer with a lot of equipment doing a job, but of a casual visitor, who incidentally brought a Leica, three lenses and a little tripod along.... The longest time I spent with each was 28 minutes...."[5]

The most telling and dramatic photographs of World War II were made by magazine photographers or under their influence. *Life* ran a school for army photographers, and sent its own cameramen to the front: Eliot Elisofon was in North Africa; William Vandivert was in London during the Blitz and in

AVEDON: Marian Anderson, 1955. From *Observations: Photographs* by Richard Avedon, Comments by Truman Capote, New York, 1959. MOMA GEH

Opposite page top: PENN: George Jean Nathan and H. L. Mencken, New York, 1947. From *Moments Preserved*, New York, 1960. MOMA

Opposite page bottom: NEWMAN: Max Ernst, 1942. GEH

India; Margaret Bourke-White was in Italy and Russia; Eugene Smith was in the Pacific where, at the cost of serious injury, he produced some of the finest war photographs; Robert Capa — who was to die in combat in Indo-China — covered the invasion and landed with paratroopers. Captain Edward Steichen, U.S.N.R., served as Director of Navy Combat Photography; under his command were many photographers who had received their training on magazine assignments.

The bitter and disastrous Korean War was photographed by David Douglas Duncan. He concentrated upon the troops, with close-ups of biting intensity which revealed the battle not only against the enemy but the cold. These photographs he published in 1951 in *This Is War!*, a picture book with a short introduction but no captions. He later joined *Life's* staff, then turned to the production of picture books; he used a photojournalistic approach in a detailed, day-by-day account of the life of the artist in *The Private World of Pablo Picasso* (1958).

Fashion magazines were among the earliest to make regular editorial use of photographs. *Vogue* in 1913 began to publish photographs taken for them by Baron A. De Meyer; he founded a style in which the elegance of fashions is displayed with photographic feeling for textures. In 1923 Edward Steichen – who had taken fashion photographs both in black and white and color for *Art et Décoration* as early as 1911 – joined the staff of Condé Nast. In addition to photographing fashions he produced a great quantity of portraits of celebrities, which appeared regularly in *Vogue* and in *Vanity Fair*. These photographs are brilliant and forceful; they form a pictorial biography of the men of letters, actors, artists, statesmen of the 1920's and 1930's, doing for that generation what Nadar did for the mid-nineteenth century intellectual world of Paris. Steichen's work is straightforward photography which relies for its effectiveness on the ability to grasp at once the moment when a face is lighted up with character, on the dramatic use of artificial lighting, and a solid sense of design. He succeeded best with people of the theatre. In *U. S. Camera Magazine* he showed how he photographed Paul Robeson as "Emperor Jones" by reproducing twenty-eight of the exposures made during one sitting. His account is revealing:

I have almost invariably found that the sitter acted as a mirror to my own point of view, so that the first step was to get up full steam on my own interest and working energy.... If everything moves swiftly and with enthusiasm, the model gains courage in the belief that he or she is doing well, and things begin to happen. The model and the photographer click together.... In photographing an artist, such as Paul Robeson, the photographer is given exceptional material to work with. In other words, he can count on getting a great deal for nothing, but that does not go very far unless the photographer is alert, ready and able to take full advantage of such an opportunity.[6]

The most challenging portraiture of the past decades has been done for magazines, on assignment, rather than for the sitter himself, his family and his friends. The portrait studio, with its set lighting, standard backgrounds and props, depending for income solely on the sale of photographs printed by the dozen from heavily retouched negatives and enclosed in deckle-edged folders, is fast becoming obsolete.

Yousuf Karsh, trained in the Boston studio of John H. Garo, travels the world around to photograph great leaders and personalities. He carries a battery of studio lights with him, along with an 8 by 10-inch camera. He thus can convert any available room into a studio, where he can light his subjects in the classical way which is so distinctive of his style.

Another approach has been taken by Cecil Beaton, in which there is an emphasis upon the setting, often of an elaborate nature, specially built for the occasion. Beaton, who is a painter as well as a photographer, has produced stage sets for theatrical productions, and this interest is reflected in his camera work. His friend, the late George Platt Lynes, showed striking ingenuity in working out poses and new uses of materials to express the character of the sitter. Arnold Newman follows in this tradition: his portraits are distinguished by the way he has introduced into them objects symbolical of the profession or interest of the sitter. Philippe Halsman, Irving Penn and Richard Avedon are concerned not only with interpreting the personality of the sitter, but in exploring those visual possibilities that will give the photograph that arresting and appealing quality so essential to the reproduction on the printed page.

When Niépce described his photographic researches to his brother Claude, he said, "But I must succeed in fixing the colors," and when he visited Daguerre in 1827 he was especially interested in the latter's researches into this problem. He wrote enthusiastically to his son:

M. Daguerre has arrived at the point of registering on his chemical substance some of the colored rays of the prism; he has already reunited four and he is working on combining the other three in order to have the seven primary colors. But the difficulties which he encounters grow in proportion to the modification which this same substance must undergo in order to retain several colors at the same time.... After what he told me, he has little hope of succeeding and his researches can hardly have any other object than that of pure curiosity. My process seemed to him much preferable and more satisfatory, because of the results which I have obtained. He felt that it would be very interesting to him to procure views with the aid of a similar simple process which would also be easy and expeditious. He desired me to make some experiments with colored glasses in order to ascertain whether the impression produced on my substance would be the same as on his.[1]

Apparently Niépce had no better results than Daguerre, but the immediate possibilities of daguerreotypes in monochrome outweighed the fact that the colors were not recorded. It was not long, however, before the lack was sensed, and daguerreotypists began to color their plates by hand. In the meantime experimenters sought for some substance which, chameleon-like, would assume whatever color was shining upon it.

The loudest voice was that of Levi L. Hill, a Baptist minister of Westkill, N. Y., who announced in the public press in 1850 that he had succeeded in fixing the colors of nature. He showed examples of his work to leading American daguerreotypists. The editor of the *Daguerreian Journal* was so impressed that he said "Could Raphael have looked upon a *Hillotype* just before completing his Transfiguration, the palette and brush would have fallen from his hand, and his picture would have remained *unfinished*."[2]

The profession demanded to know the technique. They were prepared to pay roundly for the secret, but Hill fended them off by saying that "$100,000 would not purchase my discovery," and declaring that he would publish his results "when I think proper." Months went by, and not a word from Hill. In a pamphlet dated 1852 and addressed "To the Daguerreotypists of the United States and the Public at Large," Hill stated that the invention was all that he had claimed for it, but that he was faced with difficulties beyond his control in perfecting it, by "the invisible goblins of a new photogenic process." The profession became impatient, for their business had been hurt by Hill's premature announcement. They denounced him in the press as a humbug and as an impostor. He finally published in 1856 his *Treatise on Heliochromy*, a confused and complicated piece of writing, which contained, in place of specific workable directions, an autobiography and an account of endless experiments.

That Hill achieved some kind of result cannot be doubted; the evidence of daguerreotypists and particularly of so notable an artist and scientist as Samuel F. B. Morse, is too convincing to be dismissed. More than once daguerreotypists had, by accident, found colors upon their plates; Niepce de Saint-Victor, nephew of the inventor, in 1851 secured colored daguerreotypes by sensitizing silver plates with chlorides. They received acclaim in their day but, alas, could not be made permanent. Only a few examples, carefully kept in darkness over the years, exist.[3] Hill had perhaps stumbled upon the same path which these other experimenters had struck out upon, but we can form no more definite conclusion about his work than what was written about him after his death in 1865: "He always affirmed that he *did* take pictures in their natural colors, but it was done by an *accidental* combination of chemicals which he could not, for the life of him, again produce!"[4]

The search for a direct color-sensitive medium continued. In 1891, Gabriel Lippmann, professor of physics at the Sorbonne, perfected his interference process, which relied upon the phenomenon that a thin film, such as oil upon water, will produce all the colors of the rainbow. The results were startling. Steichen in 1908 wrote Stieglitz:

Professor Lippmann has shown me slides of still-life subjects by projection, that were as perfect in color as in an ordinary glass-positive in the rendering of the image in monochrome. The rendering of white tones was astonishing, and a slide made by one of the Lumière brothers, at a time when they were trying to make the process commercially possible, a slide of a girl in a plaid dress on a brilliant sunlit lawn, was simply dazzling, and one would have to go to a good Renoir to find its equal in color luminosity.[5]

Unfortunately the Lippmann process was not a practical technique, and is now obsolete.

The practical solution of photography in color was found in an indirect approach.

The British physicist James Clerk Maxwell performed a dramatic experiment at the Royal Institution of London in 1861. To prove that any color can be recreated by mixing red, green and blue light in varying proportions, he projected three lantern slides of a tartan ribbon upon a screen. In front of each projector was a glass cell filled with colored solution: one was red, a second, blue and a third, green. Each slide had been made from a negative which Thomas Sutton had taken through the identical glass cells or filters; each was theoretically a record of the red, blue and green rays reflected by the ribbon. The result was a color photograph – crude, but prophetic of the future.

Because Clerk Maxwell *added* red, green and blue light together, this technique is called *additive*. An equal addition of the three colors forms white; red and green add to form yellow; red and blue, magenta; green and blue, the blue-green known by photographers as cyan. It is important to bear in mind that this theory holds true only for colored *light*; the mixture of pigments is another matter.

The iodized collodion emulsion which Sutton used was not sensitive to red rays, and it long puzzled scientists how he got any result. On the occasion of the centenary of Clerk Maxwell's classic experiment, Ralph Evans proposed an ingenious explanation, which he proved by recreating the experiment. The red dyes used by ribbon makers of the day not only reflected red rays but also fluoresced, and it was this fluorescence which Sutton obtained as his "red" record. When panchromatic emulsion was perfected, Clerk Maxwell's system was put to practice with success. It is inconvenient to set up three magic lanterns whenever a color photograph is to be looked at. A portable apparatus, the *Kromskop*, was devised in 1892 by Frederic E. Ives of Philadelphia, which optically reunited three stereoscopic transparencies so they could be viewed in register. Each transparency was illuminated through a filter of the appropriate primary color: red, green, blue. The result was a brilliant color photograph in three dimensions, of startling realism.

But looking through the eyepiece of an instrument, or at a screen in a darkened room, was not like looking at a photograph which could be held in the hand. The first practical method of making a single picture to be viewed without any apparatus was invented in 1893 by John Joly of Dublin. Instead of taking three separate pictures through three colored filters, he took one negative through a screen checkered with microscopic areas of red, green and blue. The screen was the exact size of the photographic plate and was placed in contact with it in the camera. After the plate had been developed, a transparency was made from it and bound permanently to the color screen. The black, gray and white areas of the picture allowed more or less light to shine through the filters; viewed from a normal reading distance the primary colors so modulated blended to form combinations reproducing the colors of the original scene. In 1903 the same principle was used by the brothers Lumière in their *autochromes* which were put on the market in 1907. The photographic plate itself was covered with minute grains of starch which had been dyed. One third were red, one third green and one third blue, and they were mixed together so that the three primary colors were evenly distributed over the surface of the plate which was then coated with emulsion. Exposure was made through the back of the plate. After development the negative was turned into a positive by the reversal process, and a transparency resulted which reproduced the original colors. Steichen was privileged to obtain a supply of the new Lumière color plates before they were put on the market, and as a result the first public demonstration in the United States was held at the Little Galleries of the Photo-Secession in New York during November, 1907, of autochromes by Steichen, Frank Eugene and Stieglitz. Manufacture of the plates was discontinued in 1932. *Dufaycolor, Agfacolor,* and the Lumières' *Filmcolor* and *Alticolor* combined these two techniques: film base was ruled to form a multiple filter somewhat similar to the Joly screen, and the image was reversed as in the autochrome process.

These methods have given way to techniques based on the *subtractive* theory.

A black object absorbs, or subtracts, all of the light falling upon it: nothing is reflected to the eye, and hence it looks black. A white object reflects all of the light rays falling upon it. If white light shines upon it, white light is reflected; if red alone shines upon it, red is reflected. A colored object, however, absorbs, or subtracts, some of the rays and reflects others. When white light falls upon a red object, the red rays are reflected, while the blue and green are subtracted. But when red light falls upon a cyan object there are no blue or green rays to be reflected and the red rays are entirely subtracted. No light reaches the eye, and the object appears black.

Transparencies printed from negatives taken through red, blue, and green filters will, if tinted in the respective complementary colors (cyan, yellow, and magenta), superimposed in register, and held against light, reproduce all the natural colors in the scene which was in front of the photographer's camera.

By one of the strangest coincidences in the history of photography, this subtractive technique was announced simultaneously in 1869 by two Frenchmen, Louis Ducos du Hauron and Charles Cros. Neither knew the other; both sent communications to the Société Française de Photographie at the same time; the secretary described their almost identical techniques at the meeting of May 7, 1869, and showed examples submitted by Ducos du Hauron. What is even more extraordinary, the two inventors, instead of disputing priority, became friends. Cros, who was a friend of the Impressionists and more interested in the theory of color than in working out a practical photographic technique, did not pursue his invention, but Ducos du Hauron began extensive research. As soon as Vogel had shown how photographic emulsions could be sensitized to all colors he perfected his technique, and was able to make quite acceptable prints by the carbon process in 1877.

Many variations of this basic principle have been devised. Separate black-and-white prints can be made from each of the three color-separation negatives, as they are called, and the developed emulsions converted to images formed of cyan, magenta, and yellow pigments respectively. The gelatin bearing the pigments is stripped from each print and the three are superimposed in register on a fresh piece of paper. This technique, a modification of the carbon process, is called *carbro*. Another method of superimposing the three images is by *dye transfer*. A gelatin matrix is prepared which will absorb dye in proportion to the lights and shadows, and which will yield up this colored image when pressed in contact with paper.

These techniques require three separate negatives. Where the subject is stationary, the exposures can easily be made in succession, but in photographing moving objects they must be made simultaneously. "One-shot" cameras have been devised, fitted with half-silvered mirrors, which will allow this to be done. But this apparatus is cumbersome, and inefficient.

In 1935 subtractive color films were introduced which eliminated the necessity of making more than one exposure and which could be used in any camera. The first to be announced was *Kodachrome film*, invented by Leopold Mannes and Leopold Godowsky in collaboration with the staff of the Research Laboratories of the Eastman Kodak Company. It is based upon the 1912 invention by Rudolf Fischer of *dye-coupling*.

A special film is prepared, consisting of three separate emulsions on one support. The top emulsion is sensitive to blue light only. Beneath it is a layer of yellow dye which absorbs the unrecorded blue rays, allowing the red and green rays to penetrate to the two emulsions beneath it, one of which is sensitive to green rays only, and the other to red. Thus, upon exposure, a simultaneous record, in latent image form, is obtained of the three primary colors in the scene. The film is first developed to a negative and then, by reversal processing, to a positive. During the second development dyes of the complementary colors of yellow, cyan and magenta are formed in the appropriate areas, and the silver is bleached away. At first the processing required complex machinery and precise control and, consequently, was done exclusively by the manufacturer. To answer the demand for a film which the photographer could process himself, Ansco brought out in 1942 its *Ansco-Color film*, which was followed by Kodak's *Ektachrome film*; in both of these dye-couplers were incorporated in the separate emulsions.

These techniques have the same limitation as the daguerreotype and the tintype; each color photograph is unique. The negative-positive principle was introduced in *Kodacolor film* (1941), which is similar in general principle to Kodachrome film, except that the image is not reversed to a positive. Dye-coupling development directly converts each emulsion to an image complementary to the color which it records. Thus a color negative shows not only reversal of the lights and shades, but also of color. A blonde will appear with blue hair and green lips. From this negative any number of prints can be made by repeating the process with identical triple emulsion coated on a white base.

Using *Ektacolor film*, announced by the Eastman Kodak Company in 1947, the photographer can process his own color negatives. An important feature of this color process is the incorporation in the film of a mask which automatically compensates for inaccuracies in color rendition. Theoretically it should be possible to choose dyes which will completely absorb each of the primary colors. In practice this cannot be done. To correct these errors, the dye couplers added to the emulsion are themselves colored, absorbing the very rays which are incorrectly absorbed by the dyes. From the Ektacolor negative three gelatin matrices can be made directly for printing by dye transfer; or prints can be made on positive material.

For reproduction on the printed page, transparencies are rephotographed by normal means and through the primary filters: from each negative a printing plate is made, usually by the halftone process. The paper is run through the press four times, with cyan, yellow, magenta, and black inks —as printers say, "in four colors."

The greatest users of color film are amateurs: it is estimated that 71% of all snapshots are in color. To the commercial photographer color has long been indispensable in meeting the requirements of advertisers. Magazines are using more and more color editorially. Newspapers are overcoming the great technical difficulty of printing color on newsprint in high speed presses. Surprisingly few photographers, however, have chosen color as a means of personal expression, favored above other media.

There are exceptions. In the tradition of straight photography, Eliot Porter, whose sensitive black-and-white photographs were shown by Stieglitz at An American Place in 1938, has brilliantly photographed the natural scene. Unlike most photographers, Porter makes his own prints from color transparencies, and can thus control his final image. Ernst Haas has chosen to depart from the naturalistic. By deliberately double exposing the film, by moving the camera while the lens is open, by choosing abnormal exposures, he produces images which are often of great intrinsic value. Eliot Elisofon, the *Life* photographer, has experimented with the use of colored filters over the lens or light source. He has been consultant to Hollywood in the distortion of color for emotional effect, as in the motion picture *Moulin Rouge*.

The color photographer is faced with many esthetic problems. The eye does not see color the way the camera does. Should he choose the naturalistic approach and, as P. H. Emerson did in black and white, limit himself to reproducing what the eye sees? Or should he follow the camera's lead, exploiting its potentials and respecting its limits? There seem to be colors which

exist only in photographs: Kodachrome film, for example, gives blue of a richness and depth which can validly be used for its own sake with no attempt at realism. Already work has been done in every field with color; practically every photographer has worked with the new techniques; and although the complexity of processing and the expense of materials has been a deterrent to free experimentation, the esthetic capabilities are being explored.

The temptation is to choose subjects which are themselves a blaze of color, and to ignore the fact that color is everywhere, and that it is not the colorful subject itself, but the photographer's handling of it, which is creative. The most satisfying results appear to be of subjects which are basically of subdued colors, with here and there a brilliant, telling accent.

The line between the photographer and the painter is no more clearly drawn than in color photography. Imitation is fatal. By the nature of his medium, the photographer's vision must be rooted in reality; if he attempts to create his own world of color he faces a double dilemma: his results no longer have that unique quality we can only define as "photographic," and he quickly discovers that with only three primary colors, modulated in intensity by three emulsions obeying sensitometric laws, he cannot hope to rival the painter with the range of pigments which he can place at will upon his canvas. On the other hand the painter cannot hope to rival the accuracy, detail, and above all the authenticity of the photograph. The esthetic problem is to define that which is essentially *photographic* in color photography, to learn what is unique about the process, and to use it to produce pictures which cannot otherwise be obtained. Edward Weston clearly stated the problem, writing about the work he did in 1947:

So many photographs – and paintings, too, for that matter – are just tinted black-and-whites. The prejudice many photographers have against color photography comes from not thinking of *color as form*. You can say things with color that can't be said in black-and-white.... Those who say that color will eventually replace black-and-white are talking nonsense. The two do not compete with each other. They are different means to different ends.[6]

When Hurter and Driffield described their system of exposure determination in 1890, they met with unexpected opposition. They felt that by limiting variables, and providing the photographer with a relatively few factors to estimate, they were doing him a service. But a certain Colonel Noverre, apparently an amateur, was not satisfied. In a series of letters to the editor of *The Amateur Photographer* he asked for the elimination of all estimation. Stung, Hurter replied in the March 25, 1892, issue: "If Col. Noverre waits for an instrument with hands like a clock, which will point infallibly to the correct exposure, or for some other automatic machine which will cap and uncap his lens at the right moment, he will probably have to wait a long time."

The wait was precisely thirty-nine years. In 1931 the first photoelectric exposure meter was offered to photographers by J. Thomas Rhamstine, of Detroit, as the *Electrophot*. Current, generated by a battery, was measured by an ammeter. A photoelectric cell in the circuit modulated the amount of current passed to the meter, according to the light falling upon it. Thus the meter recorded the overall luminance of the scene. The dial was calibrated in *f*/stops for the proper exposure with what was described as "regular panchromatic" film at 1/32 second, the standard speed of the shutter of a motion picture camera. It weighed a pound and was 3½ inches in diameter. In 1932 the *Weston Exposure Meter* was put on the market. It was similar to the Electrophot, but required no battery: the photocell generated current in proportion to light falling upon it. The dial was marked in units of illumination (candles per square foot), and a circular slide rule attached to the instrument enabled the photographer to compute the *f*/stop and shutter speed settings for a variety of films which the company rated according to sensitivity. The meter not only gave direct readings of average illumination, but could be used to make more precise calculations of exposure by measuring the luminance of various areas of the scene and computing the tonal range.

Photoelectric exposure meters made by others soon appeared in great quantities, and quickly became standard equipment for photographers. They have recently become more sensitive and compact and have been built into cameras; they have even been coupled mechanically with the lens settings. A new era in camera technology began in 1938 when the Eastman Kodak Company announced the *Super Six-20 Kodak camera*. On pressing the shutter release, the diaphragm was opened to a size determined by an index actuated by current from a photoelectric cell.

After World War II the system was revived for amateur motion picture cameras and in 1956 Agfa brought out its *Automatic 66 camera* for roll film, fitted with a shutter controlled by the photocell. Today most camera manufacturers offer automatic cameras. In some of them the photoelectric cell controls the size of the diaphragm; in others, the shutter speed. The shutter of the *Polaroid Automatic 100 Land camera* (1963), for example, opens when the operator presses the button and closes at the command of the photocell. The periods of exposure range from approximately 1/1000 second in brilliant light to several seconds in dull light.

The system operates rapidly. During the brief period that a flash bulb emits its peak illumination – approximately the hundredth of a second – it measures the luminance of the scene and makes the exposure. The camera is precisely the "automatic machine" which Hurter sarcastically prescribed for uncapping and capping Col. Noverre's lens at the right moment.

Along with the perfection of cameras there has been marked progress in making films of greater sensitivity than ever. In 1942, when the American Standards Association adopted its system of film rating, the most sensitive film had their Speed Number of 100. In 1954 the speed was officially increased to ASA 400, although photographers found they could expose satisfactorily at ASA 1,280. In 1959 the speed shot up to ASA 3,000 and, for special purposes, even 10,000.

One of the most notable contributions is the Polaroid-Land process, invented in 1947 by Edwin H. Land, which not only permits the photographer to process a brilliant, high quality picture on the spot, inside a special camera in a matter of seconds, but opens up a new approach to photographic esthetics. With the obsolete techniques of the daguerreotype, the ambrotype, and the tintype, the photographer saw a finished positive a few minutes after he had made the exposure. But the conventional negative-positive system necessitates a division of processing: the negative is commonly developed some length of time after exposure, and the positive – the end result and the most critical part of the entire process – is usually made at an even later date, when the memory of the subject has dulled or faded. With Land's one-step process the photographer can work towards perfection by inspecting finished prints in the presence of the subject.

In a demonstration at the Royal Photographic Society in London in 1949 Land stated:

The purpose of this investigation is essentially esthetic, although the realm of investigation is, of course, scientific and technical. The esthetic purpose is to make available a new medium of expression to the numerous individuals who have an artistic interest in the world around them, but who are not given to drawing, sculpture, or painting. For most people photography cannot compete with these arts, partly because of the intricacies of photographic manipulations and partly because of an important fundamental difference in the approach to the creative problem. In the earlier arts the artist initiates his activity by observing his subject matter and then responds, as he proceeds, to a twofold stimulus: the original subject matter and his own growing but uncompleted work. With photography, except for those who combine long training, high technical ability, and splendid imagination, this important kind of double stimulus – original subject and partly finished work – cannot exist. Consequently, for most people it has been of limited and sporadic interest and has not been a source of deep artistic satisfaction, and there has arisen a gulf between the majority who make snapshots as a record and as a gamble, and the minority who can reveal beauty in this medium....

By making it possible for the photographer to observe his work and his subject matter simultaneously, and by removing most of the manipulative barriers between the photographer and the photograph, it is hoped that many of the satisfactions of working in the early arts can be brought to a new group of photographers.[1]

Land then went on to state the criterion of the system. "The process must be concealed from – non-existent for – the photographer, who by definition need think of the art in the *taking* and not in *making* photographs.... In short, all that should be necessary to get a good picture is to *take* a good picture, and our task is to make that possible."

In the conventional negative-positive system, silver halide grains are suspended in gelatin. Those grains which are exposed to light are converted to silver by the action of the developer. Those not exposed to light are dissolved in hypo (sodium thiosulfate) and washed away. In the diffusion process the unexposed silver salts dissolved by the hypo are not washed away, but are transferred to a receiving sheet and there convert-

ed to silver by the developer. The negative and positive are simultaneously processed inside the camera. The processing agents, in jelly form, are spread between the negative and positive sheets when they are pulled through a pair of rollers. In ten seconds the processing is completed, and the finished print is peeled from the negative in light. At first the negative was destroyed by this operation, but in 1961 a modification of the process was introduced by which sheet film can be used in a special holder fitting any standard 4 by 5-inch camera; both a positive for immediate evaluation and a negative for future printing by conventional means are obtained. In 1963 the Polaroid Corporation introduced color film for use in its cameras. The film is a multilayer emulsion with yellow, cyan and magenta dyes in the layers sensitive to blue, red and green light. On processing, the dyes are diffused to the positive sheet.

The success of the Polaroid-Land process depends not only on rapid processing, but also on the quality of its rendition of the tonal scale. It has been used successfully for all kinds of photography. A portfolio of outstanding photographs by himself and other professionals appears in the *Polaroid Land Photography Manual* by Ansel Adams.

Never has the photographer had more flexible materials, more precise tools, and more technical control than at present. There is evidence everywhere that photography has never been so popular, nor has it seen such widespread uses. Its boundaries are daily being pushed farther and farther.

The world of art, however, does not progress in the cumulative way so characteristic of science and technology: our painting, music, and architecture differ from those of other generations not in quality, but in style, approach, content and form. Technique gives an age the means to paint, to compose, and to build; man's spirit, his will to form, shapes its vision. Like the other arts, the art of photography has its progression of style. The present style seems based on four trends which have dominated photography in Europe and America since 1910, when the painterly approach fostered by the pictorialists lost its significance and force.

(1) *Straight photography*, explored as an esthetic approach by Stieglitz, Strand, Weston, Adams and others, in which the ability of the camera to record exact images with rich texture and great detail is used to interpret nature and man, never losing contact with reality. The final image is characteristically previsualized. Technique is the realization of the image, without alteration. This approach has become classical. The fine print is presented as an experience in itself.

MINOR WHITE: Pacific, 1948. MOMA GEH

(2) *The formalistic*, a product of the restless search in the arts for a means of isolating and organizing form for its own sake, pioneered largely by Man Ray and Moholy-Nagy, in which certain phenomena of the photographic process are exploited, such as deliberate narrowing of the tonal scale, edge reversal ("solarization") of the image, the appreciation of the negative as the final image, and the creation of images on sensitized materials without the use of the camera. Subject is of no concern, and if indeed it exists, is often distorted beyond recognition. The image is seldom previsualized, but characteristically is produced accidentally. New, challenging forms and space relationships are recognized in the final product by a vision highly conditioned by abstract painting. The photograph is rarely considered for its own sake, but as a tool for vision.

(3) *Documentary*, essentially a desire to communicate, to tell about people, to record without intrusion, to inform honestly, accurately, and above all, convincing-ly. Subject is paramount. The final print is usually not the end product, but the intermediate step toward the picture on the printed page.

(4) *The equivalent*, to borrow the word used by Alfred Stieglitz to define the photograph as symbol, or metaphor. The subject is recognizable, but it is only the starting point, for it is charged with meaning by the vision of the photographer. Stieglitz photographed clouds not because they were clouds but, as he said, because through them he could put down his philosophy of life. His "equivalents" are photographs charged with emotional significance and inner meaning, but first of all, photographs. "My aim," he wrote in 1923, "is increasingly to make my photographs look so much like photographs that unless one has *eyes* and *sees*, they won't be seen – and still everyone will never forget them having once looked at them."[2]

The photograph as metaphor can be found throughout photography. In the early days of the motion pic-

MINOR WHITE: Ritual Branch, 1958. GEH

STEINERT: Saar Landscape, 1953. GEH

ture the visual photographic metaphor was common: D. W. Griffith's *Intolerance* (1916), in which the theme is unfolded by four disparate sequences of images that are suddenly intermingled in a wholly realistic yet utterly non-literal way, is an example. Erich von Stroheim's *Greed* (1924) carries symbolism almost to an excess; the camera lingers on everything gold (actually tinted in gold on the release print); a caged canary, freed at the hero's death, symbolizes his soul. The Russians, expecially Sergei Eisenstein and Vsevolod I. Pudovkin, not only showed again and again the power of the visual metaphor in their films, but wrote extensively about it.

Photographs have been put with words, not as literal illustrations, but to reinforce one another, so that new meanings can be read in each. Thus in the book *Time in New England*, an anthology of New England writing with Paul Strand's photographs, Nancy Newhall put a photograph of a blasted tree with an account of witchcraft, a stern detail of rock with eye-witness accounts of the Boston Massacre, the spire of a meeting house with a statement on abolition, an infinite seascape with the chronicle of the loss of a ship at sea. In the exhibition *The Family of Man* at The Museum of Modern Art, and in the book made from it, Edward Steichen chose not only photographs of family life the world over to put in juxtaposition, but also photographs as metaphor: the photograph *Mount Williamson* by Ansel Adams expressed the creation of earth; a photograph by Wynn Bullock of a child asleep in a forest glade, the creation of man.

Minor White, whose photographic style was formed during his association with Stieglitz, Weston and Adams, and who has had long experience as a teacher, has explored the equivalent as a photographic approach in his own camera work, in his teaching, and in his extensive writing. He has defined the photograph as a mirage and the camera as a metamorphosing machine:

To get from the tangible to the intangible (which mature artists in any medium claim as part of their task) a paradox of some kind has frequently been helpful. For the photographer to free himself of the tyranny of the visual facts upon which he is utterly dependent, a paradox is the only possible tool. And the talisman paradox for unique photography is to work "the mirror with a memory" as if it were a mirage, and the camera a metamorphosing machine, and the photograph as if it were a metaphor.... Once freed of the tyranny of surfaces and textures, substance and form [the photographer] can use the same to pursue poetic truth.[3]

By this definition, then, the equivalent has become something both rooted in the subject and yet beyond it;

surface appearance, though of secondary importance, is essential: and the photograph must be transformed into a new event, to be interpreted, or read. To find the inner meaning discovered by the photographer is not easy. In *Aperture*, the quarterly which he has edited and published since 1952, White has published frequent discussions on this problem.

White is a brilliant technician, and insists upon the mastery of straight photography by his students, both in technique and especially in previsualization. He has written a *Zone System Manual*, an adaptation and explanation of the technical and esthetic approach founded by Ansel Adams. He photographs the world with great sensitivity, always using the camera faithfully. Rock is rock, sand is sand, frost on the window pane is frost. But the resulting image may seem equivocal: a rock becomes a landscape, frost becomes a sea wave. He often presents his work in sequences of images chosen to reinforce one another, sometimes accompanied by his own poetic text.

Aaron Siskind, who teaches photography at the Institute of Design of Illinois Institute of Technology, began his photographic career as a documentarian in 1935. Around 1944 he became concerned with the structure of form, and has worked out a unique, powerful style. He described as his primary concern

a concentration on the world within the frame of the picture. For my material I have gone to the "commonplace", the "neglected", the "insignificant" – the walls, the pavements, the iron work of New York City, the endless items once used and now discarded by people, the concrete walls of Chicago and the deep subways of New York on which water and weather have left their mark – the detritus of our world which I am combing for meaning. In this work fidelity to the object and to my instrument, the clear-seeing lens, is unrelenting; transformation into an esthetic object is achieved in the act of seeing, and not by manipulation.[4]

He emphasizes the linear. Edges are sharp, contrasts are great. Everything seems on a single plane, with little depth. Often the image is ambiguous, creating in the beholder a tension between what is obvious and what is revealed.

In the introduction to a book of Siskind's photographs, the critic Harold Rosenberg wrote: "Instead of scenes that seem like paintings, Siskind's pictures ARE paintings as they appear on the printed page – which is where people today see most of the paintings that they see. They are reproductions that have no originals."[5]

Reviewing the book, White took issue with this confused appraisal:

SISKIND: Chicago, 1949

"This disfigured 'R' doesn't seem important to me as a letter—but the fact that this shape *is* a letter lends a kind of pathos to it. I think that you find that there is a heroic quality about the picture too, and there is virility. To me, signs are like this. Perhaps it is that the forms, the shapes in them, communicate more, and are more important than what was originally said on them."—Aaron Siskind in *Modern Photography*, Feb., 1958.

SISKIND: Gloucester, Massachusetts, 1944

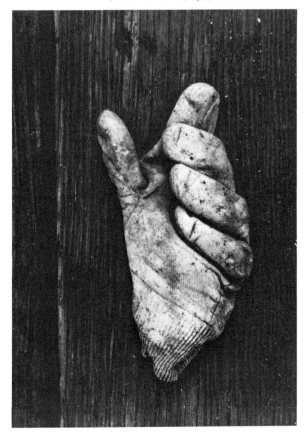

FRANK: Chicago. 1956. From *Les Américains*, Paris, 1958.

straight photography has sharpened and made convincing the formalistic. The formalists, in turn, have stimulated the straight photographers and the documentarians to the discovery of new spatial organization. The documentarian has helped the photojournalist to make his report more convincing. Robert Frank, who was on the staff of *Harper's Bazaar* magazine, traveled across America under a Guggenheim Fellowship in 1956 and 1957. His harsh, often bitter, photographs, first published in France as *Les Américains*, owe much to the example of the Farm Security Administration photographers without, unfortunately, the sense of compassion which distinguished their work. Walker Evans has written:

That Frank has responded to America with many tears, some hope, and his own brand of fascination, you can see in looking over... his pictures of people, of roadside landscapes and urban cauldrons and of semi-living, i.e. semi-satanic children. He shows high irony towards a nation that generally speaking has it not....[7]

A similar interchange characterizes recent photography in Europe. After World War II several groups of photographers, concerned with the loss of standards during the war years, groped towards the esthetic rehabilitation of photography. Otto Steinert, a German physician, who after army service renounced medicine for photography, began with a few friends to re-explore photography's potentials. Under the name "fotoform" they exhibited their work first in Milan and then at the 1950 "photokina" international photographic trade exposition in Cologne. The show was a revelation. Photographers as well as the public had lost touch during the Hitler regime with the fruitful experiments which had been conducted at the Bauhaus. A whole generation knew nothing of modern art and modern photography. Encouraged with the success of "fotoform," Steinert organized in 1951 an international exhibition at the City Art School in Saarbrücken, of which he had become director. He called it "Subjektive Fotografie" and explained:" 'Subjective Photography' means humanized and individualized photography, and implies the handling of the camera in order to win from the single object the views expressive of its character."[8] He took care to point out that this was a concept "embracing all aspects of individual creation from the non-objective photogram to profound and aesthetically satisfying reportage." A book with one hundred and twelve reproductions was made of the exhibition. It included three essays: one by Steinert defining and outlining the scope of the work, and two on photographic esthetics, by the art

Such photographs, because they suggest the work of non-objective or abstract painters, are often referred to as "abstractions." Yet, because photographs which perpetrate the hieroglyphics of accident and chance are made during a state of photographic selection instead of a mental condition of painterly organization, another name NOT from painting should be applied.... So here we will use the term "Equivalent" to name these 50 photographs which are moments of finding in a continual search for the significance behind surfaces.[6]

White and Siskind independently by their teaching and the example of their work have greatly influenced younger photographers in an approach to the photograph "not as a window, but as an event for its own sake," an attitude closely akin, yet separate from, the esthetic of abstract expressionist, or action, painting. Indeed, it may be argued that the painter has learned much from the photographer, particularly when he abandons the brush, and by assemblage physically puts natural objects and artifacts within a frame.

The four trends we have described are by no means strict categories, and in recent years there has been a lively and beneficial interchange between these differing viewpoints. Harry Callahan, with the discipline of

CALLAHAN: Multiple
exposure, Chicago, 1956.
MOMA

historians J. A. Schmoll genannt Eisenwerth and Franz Roh. The latter was the author of *Foto-Auge*, a book made of the 1929 Film und Foto exhibition at Stuttgart, and the influence of that famous show is proclaimed by the inclusion in *Subjektive Fotografie* of photographs by Moholy-Nagy, Man Ray, and Herbert Bayer. All of the recent photographs showed a strong graphic sense, often linear, sometimes mere pattern making: the formalistic dominated despite Steinert's stated desire to cover all approaches. A second show was held in 1954, followed by a book with an essay by Schmoll gen. Eisenwerth classifying photography according to the photographer's concern with subject matter, from its destruction (photogram) to its passive recording. Again the formalistic dominated. A third and final exhibition was held in 1958, but no book was published. Steinert stated to an interviewer that what seemed in 1950 to be new had already become a formula; "the revolution ended in evolution."

In his own photography Steinert has wavered between the formalistic (photograms, montages) and straight photography (stark landscapes, portraits). As director of the photography department of the Folk-

wangschule in Essen, he has organized several important exhibitions in the Folkwangmuseum.

Everywhere progress is being made in the acceptance of photography as a valid, vital and needful art form. The formation of a department of photography at The Museum of Modern Art in 1940; the founding of the George Eastman House in 1949; the scheduling of major photographic exhibitions by leading art museums in Europe and America; the inclusion of courses in photographic arts by universities and art schools; these are steps towards the ultimate unquestioned acceptance of the esthetic potentials of the camera.

More and more are turning to photography as a medium of expression as well as communication. The leavening of esthetic approaches which we have noted continues. While it is too soon to define the characteristic of the photographic style of today, one common denominator, rooted in tradition, seems in the ascendancy: the direct use of the camera for what it can do best, and that is the revelation, interpretation and discovery of the world of man and of nature. The greatest challenge to the photographer is to express the inner significance through the outward form.

Notes

1. THE ELUSIVE IMAGE

1. D. Barbaro, *Pratica della Perspettiva*, Venice, 1568–69; transl. by A. H. Mayor in *Bul. Metropolitan Mus. of Art*, Summer, 1946, p. 18.
2. Vol. I, p. 170–74; repr. in B. Newhall, *On Photography*, 1956, p. 9–13.
3. V. Fouque, *La Verité sur l'invention de la photographie; Nicéphore Niépce*, Paris, 1867, p. 61.
4. *Ibid.*, p. 62.
5. *Ibid.*, p. 64–65.
6. *Ibid.*, p. 129–30.
7. *Ibid.*, p. 130–31.
8. *Ibid.*, p. 140–42.
9. Niépce to Lemaître, Oct. 12, 1829. The letter is in the Soviet Academy of Sciences, and is published in P. Kravets, ed., *Dokumenti po Istorici Izobreteniya Fotografii*, Moscow, 1949, p. 286; the translation is from *Brit. Jour. Phot.*, Nov. 14, 1930, p. 687.
10. Fouque, *op. cit.*, p. 157–58.

2. THE MIRROR WITH A MEMORY

1. Transl. by C. W. Canfield in *Phot. Times*, Jul., 1895, p. 47.
2. *Idem.*
3. Fouque, *op. cit.*, p. 222.
4. Broadside publ. by Daguerre in 1838. Coll. George Eastman House; repr. in *Image*, Mar., 1959, p. 32–36.
5. *Mechanic's Mag.*, 1839, p. 320.
6. M. A. Gaudin, *Traité pratique de photographie*, Paris, 1844, p. 6–7.
7. *New York Star*, Oct. 14, 1839.
8. *Edinburgh Rev.*, 1843, p. 332.
9. J. F. Soleil, *Guide de l'amateur de photographie*, Paris, 1840, p. 70–71.
10. In a letter dated Feb. 10, 1855, to M. A. Root, who published it in his *Camera and Pencil*, Phila., 1864, p. 346–47.
11. *Amer. Jour. Phot.*, 1861, p. 42.
12. Letter from Daguerre to Edward Anthony and J. R. Clark, Feb. 15, 1847. Coll. Kodak-Pathé, Vincennes.
13. *Phot. Art Jour.*, 1851, p. 358.

3. PRINTS FROM PAPER

1. H. F. Talbot, *The Pencil of Nature*, London, 1844 [unpaged].
2. *Athenaeum*, Feb. 9, 1839, p. 116.
3. *Literary Gazette*, Apr. 13, 1839, p. 235.
4. *Ibid.*, p. 72.
5. Reported by an eyewitness, J. D. Harding, in a letter to Baron Isidore Taylor, Jan. 31, 1839. Coll. George Eastman House.
6. *Athenaeum*, Feb. 9, 1839, p. 116–17.
7. *L'Artiste*, 2e série, tome 3, 1839, p. 64.
8. *Art Union*, 1854, p. 84.
9. Talbot, *Pencil of Nature*.
10. *Art Jour.*, Feb. 1, 1855, p. 51.
11. Letter from D. O. Hill to Mr. Bicknell, Jan. 17, 1848. Coll. George Eastman House.
12. *Phot. Notes*, 1857, p. 103–04.
13. Lo Duca, *Bayard*, Paris, 1943, plate I.

4. PORTRAITS FOR THE MILLIONS

1. Reese & Co., *Daguerreotype Directory*, New York, 1854.
2. E. Liesegang, quoted in *Geschichte der Firma Ed. Liesegang*, 1929, p. 8.
3. "He took the tide of the 'cardomania' at the height of the flood." Obituary of a Mr. Clarkington in *Phot. News*, Nov. 8, 1861, p. 538.
4. *Anthony's Phot. Bul.*, Feb. 1884, p. 65.
5. *Gazette des Beaux-Arts*, 1859, p. 215–16.
6. *Phot. Jour.*, May, 1954.
7. *Wilson's Phot. Mag.*, Jan., 1893, p. 11.
8. *Op. cit.*, Jan., 1897, p. 65–75.
9. *Op. cit.*, Jan., 1893, p. 11.

5. PICTORIAL EFFECT

1. C. Jabez Hughes in *Phot. Notes*, VI (1861), 56–60.
2. N. P. Lerebours, *A Treatise on Photography*, London, 1843, p. 5.
3. *Humphrey's Jour. Phot.*, Jul. 15, 1857, p. 92–93.
4. *Ibid.*, p. 93.
5. *Phot. Jour.*, Apr. 21, 1858, p. 193.
6. *Brit. Jour. Phot.*, VII (1860), 95.
7. Quoted in *Practical Phot.*, Mar., 1895, p. 65.
8. Letter reproduced: *Ibid.*
9. H. P. Robinson, *Art Photography in Short Chapters*, London, 1890, p. 1.
10. H. P. Robinson, *Pictorial Effect in Photography*, London, 1869, pp. 51, 78, 109.
11. A. de Lamartine, *Cours familier de littérature*, Paris, 1859, VII, p. 43.
12. Robinson, *Pictorial Effect*, p. 109.
13. *Ibid.*, p. 51.
14. *Phot. Notes*, 1861, p. 56–60.
15. *Phot. Jour.*, Jul., 1927, p. 297 (facsimile of MS), p. 300.
16. *London Quarterly Rev.*, Amer. ed., 1857, p. 456.
17. R. C. Bayley, *The Complete Photographer*, London, 1906, p. 392.

6. THE FAITHFUL WITNESS

1. Quoted by H. Milhollen in *Library of Congress Quarterly Jour.*, Aug., 1946, p. 11.
2. Quoted by L. R. Fenton in *Illus. London News*, Nov. 8, 1941, p. 590.
3. Repr. in *Amer. Jour. Phot.*, Oct. 1, 1862, p. 145.
4. Mar. 15, 1851, p. 320.
5. Quoted in E. & H. T. Anthony, *Catalogue of Card Photographs*, New York, Nov., 1862, p. 2.
6. J. Cobb, "Photographers of the Civil War," *Military Affairs*, Fall, 1962, p. 127–35.
7. *Atlantic Monthly*, June, 1859, p. 746.
8. *Ibid.*, Jul., 1863, p. 12.
9. F. S. Dellenbaugh, *A Canyon Voyage*, New York, 1908, p. 58.
10. *Ibid.*, p. 179.
11. G. M. Wheeler, *Preliminary Report... Explorations and Surveys Principally in Nevada and Arizona*, Washington, D.C., 1872, p. 18.

7. THE CONQUEST OF ACTION

1. *Foreign Quarterly Rev.*, 1839, p. 213–18.
2. *Phot. Notes*, Oct. 1, 1859, p. 239–40.
3. *Ibid.*
4. *Ibid.*, Jan. 1, 1860, p. 12–13.
5. *Phot. News*, May 24, 1861, p. 242.
6. Repr. in *Phot. News*, Sep. 21, 1877, p. 456.
7. *Brit. Jour. Phot.*, 1891, p. 677.
8. *Intl. Annual of Anthony's Phot. Bul.*, 1889, p. 285–87.
9. *Ibid.*, p. 196–98.
10. P. H. Emerson, *Naturalistic Photography*, London, 1889, p. 161.
11. From the rhyme "Gelatine" by Marc Oute in *Brit. Jour. Phot. Almanac*, 1881, p. 213.
12. A. Black, *Time and Chance*, New York, 1937, p. 103.
13. *Scribner's*, 1895, p. 348.
14. Quoted by W. B. Ferguson, *Photographic Researches of Ferdinand Hurter and Vero C. Driffield*, London, 1920, p. 6.
15. *Phila. Photog.*, Jan. 1874, p. 29.
16. Letter from George Eastman to Myron G. Peck, Jan. 19, 1892. Coll. George Eastman House.
17. *Photo-Miniature*, No. 21 (Dec. 1900), p. 396.

8. PHOTOGRAPHY AS AN ART

1. By R. C. Bayley in his *Complete Photographer*, London, 1906, p. 357.
2. Principally *Brit. Jour. Phot.* Aug. 16–Oct. 11, 1889; pp. 343, 563, 579, 595, 610, 658, 674; see N. Newhall, "Dr. Emerson's Bombshell," *Photography* [Ziff Davis Publ. Co.], Winter, 1947, p. 114.
3. July, 1890, p. 268.
4. J. T. Keiley, "The Linked Ring," *Camera Notes*, Oct. 1901, p. 113.
5. *Photograms of '95*, London, p. 14.
6. The editor proposed the word *photogram* in the belief that it was a more correct derivation from the Greek than *photography* and insisted on its use editorially. He had no idea that the word would come to be used to designate a photograph made without a camera.
7. *Photograms of '97*, p. 94.
8. *Bul. du Photo-Club de Paris*, Feb. 1894, p. 33–34.
9. In his introduction to F. Matthies-Masuren, *Künstlerische Photographie*, Berlin, 1907, p. 2–3.
10. *Ibid.*, p. 11.
11. The date was thus given by Stieglitz in *The American Annual of Photography for 1897*. He later stated that the picture was taken on February 22 of 1892. On this date, however, no snow fell in New York City. Four inches were recorded by the Weather Bureau on February 22, 1893.
12. Feb., 1896, p. 13.
13. *Amer. Annual Phot.*, 1895, p. 27–28.
14. *Amer. Amateur Photog.*, Apr., 1896, p. 145.
15. *Camera Notes*, Jul., 1898, p. 23.
16. *Photograms of the Year 1900*, p. 35–42.
17. *Ibid.*
18. Quoted by J. F. Strauss in *Camera Notes*, July, 1902, p. 34.
19. *New York Evening Sun*, repr. in *Camera Notes*, Jul., 1902, p. 39.
20. Stieglitz conversation recorded in *Twice A Year*, No. 8–9 (1942), p. 117.
21. *The Photo-Secession*, No. 1 (1902).
22. *Camera Work*, No. 12 (1905), p. 59.
23. *Ibid.*, No. 30, (1910), p. 47.
24. *Ibid.*, No. 42–43.
25. *Ibid.*, No. 32, (1910), p. 47.
26. *Ibid.*, No. 37, (1912), p. 43.
27. Jan., 26, 1913.
28. *Photo-Miniature*, No. 124, (Mar. 1913), p. 220.

9. STRAIGHT PHOTOGRAPHY

1. *New York Times*, Oct. 13, 1912, Part VII, p. 7.
2. C. H. Caffin, *Photography as a Fine Art*, New York, 1901, p. 39.
3. Stieglitz conversation recorded in *Twice A Year*, No. 8–9, 1942, p. 128.
4. *PSA Jour.*, Nov. 1947, p. 721.
5. *Photo-Miniature*, No. 183 (1921), p. 138–39.
6. *Amateur Phot.*, Sep. 19, 1923, p. 255.
7. *Seven Arts*, II (1917), 524–25.
8. Quoted by C. Rourke, *Charles Sheeler*, New York, 1938, p. 120; by permission of Harcourt, Brace and World.
9. Edward J. Steichen; he changed the spelling of his Christian name, and dropped his middle initial around 1918.
10. E. Weston, *Daybooks: Vol. I, Mexico*, Rochester, N.Y., 1961, pp. 55, 102, 80, 118.

10. DOCUMENTARY

1. Oct. 11, 1889, p. 668.
2. *Camera Work*, No. 24 (1908), p. 22.

3. *Art Jour.*, Nov. 1, 1862, p. 227.

4. *New York Sun*, Feb. 12, 1888.

5. *Ibid.*

6. Introduction to P. Rotha, *Documentary Film*, London, 1936, p. 5; by permission of Faber & Faber.

7. p. 189.

8. J. Grierson, *On Documentary*, London, 1946; by permission of Collins.

9. *U. S. Camera Mag.*, No. 1 (1938), p. 47, 67.

10. Vol. I, p. 93–116.

11. *The Complete Photographer*, New York, 1942, II, p. 1364–71.

12. *Ibid.*, p. 1394.

11. INSTANT VISION

1. *Amer. Repertory of Arts, Sciences and Manufacturers*, 1840, p. 401–402.

2. C. Piazzi Smyth, *A Poor Man's Photography at the Great Pyramid*, London, 1870, p. 15.

3. *Amer. Annual of Phot. for 1897*, p. 27.

4. *Brit. Jour. Phot. Almanac*, 1894, p. 1008.

5. One of Sigriste's cameras in the George Eastman House collection was recently tested; after half a century the shutter still operated at this remarkably high speed.

6. Catalogue, Ernemann Werke, Dresden, n.d., [1925?], p. 6.

7. Quoted by *Letters* (Time Inc.), Mar. 18, 1935, p. 1–2.

8. By Peter Lloyd, in announcement of Cartier-Bresson exhibition at Julien Levy Gallery, New York, 1933.

9. Letter to B. Newhall, June 28, 1937.

10. In W. D. Morgan & H. M. Lester, eds., *Graphic-Graflex Photography*, 8th ed., New York, 1948, p. 218.

12. THE QUEST FOR FORM

1. Letter to B. Newhall, Apr. 11, 1947.

2. *Athenaeum*, Feb. 9, 1839, p. 115.

3. *The Listener*, 1938, p. 686.

4. *Aperture*, III, No. 1 (1955), p. 12.

5. W. B. Woodbury, *Photographic Amusements*, New York, 1896.

6. *transition*, No. 25 (1936), p. 97.

7. No. 12, 1940, pp. 38, 73–74.

8. *Athenaeum*, Feb. 9, 1839, p. 116.

9. Introduction to E. S. King, *Manual of Celestial Photography*, Boston, 1931.

10. Le Corbusier, *L'Art décoratif d'aujourd'hui*, Paris, 1925, p. 127.

13. FOR THE PRINTED PAGE

1. *Penrose's Pictorial Annual, the Process Year Book for 1898*, London, p. 2.

2. *New York Post*, May 7, 1937.

3. J. R. Whiting, *Photography Is a Language*, Chicago, 1946, p. 98.

4. N. Newhall, in *Aperture*, I, No. 1 (1952), p. 22.

5. Letter to B. Newhall, Jan. 28, 1952.

6. *U. S. Camera Mag.*, Oct. 1938, p. 15–16.

14. IN COLOR

1. V. Fouque, *La Vérité sur l'invention de la photographie*, Paris, 1867, p. 140–42.

2. *Daguerreian Jour.*, II (1851), p. 17.

3. Eastman House possesses one of these color photographs. It is from the collection of J. M. Eder, and was reproduced by him in his *Geschichte der Photographie*, II, pl. III.

4. *Humphrey's Jour. Phot.*, XVI (1865), p. 315–16.

5. *Camera Work*, No. 22 (1908), p. 14.

6. *Modern Photography*, Dec., 1953, p. 54.

15. RECENT TRENDS

1. *Phot. Jour.*, Jan. 1950, p. 7–15.

2. *Amateur Phot.*, Sep. 19, 1923, p. 255.

3. *Art in America*, Vol. 46, No. 1 (1958), p. 52–55.

4. Unpublished statement to B. Newhall, 1954.

5. *Aaron Siskind Photographs*, New York, 1959.

6. *Aperture*, VII, No. 3 (1960), 124.

7. *U. S. Camera 1958*, N.Y., 1957, p. 90.

8. Preface to *Subjektive Fotografie*, Bonn, 1952, p. 26.

Bibliography

This bibliography is intended as a guide for further reading, and is not inclusive. The place of publication, when not indicated, is the same as that of the immediately preceding work. References for individual photographers are divided into two groups: publications by the individual (marked PUBL.) and literature about the individual and his work (marked BIBL.). Further references can be found in *Photographic Literature*, edited by Albert Boni (New York, 1963), a bibliography so comprehensive that it is an indispensable reference work for all students.

1. GENERAL WORKS

Baier, W., *A Source Book of Photographic History*, London, 1964(?) (introduction in English; text in German).

Bensusan, A. D., *Silver Images; History of Photography in Africa*, Cape Town, 1966.

Braive, M., *The Age of Photography*, New York, 1966.

Cato, J., *The Story of the Camera in Australia*, Melbourne, 1955.

Christ, Y., *L'Age d'or de la photographie*, Paris, 1965.

Coke, V. D., *The Painter and the Photograph*, Albuquerque, N. M., 1964.

Darrah, W. C., *Stereo Views; a History of Stereographs in America*, Gettysburg, Pa., 1964.

Doty, R., *Photo-Secession; Photography as a Fine Art*, Rochester, N.Y., The George Eastman House, 1960.

Eder, J. M., *History of Photography*, New York, 1945 (unillus. transl. of *Geschichte der Photographie*, 2 vols., Halle, 1932).

Museum Folkwang, *Die Kalotypie in Frankreich*, Essen, 1965–66 (exhibition catalogue; essays by O. Steinert & A. Jammes).

—. *Kunstphotographie um 1900*, 1964 (exhibition catalogue; essays by O. Steinert, F. Kempe, H. Speer, D. Masclet, L. F. Gruber, H. Freytag, H. Spielman).

Faber, J., *Great Moments in News Photography*, New York, 1960.

Focal Encyclopedia of Photography, London, 1956 (2d ed., 2 vols., 1965).

Freund, G., *La Photographie en France au dix-neuvième siècle*, Paris, 1936.

Friedman, J. S., *History of Color Photography*, Boston, 1944.

George Eastman House, *Photography in the Twentieth Century*, Rochester, 1967.

Gernsheim, H., *Creative Photography; Aesthetic Trends, 1839–1960*, London, 1962 (also Boston, 1962).

—. *The History of Photography*, London, 1955.

—. *A Concise History of Photography*, New York, 1965.

Greenhill, R., *Early Photography in Canada*, Toronto, 1965.

Gruber, L. Fritz, *Grosse Photographen unseres Jahrhunderts*, Düsseldorf, 1964.

Hicks, W., *Words and Pictures; an Introduction to Photo-journalism*, New York, 1952.

Lacey, P., *The History of the Nude in Photography*, 1964.

Lecuyer, R., *Histoire de la photographie*, Paris, 1945.

Lyons, N., ed., *Photographers on Photography*, Englewood Cliffs, N. J. & Rochester, N. Y., 1966.

Newhall, B., *The Daguerreotype in America*, New York, 1961.

—. *Latent Image; the Discovery of Photography*, Garden City, N.Y., 1967.

—. "Looking Back at Stereo," in *Stereo-Realist Manual* by W. D. Morgan, H. M. Lester and others, New York, 1954.

—. ed., *On Photography; a Source Book of Photo History in Facsimile*, Watkins Glen, N.Y., 1956.

Newhall, B. & N., *Masters of Photography*, New York, 1958.

Pollack, P., *The Picture History of Photography*, 1958.

Potonniée, G., *History of the Discovery of Photography*, New York, 1936 (unillustrated translation of *Histoire de la découverte de la photographie*, Paris, 1925).

Rothstein, A., *Photojournalism*, New York, 1956 (2d ed. 1965).

Scharf, A., *Creative Photography*, London & New York, 1965.

Sipley, L. W., *A Half Century of Color*, New York, 1951.

—. *A Collector's Guide to American Photography*, Philadelphia, 1957.

—. *Photography's Great Inventors*, 1965.

Skopec, R., *Photographie im Wandel der Zeiten*, Prague, 1964.

Steichen, E., ed., *The Bitter Years, 1935–41; Rural America as Seen by the Photographers of the Farm Security Administration*, New York, Museum of Modern Art, 1962.

Stenger, E., *The March of Photography*, London, 1958 (unillustrated transl. of *Siegeszug der Photographie*, Seebruck am Chiemsee, 1950).

Szarkowski, J., *The Photographer's Eye*, New York, 1966.

Taft, R., *Photography and the American Scene*, New York, 1938 (repr. without change, 1942, 1964).

Vigneau, A., *Une brève histoire de l'art de Niepce à nos jours*, Paris, 1963.

Wall, E. J., *The History of Three-Color Photography*, Boston, 1925 (not illustrated; mainly technical).

Weimar, W., *Die Daguerreotypie in Hamburg*, Hamburg, 1915.

2. INDIVIDUAL PHOTOGRAPHERS

ABBOTT, BERENICE
PUBL. *Changing New York*, New York, 1939 (text by E. McCausland); *A Guide to Better Photography*, 1941 (2d ed., 1953); *The View Camera Made Simple*, 1948; *Greenwich Village Today and Yesterday*, 1949 (with H. W. Lanier); "The Image of Science," *Art in America*, 1959, No. 4, p. 76–79.
BIBL. E. McCausland, "Berenice Abbott... Realist," *Photo Arts* (Ziff Davis Publ. Co.), Spring, 1948, 46–50+.

ADAMS, ANSEL
PUBL. *Taos Pueblo*, San Francisco, 1930 (text by Mary Austin); *Making a Photograph*, London, 1935 (rev. ed., 1939; reprinted, 1948); *Sierra Nevada; the John Muir Trail*, Berkeley, Calif., 1938; *Born Free and Equal; Photographs of the*

Loyal Japanese-Americans at Manzanar Relocation Center, Inyo County, California, New York, 1944; *Yosemite and the High Sierra*, Boston, 1948 (text by John Muir); *Basic Photo Series*, New York, 1948–56 (1. *Camera & Lens*; 2. *The Negative*; 3. *The Print*; 4. *Natural-Light Photography*; 5. *Artificial-Light Photography*); *The Land of Little Rain*, Boston, 1950 (text by Mary Austin); *My Camera in Yosemite Valley*, Yosemite National Park, Calif., & Boston, 1950 (rev. ed., *These We Inherit*, San Francisco, 1962); *My Camera in the National Parks*, Yosemite National Park, Calif., & Boston, 1950; *Death Valley*, San Francisco, 1954 (3d ed., 1963; text by N. Newhall); *Mission San Xavier del Bac*, 1954 (text by N. Newhall); *The Pageant of History in Northern California*, 1954 (text by N. Newhall); *The Islands of Hawaii*, Honolulu, 1958 (text by E. Joesting); *Yosemite Valley*, San Francisco, 1959 (ed. by N. Newhall); *This Is the American Earth*, 1960 (text by N. Newhall); *Death Valley and the Creek Called Furnace*, Los Angeles, 1962 (text by E. Corle); *Polaroid-Land Photography Manual*, New York, 1963; *Fiat Lux, The University of California*, 1967 (text by N. Newhall).

BIBL. N. Newhall, *Ansel Adams; Vol. I: The Eloquent Light*, San Francisco, 1963. N. Newhall, *Ansel Adams Photographs 1923–1963, The Eloquent Light*, 1963 (pamphlet, with chronology and extensive bibl.). B. & N. Newhall, "Ansel Adams," in their *Masters of Photography*, New York, 1958, p. 172–87.

ADAM-SALOMON, ANTONY SAMUEL
Obituary, by his admirer, E. L. Wilson in *Phila. Phot.*, Jul., 1881, p. 193–96.

ARCHER, FREDERICK SCOTT
PUBL. *A Manual of the Collodion Process*, London, 1852 (2d ed., 1854); *Photographic Views of Kenilworth*, 1851.

BIBL. W. J. Harrison, *History of Photography*, New York, 1887, p. 39–40.

ATGET, EUGÈNE
Atget, Photographe de Paris, New York, n. d. (c. 1930, French preface by P. MacOrlan). B. Abbott, *The World of Atget*, New York, 1964. A. D. Trottenberg, *A Vision of Paris; The Photographs of Eugène Atget; The Words of Marcel Proust*, New York, 1963. B. & N. Newhall, "Eugène Atget," in their *Masters of Photography*, 1958, p. 92–101.

AVEDON, RICHARD
PUBL. *Observations*, New York, 1959 (text by T. Capote); *Nothing Personal*, 1964 (text by J. Baldwin).

BARNARD, GEORGE N.
PUBL. *Photographic Views of Sherman's Campaign*, New York, 1866.

BAYARD, HIPPOLYTE
BIBL. Lo Duca, *Bayard*, Paris, 1943. Folkwang Museum, Essen, *Hippolyte Bayard, ein Erfinder der Photographie*, 1960 (exhibition catalogue; German essay by O. Steinert; French essay by P. Harmant).

BLACK, ALEXANDER
PUBL. Picture plays in book form: *Miss Jerry*, New York, 1895; *A Capital Courtship*, 1897; *Miss America*, 1898. Autobiography: *Time and Chance; Adventures with People and Print*, 1937.

BLANQUART-EVRARD, LOUIS DÉSIRÉ
PUBL. *Traité de photographie sur papier*, Paris, 1851 (the historical intro., by Georges Ville, is translated in *Amer. Photo Engraver*, Jan.-Mar., 1939); *Les Origines de la photographie*, Lille, 1869 (with original prints by various techniques).

BIBL. G. Peterich, "L. D. Blanquart-Evrard, Gutenberg of Photography," *Image*, Apr., 1957, p. 80–87.

BOURKE-WHITE, MARGARET
PUBL. *Eyes on Russia*, New York, 1931; *You Have Seen Their Faces*, 1937 (text by E. Caldwell); *North of the Danube*, 1939 (text by E. Caldwell); *Say, Is This the U.S.A.*, 1941 (text by E. Caldwell); *Shooting the Russian War*, 1942; *Purple Heart Valley*, 1944; *Dear Fatherland, Rest Quietly*, 1946; *Halfway to Freedom; A Study of the New India*, 1949; *Report on the American Jesuits*, 1956 (with John Lafarge); *Portrait of Myself*, 1963.

BRADY, MATHEW B.
PUBL. *The Gallery of Illustrious Americans*, New York, 1850 (lithographs after daguerreotypes).
BIBL. J. D. Horan, *Mathew Brady, Historian with a Camera*, New York, 1955. R. Meredith, *Mr. Lincoln's Camera Man, Mathew B. Brady*, 1946. Library of Congress, *Civil War Photographs 1861-1865; a Catalogue*, compiled by H. D. Milhollen & D. H. Mugridge, Washington, D.C., 1961.

BRAGAGLIA, ANTON GIULIO
PUBL. *Fotodinamismo Futurista*, Rome, 1912.
BIBL. P. Racanicchi, "Fotodinamismo Futurista," *Popular Phot. Edizione Italiana*, Jan., 1963, p. 43-54.

BRANDT, BILL
PUBL. *The English at Home*, London 1936; *A Night in London*, 1938; *Camera in London*, 1948; *Literary Britain*, 1951; *Perspectieve of Nudes*, 1961; *Shadow of Light*, 1966.
BIBL. R. Doty, "The Photographs of Bill Brandt," *Image*, Vol. 12, No. 2 (1963), p. 5–6.

BRASSAÏ
PUBL. *Paris de Nuit*, Paris, 1933 (text by Paul Morand); *Camera in Paris*, London, 1949; *Seville en fête*, Paris, 1954; *Graffiti, 105 Schwarzweiss Fotos*, Stuttgart, 1960; *Picasso & Co.*, Garden City, N.Y., 1966.
BIBL. H. Miller, *Brassaï*, Paris, 1952. N. Newhall, "Brassaï," *Camera* (Lucerne), May, 1956, p. 185–215.

CALLAHAN, HARRY M.
PUBL. "An Adventure in Photography," *Minicam*, Feb., 1946, p. 28–29; *The Multiple Image*, Chicago, 1961; *Photographs: Harry Callahan*, Santa Barbara, 1964.

CAMERON, JULIA MARGARET
PUBL. "The Annals of My Glass House," *Phot. Jour.*, Jan., 1927 (repr. Gernsheim, *Cameron*).
BIBL. H. Gernsheim, *Julia Margaret Cameron*, London, 1948. V. Woolf & R. Fry, *Victorian Photographs of Famous Men and Fair Women*, 1926. B. & N. Newhall, "Julia Margaret Cameron," in their *Masters of Photography*, New York, 1958, p. 46–53.

CAPA, ROBERT
PUBL. *Slightly Out of Focus*, New York, 1947 (autobiography); *Death in the Making*, 1938; *Images of War*, 1964.
BIBL. Magnum Photos, *Robert Capa War Photographs*, New York, 1960 (bibl.; chronology).

CARROLL, LEWIS (Pseudonym of Charles Lutwidge Dodgson)
H. Gernsheim, *Lewis Carroll, Photographer*, London, 1949.

CARTIER-BRESSON, HENRI
PUBL. *The Decisive Moment*, New York, 1952; *D'une Chine à l'autre*, Paris, 1954 (text by J.-P. Sartre); *The Europeans*, New York, 1955; *The People of Moscow*, 1955; *China*, 1964 (with B. B. Miller).
BIBL. The Museum of Modern Art, *The Photographs of Cartier-Bresson*, New York, 1947 (essays by L. Kirstein and B. Newhall; bibliography, chronology; new ed., with different selection of plates, new essays by Kirstein and Newhall, without bibl., New York, Grossman Publishers, 1963). B. Newhall, "The Instantaneous Vision of Cartier-Bresson,"

Camera (Lucerne), Oct., 1955, p. 485–89. B. & N. Newhall, "Henri Cartier-Bresson," in their *Masters of Photography*, New York, 1958, p. 160–71.

COBURN, ALVIN LANGDON
PUBL. *London*, London, 1909 (intro. by H. Belloc); *New York*, 1910 (intro. by H. G. Wells); *Men of Mark*, 1913; *Moore Park, Rickmansworth*, 1915; *More Men of Mark*, 1922; *Autobiography*, 1966.
BIBL. The George Eastman House, *A Portfolio of Sixteen Photographs by Alvin Langdon Coburn*, Rochester, N.Y., 1962 (with essay by Nancy Newhall, extensive bibl.).

CUTTING, JAMES A.
U. S. Patents 11, 213, July 4, 1854; 11, 266 and 11, 267, July 11, 1854.

DAGUERRE, LOUIS JACQUES MANDÉ
PUBL. *Historique et description des procédés du Daguerréotype et du Diorama*, Paris, 1839 (for bibl. of all editions and translations see below, Gernsheim. English transl. of technical specifications in Newhall, *On Photography*).
BIBL. H. & A. Gernsheim, *L. J. M. Daguerre*, London, 1956 (also, Cleveland & New York, 1956). G. Potonniée, *Daguerre peintre et décorateur*, Paris, 1935.

DEGAS, HILAIRE GERMAIN EDGAR
B. Newhall, "Degas, photographe amateur; huit lettres inédites," *Gazette des Beaux-Arts*, Jan., 1963, p. 61–64 (Engl. transl. of letters: *Image*, June, 1956, p. 124–26).

DISDÉRI, ANDRÉ ADOLPHE EUGÈNE
PUBL. French patent 21, 502, Nov. 27, 1854 (carte-de-visite system); *Renseignements photographiques indispensables à tous*, Paris, 1855; *L'Art de la photographie*, 1862 (Engl. transl., London, 1864).

DODGSON, CHARLES LUTWIDGE. See CARROLL, LEWIS (Pseud.).

DU CAMP, MAXIME
PUBL. *Egypte; Nubie, Palestine et Syrie; dessins photographiques*, Paris, 1852; *Le Nil*, Paris, 1854.
BIBL. J. M. Carré, *Voyageurs et écrivains français en Egypte*, 2 vols., Cairo, 1932 ("Flaubert et Maxime Du Camp," II 77–128).

DUCOS DU HAURON, LOUIS
PUBL. *Les Couleurs en photographie*, Paris, 1869.
BIBL. Alcide Ducos du Hauron, *La Photographie des couleurs et les découvertes de Louis Ducos du Hauron*, Paris, n.d. (1898 or later). G. Potonniée, "Louis Ducos du Hauron," *Bul. de la Soc. Française de Phot.*, May, 1914, p. 149–63; Feb., 1938, p. 17–21 (Engl. transl., *Photo-Engravers' Bul.*, Feb., 1939, p. 18–20; Mar., 1939, p. 35–46). B. Newhall, "An 1877 Color Photograph," *Image*, May, 1954, p. 33–34.

DUNCAN, DAVID DOUGLAS
PUBL. *This Is War!*, New York, 1961; *The Private World of Pablo Picasso*, 1958; *Yankee Nomad, a Photographic Odyssey*, 1966.

EAKINS, THOMAS
PUBL. Description of his chronophotographic experiments, with illustration, in E. Muybridge, *Animal Locomotion: the Muybridge Work at the University of Pennsylvania; the Method and the Work*, Philadelphia, 1888.
BIBL. C. Bregler, "Photos by Eakins," *Mag. of Art*, Jan., 1943, p. 28–29. W. I. Homer, "Eakins, Muybridge and the Motion Picture Process," *Art Quarterly*, Summer, 1963, p. 194–216.

EASTMAN, GEORGE
C. W. Ackerman, *George Eastman*, Boston, 1930. B. Newhall, "The Photographic Inventions of George Eastman," *Jour. Phot. Sci.*, Mar.-Apr., 1955, p. 33–40.

EDGERTON, HAROLD, E.
PUBL. *Flash! Ultraspeed Photography*, 2d ed., Boston, 1945 (with J. R. Killian; bibl.).

EISENSTAEDT, ALFRED
PUBL. *Witness to Our Time*, New York, 1966.
BIBL. S. Rayfield, "The Wonderful Eye of Alfred Eisenstaedt," *Popular Phot.*, Oct., 1955, p. 82–93+. M. White, "Alfred Eisenstaedt — Horizon: People," *Leica Phot.*, 1955, No. 3, p. 4–7.

ELISOFON, ELIOT
PUBL. "Color Control," *Popular Phot.*, Dec., 1958, p. 73–93; *Color Photography*, New York, 1961.

EMERSON, PETER HENRY
PUBL. "Photography, a Pictorial Art," *Amateur Phot.*, Mar. 19, 1886, p. 138–39; *Life and Landscape on the Norfolk Broads*, London, 1886; *Idylls of the Norfolk Broads*, 1887; *Pictures from Life in Field and Fen*, 1887; *Pictures of East Anglian Life*, 1888; *Naturalistic Photography for Students of the Art*, 1889 (2d ed., 1890; 3d rev. ed., 1899); *Wild Life on a Tidal Water*, 1890; *The Death of Naturalistic Photography*, 1890; *On English Lagoons*, 1893; *Marsh Leaves*, 1895.
BIBL. B. & N. Newhall, "Peter Henry Emerson," in their *Masters of Photography*, New York, 1958, p. 54–59. N. Newhall, "Emerson's Bombshell," *Photography* (Ziff Davis Publ. Co.), Winter, 1947, p. 50–52+.

EVANS, FREDERICK H.
B. Newhall, *Frederick H. Evans*, Rochester, N.Y., 1964.

EVANS, WALKER
PUBL. *The Bridge, a poem by Hart Crane*, illus. with three photographs, Paris, 1930; *The Crime of Cuba*, Philadelphia, 1933 (with Carleton Beals); *Let Us Now Praise Famous Men*, Boston, 1941 (with J. Agee; new ed. with 62 photographs, 1960); *Many are Called*, 1966; *Message from the Interior*, New York, 1966.
BIBL. The Museum of Modern Art, *American Photographs*, New York, 1938 (with essay by L. Kirstein; repr., 1962). B. & N. Newhall, "Walker Evans," in their *Masters of Photography*, 1958, p. 150–59.

FENTON, ROGER
PUBL. "Narrative of a Photographic Trip to the Seat of War in the Crimea," *Jour. of the Photographic Soc.*, Jan. 21, 1856, p. 284–91.
BIBL. H. & A. Gernsheim, *Roger Fenton, Photographer of the Crimean War*, London, 1954.

FISCHER, RUDOLF
PUBL. German patents 253335, Nov. 12, 1912, "Verfahren zur Herstellung farbiger photographischer Bilder," and 257160, Apr. 17, 1913, "Verfahren zur Herstellung von Farbenphotographien."
BIBL. E. Stenger, "Dr. Rudolf Fischer 70 Jahre alt," *Zeitschrift für wissenschaftliche Photographie*, 1951, p. 118–20.

FIZEAU, HIPPOLYTE LOUIS
BIBL. *Notice sur les travaux de M. H. Fizeau*, Paris, 1859. A. E. Marshall, "Fizeau Gravure Process," *The Complete Photographer*, No. 28 (1942), p. 1782–84.

FRANK, ROBERT
PUBL. *U. S. Camera 1958*, p. 90–115 (33 reproductions; statements by Frank and Walker Evans); *Les Américains*, Paris, 1958 (text ed. by A. Bosquet: publ. in New York, 1959, as *The Americans*, with text by Jack Kerouac).

GARDNER, ALEXANDER
PUBL. *Catalogue of Photographic Incidents of the War from the Gallery of Alexander Gardner*, Washington, D.C., 1863; *Photographic Sketch Book of the War*, 2 vols., 1865–66 (repr. in one

vol., New York, 1959); *Rays of Sunlight from South America,* Washington, D.C., 1865.

BIBL. J. Cobb, "Alexander Gardner," *Image,* June, 1958, p. 124–36. B. & N. Newhall, "Alexander Gardner," in their *Masters of Photography,* New York, 1958, p. 38–42.

GODOWSKY, LEOPOLD. See MANNES, LEOPOLD

HAAS, ERNST
PUBL. "On Color Photography," *Popular Photography Color Annual,* 1957, p. 30.

BIBL. B. Dobell, "Ernst Haas, Master of Color," *Ibid.,* p. 28.

HALSMAN, PHILIPPE
PUBL. "On Psychological Portraiture — Technique and Emotion," *Popular Phot.,* Dec., 1958, p. 118–41+; *Halsman on the Creation of Photographic Ideas,* New York, 1961.

BIBL. B. Downes, "Philippe Halsman," *Popular Phot.,* Feb., 1946, p. 2–31+.

HERSCHEL, SIR JOHN FREDERICK WILLIAM
PUBL. "Note on the Art of Photography," *Proceedings, Royal Soc.,* 1839, IV, 131–33; "On the Chemical Action of the Rays of the Solar Spectrum on Preparations of Silver, etc.," *Philosophic Transactions, Royal Soc.,* 1840, Part I, p. 1–59.

BIBL. B. Newhall, "Sir John Herschel," *The Encyclopedia of Photography* (Greystone Press). H. Gernsheim, "Talbot's and Herschel's Photographic Experiments in 1839," *Image,* Sept., 1959, p. 133–37.

HILL, DAVID OCTAVIUS, & ROBERT ADAMSON
BIBL. H. Schwarz, *David Octavius Hill,* New York, 1931 (also London, 1932). B. & N. Newhall, "David Octavius Hill and Robert Adamson," in their *Masters of Photography,* New York, 1958, p. 14–21. Folkwang Museum, Essen, *David Octavius Hill, Robert Adamson, Inkunabeln der Photographie,* 1963 (exhibition catalogue; intro. by Otto and Marlis Steinert).

HILL, LEVI L.
PUBL. *Treatise on Heliochromy,* New York, 1856.

BIBL. B. Newhall, *The Daguerreotype in America,* New York, 1961, p. 96–106.

HINE, LEWIS W.
PUBL. *Men at Work,* New York, 1932.

BIBL. R. Doty, "The Interpretive Photographs of Lewis Hine," *Image,* May, 1957, p. 112–19. E. McCausland, "Boswell of Ellis Island; Lewis Hine," *U. S. Camera Mag.,* No. 2 (1939), p. 58–62. B. Newhall, "Lewis W. Hine," *Mag. of Art,* Nov., 1938, p. 636–37.

HUGO, CHARLES VICTOR
P. Gruyer, *Victor Hugo, photographe,* Paris, 1905.

HURTER, FERDINAND & CHARLES VERO DRIFFIELD
PUBL. Collected writings: W. B. Ferguson, ed., *The Photographic Researches of Ferdinand Hurter & Vero C. Driffield,* London, 1920.

BIBL. B. Newhall, "Hurter & Driffield," in *The Encyclopedia of Photography,* X (1963), p. 1789–92.

HUTTON, K.
PUBL. *Speaking Likeness,* London, 1947.

JACKSON, WILLIAM HENRY
PUBL. *Time Exposure,* New York, 1940. Jackson's diaries are preserved in the New York Public Library and in the State Historical Society of Colorado; those for 1866–67, 1873–74, are published by L. R. and A. W. Hafen, Glendale, Calif., 1959.

BIBL. C. S. Jackson, *Picture Maker of the Old West; William Henry Jackson,* New York, 1947.

JOLY, JOHN
PUBL. "On a Method of Photography in Natural Colours," *Nature,* 1895, p. 91–93.

KARSH, YOUSUF
PUBL. *Faces of Destiny,* Chicago, 1946; *Portraits of Greatness,* New York, 1959; *In Search of Greatness,* 1962.

BIBL. "Karsh the Worker; a Picture Close-Up of His Lighting and Posing Techniques," *Popular Phot.,* May, 1945, p. 20–33+.

KEITH, THOMAS
BIBL. A. L. Coburn, "The Old Masters of Photography," *The Century,* Oct., 1915, p. 908–20. C. S. Minto, *Thomas Keith, 1827–1895; Surgeon and Photographer,* Edinburgh, 1966.

KERTÉSZ, ANDRÉ
PUBL. *Enfants,* Paris, 1933; *Nos amis les bêtes,* 1936; *Day of Paris,* New York, 1945.

BIBL. Brassaï, "My Friend Kertész," *Camera* (Lucerne), Apr., 1963, p. 7–32. "The World of Kertész," *Show,* 1964, p. 56–61. The Museum of Modern Art, *André Kertész, Photographer,* New York, 1964 (introduction by J. Szarkowski). *André Kertész,* New York, Paragraphic Books, 1966 (essay by Anna Fárová).

LAND, EDWIN H.
PUBL. "A New One-Step Photographic Process," *Jour. of the Optical Soc. of America,* Feb. 1947, p. 61–77; "One-Step Photography," *Phot. Jour.,* Jan., 1950, p. 7–15.

LANGE, DOROTHEA
PUBL. *An American Exodus; a Record of Human Erosion,* New York, 1939 (with P. Taylor); "Photographing the Familiar," *Aperture,* Vol. I, No. 2 (1952), 4–15 (with D. Dixon); *The American Country Woman,* Fort Worth, Texas, Amon Carter Museum, 1967.

BIBL. D. Dixon, "Dorothea Lange," *Modern Phot.,* Dec., 1952, p. 68–77+. B. & N. Newhall, "Dorothea Lange," in their *Masters of Photography,* New York, 1958, p. 140–49. W. Van Dyke, "The Photographs of Dorothea Lange, a Critical Analysis," *Camera Craft,* Oct., 1934, p. 461–67. The Museum of Modern Art, *Dorothea Lange,* New York, 1966 (essay by G. P. Elliott).

LARTIGUE, JACQUES HENRI
BIBL. The Museum of Modern Art, *The Photographs of Jacques Henri Lartigue,* New York, 1963 (with essay by J. Szarkowski). *Boyhood Photos of J. H. Lartigue; The Family Album of a Gilded Age,* Paris (?), 1966.

LE SECQ, HENRY
BIBL. G. Cromer, "Henry Le Secq," *Bul. de la Soc. Française de Phot.,* 1930, p. 287–95.

LIPPMANN, GABRIEL
BIBL. A. Berget, *Photographie des couleurs par la méthode interférentielle de M. Lippmann,* Paris, 1891. C. de Watteville, in *Bul. de la Soc. Française de Phot.,* 1921, p. 325–41.

LUMIÈRE, LOUIS
PUBL. *Notice sur le cinématographe,* Lyons, 1897; Appendix to E. Wallon, *La Photographie des couleurs et les plaques autochromes,* Paris, 1907.

BIBL. E. Wallon, *Bul. de la Soc. Française de Phot.,* 1921, p. 225–49. M. Bessy & Lo Duca, *Louis Lumière inventeur,* Paris, 1948.

LYNES, GEORGE PLATT
BIBL. R. W. Marks, "George Platt Lynes, Photographer of Fantasy," *Popular Phot.,* Dec., 1939, p. 24–25+.

McCOMBE, LEONARD
BIBL. R. Mackland, "Leonard McCombe, Journalist," *Pho-*

tography (Ziff Davis Publ. Co.), Winter, 1947, p. 38–45 +.

MANNES, LEOPOLD & LEOPOLD GODOWSKY

BIBL. G. E. Matthews, "Leopold Godowsky, Jr. and Leopold Mannes," *PSA Jour.*, Oct., 1955, p. 33–34.

MAREY, ETIENNE JULES

PUBL. *La Photographie du mouvement*, Paris, 1893 (Engl. transl., London, 1895).

BIBL. A. R. Michaelis, "E. J. Marey — Physiologist and First Cinematographer," *Brit. Jour. Phot.*, Dec. 2, 1955, p. 598–601. Cinémathèque française, *Hommage à J. E. Marey*, Paris, 1963 (exhibition catalogue; essay by E. N. Bonton; chronology).

MAXWELL, JAMES CLERK

BIBL. D. A. Spencer, "The First Colour Photograph," *Penrose Annual*, 1940, p. 99–100. R. M. Evans, "Some Notes on Maxwell's Colour Photograph," *Jour. Phot. Sci.*, Jul.-Aug., 1961, p. 243–46.

MEES, CHARLES EDWARD KENNETH

PUBL. *Theory of the Photographic Process*, rev. ed., New York, 1954; *From Dry Plates to Ektachrome Film*, 1961 (autobiographical). For bibl. of principal articles, see *Image*, Oct., 1954, p. 55–56.

BIBL. W. Clark, "Charles Edward Kenneth Mees, 1882–1960," *Biographical Memoirs of Fellows of the Royal Society*, Nov., 1961, p. 173–97.

MERLIN, HENRY BEAUFOY

BIBL. K. Burke, "Gold and Silver," *Australasia Photo-Review*, Mar., 1953, p. 141–168.

MOHOLY-NAGY, LÁSZLÓ

PUBL. *Malerei, Photographie, Film*, Munich, 1925 (2d. ed., 1927); *Vom Material zur Architektur*, 1929 (transl. as *The New Vision*, New York, 1938); *Vision in Motion*, Chicago, 1947.

BIBL. F. Roh, ed., *L. Moholy-Nagy, 60 Fotos*, Berlin, 1930. S. Moholy-Nagy, *Moholy-Nagy's Experiment in Totality*, New York, 1950.

MORGAN, BARBARA

PUBL. *Martha Graham, Sixteen Dances in Photographs*, New York, 1941; *Summer's Children*, Scarsdale, N.Y., 1951; *Aperture*, Vol. XI, No. 1, 1964 (Special B. Morgan issue, chronology, bibliog.).

MUYBRIDGE, EADWEARD

PUBL. *The Horse in Motion*, Boston, 1882 (text by J. D. B. Stillman; the first book publication of the horse photographs); *Animal Locomotion*, 11 vols., Philadelphia, 1887 (basic: Muybridge reproduced many of the same photographs in his *Animals in Motion*, London, 1899, and *The Human Figure in Motion*, 1901, books not to be confused with the Dover Press publications *Animals in Motion*, 1955, and *The Human Figure in Motion*, 1957, which contain poor reproductions made from the *Animal Locomotion* collotypes, rather than from original photographs); *Descriptive Zoopraxography*, Philadelphia, 1893.

BIBL. Univ. of Pennsylvania, *Animal Locomotion, the Muybridge Work*, Philadelphia, 1888. B. Newhall, "Muybridge and the First Motion Picture," *Image*, Jan., 1956, p. 4–11 (repr. in *U. S. Camera Annual*, 1957, p. 235–42). A. Scharf, "Painting, Photography and the Image of Movement," *Burlington Magazine*, May, 1962, p. 186–195 (Reply with rejoinder by W. I. Homer, September, 1962, p. 391–392).

NADAR (Pseudonym of Gaspard Félix Tournachon)

PUBL. *Quand j'étais photographe*, Paris, n. d. (c. 1900).

BIBL. J. Prinet & A. Dilasser, *Nadar*, Paris, 1966. R. Skopec, *Nadar*, Prague, 1962 (text in German, English, French). B.

& N. Newhall, "Nadar," in their *Masters of Photography*, New York, 1958, p. 32–37. *Camera* (Lucerne), Dec., 1960 (Nadar issue: "The History and Legend of Nadar," by Michel-François Braive; "This Nadar..." by E. Sougez; 21 photographs and facsimile reproduction of the lithograph *Le Panthéon-Nadar*). Bibliothèque Nationale, *Nadar*, Paris, 1965 (exhibition catalogue).

NEFF, PETER

U. S. Patent 14, 300, Feb. 19, 1856.

NÈGRE, CHARLES

BIBL. A. Jammes, *Charles Nègre photographe*, Paris, 1963.

NEWMAN, ARNOLD

BIBL. "Arnold Newman on Portraiture, an Interview," *Popular Phot.*, May, 1957, p. 87.

NIÉPCE, NICÉPHORE

PUBL. "Notice sur l'Héliographie" in L. J. M. Daguerre, *Historique et description des procédés du Daguerréotype*, Paris, 1839.

BIBL. V. Fougue, *The Truth Concerning the Invention of Photography: Nicéphore Niépce, His Life and Works*, New York, 1935 (excerpts from letters). T. P. Kravets, ed., *Dokumenti po Istorii Izobreteniya Fotografii*, Moscow, 1949 (important coll. of letters by Daguerre, Niépce and others, given by Isidore Niépce to Russian ambassador and now in Soviet Academy of Sciences; publ. in original French with Russian transl.).

NIEPCE DE SAINT-VICTOR, CLAUDE FÉLIX ABEL

PUBL. *Recherches photographiques*, Paris, 1855 (with biogr. sketch by E. Lacan).

O'SULLIVAN, TIMOTHY H.

BIBL. H. M. Baumhofer, "T. H. O'Sullivan," *Image*, Apr., 1953, p. 20–21. B. & N. Newhall, "Timothy H. O'Sullivan," in their *Masters of Photography*, New York, 1958, p. 38–45. B. & N. Newhall, *T. H. O'Sullivan, Photographer*, Rochester, N.Y., 1966. J. D. Horan, *Timothy O'Sullivan, America's Forgotten Photographer*, New York, 1966.

PENN, IRVING

PUBL. *Moments Preserved; Eight Essays in Photographs and Words*, New York, 1960.

PETIT, PIERRE

BIBL. Article in *Le Biographe*, Paris, n.d., (c. 1880).

PETZVAL, JOSEF

BIBL. J. M. Eder, *Ausführliches Handbuch der Photographie*, Vienna, 1891, Band I, Zweite Hefte, p. 114 (original calculations of Petzval's lens, with foci of elements). R. Kingslake, "Petzval Lens and Camera," *Image*, Dec., 1953, p. 60–61.

PORTER, ELIOT

PUBL. "Chemistry, Medicine, Law and Photography," U.S. *Camera Mag.*, No. 8 (1940). p. 26–29, 64; *In Wildness Is the Preservation of the World*, San Francisco, 1962; *The Place No One Knew: Glen Canyon on the Colorado*, 1963; *Forever Wild: The Adirondacks*, Blue Mountain Lake, N.Y. & New York, 1966 (text by W. C. White). *Summer Island: Penobscot Country*, San Francisco, 1966.

RAY, MAN

PUBL. *Self Portrait*, Boston, 1963; *12 Rayographs*, Stuttgart, 1963.

BIBL. G. Ribemont-Dessaignes, *Man Ray*, Paris, c. 1929. J. T. Soby, *Photographs by Man Ray*, 1920–34, Hartford, Conn., 1934. L. F. Gruber, ed., *Man Ray Portraits*, Gutersloh, 1963 (also, with French text, Paris, 1963).

REJLANDER, OSCAR G.

PUBL. "On Photographic Composition, with a Description

of 'Two Ways of Life'," *Phot. Jour.*, Apr. 21, 1858, p. 191–97.

BIBL. A. H. Wall, "Rejlander's Photographic Art Studies," *Phot. News*, Jul. 30, 1886–Sept. 2, 1887 (ten monthly installments, illus.).

RENGER-PATZSCH, ALBERT
PUBL. *Die Welt ist schön*, Munich, 1928.

BIBL. B. Newhall, "Albert Renger-Patzsch," *Image*, Sept., 1959, p. 138–42. Ruhrland- und Heimatmuseum, *Albert Renger-Patzsch, der Fotograf der Dinge*, Essen, 1966–67 (exhibition catalogue; essay by Fritz Kempe).

RIIS, JACOB A.
PUBL. *The Battle with the Slum*, New York and London, 1902; *The Children of the Poor*, New York, 1892; *How the Other Half Lives*, New York, 1890.

BIBL. "'The Battle with the Slum,' 1887–1897," *U. S. Camera Annual*, 1948, p. 11–18+.

ROBINSON, HENRY PEACH
PUBL. *Pictorial Effect in Photography*, London, 1869; *Picture Making by Photography*, 1884 (2d ed., 1889, with chapter refuting Emerson); *Letters on Landscape Photography*, 1888; *The Elements of a Pictorial Photograph*, 1896.

BIBL. N. Newhall, "H. P. Robinson," *The Complete Photographer*, No. 49 (1943), p. 3150–53.

ROTHSTEIN, ARTHUR
PUBL. *Photojournalism*, New York, 1956 (2d ed., 1965); *Creative Color in Photography*, Philadelphia, 1963.

RUSSELL, ANDREW JOSEPH
PUBL. *Sun Pictures of Rocky Mountain Scenery*, New York, 1870 (30 photographs; text by F. V. Hayden).

BIBL. W. D. Pattison, "The Pacific Railroad Rediscovered," *Geographical Rev.*, 1962, p. 25–36.

SALOMON, ERICH
PUBL. *Berühmte Zeitgenossen in unbewachten Augenblicken*, Stuttgart, 1931; *Portrait of an Epoch*, New York, 1967 (biographical essay by P. Hunter-Salomon).

BIBL. P. Hunter, "Salomon." *Photography* (London), Jan., 1957, p. 32-37+; P. Hunter-Salomon, *Porträt einer Epoche*, Berlin, 1963. B. & N. Newhall, "Erich Salomon," in their *Masters of Photography*, New York, 1958, p. 134-39. K. Safranski, "Dr. Salomon," *Popular Phot.*, Aug., 1948 p. 56-59+.

SCHULZE, JOHANN HEINRICH
PUBL. "De Effectu Radiorum Solarium," in *Acta Physico-Medica Academiae Caesarae Leopoldino-Carolinae*, Nuremberg, 1727 (repr. in J. M. Eder, *Quellenschriften zu den frühesten Anfängen der Photographie*, Halle a. d. Saale, 1913; Engl. transl. in R. B. Litchfield, *Tom Wedgwood*, London, 1903).

BIBL. J. M. Eder, *Johann Heinrich Schulze*, Vienna, 1917.

SHEELER, CHARLES
BIBL. C. Rourke, *Charles Sheeler; Artist in the American Tradition*, New York, 1938.

SISKIND, AARON
PUBL. "The Drama of Objects," *Minicam Phot.*, June, 1945, p. 20–23+. *Aaron Siskind, Photographs*, New York, 1959.

BIBL. George Eastman House, *Aaron Siskind Photographer*, Rochester, N.Y., 1965 (essays by N. Lyons, H. H. Smith, T. B. Hess and A. Siskind).

SMITH, W. EUGENE
PUBL. Principal picture essays for *Life*: "Country Doctor" (Sept. 20, 1948); "Spanish Village" (Apr. 9, 1951); "Nurse Midwife" (Dec. 3, 1951); "A Man of Mercy" (Nov. 15,

1954). "Pittsburgh," *1959 Photography Annual*, New York, Ziff Davis Publ. Co., 1958. Interview: *Popular Phot.*, Nov., 1956, p. 48–49.

BIBL. E. A. Mack, "The Myth Named Smith," *Camera 35*, Dec. 1959–Jan. 1960, p. 45–47+. D. Vestal, "...A Great Unknown Photographer – W. Eugene Smith," *Popular Phot.*, Dec., 1966, p. 114–17+.

SMYTH, C. PIAZZI
BIBL. A. T. Gill, "Photography at the Great Pyramid; an Account of the Work of C. Piazzi Smyth," *Phot. Jour.*, Apr., 1965, p. 109–118.

SOUTHWORTH, ALBERT SANDS & JOSIAH JOHNSON HAWES
BIBL. I. N. Phelps Stokes, *The Hawes-Stokes Collection of American Daguerreotypes by Albert Sands Southworth and Josiah Johnson Hawes; a Catalogue*, New York, The Metropolitan Museum of Art, 1939. B. & N. Newhall, "Albert Sands Southworth and Josiah Johnson Hawes," in their *Masters of Photography*, New York, 1958, p. 22-31.

STEICHEN, EDWARD
PUBL. *The Family of Man*, New York, 1955 (book made from the exhibition of the same title); *A Life in Photography*, Garden City, New York, 1963.

BIBL. Museum of Modern Art, New York, *Steichen the Photographer*, 1961 (exhibition catalogue; biographical data by Grace Mayer). B. & N. Newhall, "Edward Steichen," in their *Masters of Photography*, New York, 1958, p. 76-91. C. Sandburg, *Steichen the Photographer*, 1929.

STEINERT, OTTO
PUBL. *Subjektive Fotografie*, Bonn, 1952; *Subjektive Fotografie 2*, Munich, 1955.

BIBL. J. A. Schmoll gen. Eisenwerth, "Otto Steinert, der Initiator einer fotografischen Bewegung," in catalogue of exhibition *Otto Steinert und Schüler*, Folkwang Museum, Essen, 1959. Folkwangschule für Gestaltung, *Otto Steinert und Schuler*, Essen, 1965 (exhibition catalogue; essay by F. Kempe, "Otto Steinert und die Geschichte der Photographie").

STIEGLITZ, ALFRED
PUBL. *Picturesque Bits of New York, and Other Studies*, New York, 1897; *Camera Notes*, official organ of the Camera Club of New York, managed and edited by the publications committee (Alfred Stieglitz, chairman), 1897–1902; *Camera Work*, an illustrated quarterly magazine devoted to photography, published and edited by Alfred Stieglitz, 1902–1917; "The Hand Camera — Its Present Importance," *Amer. Annual Phot. for 1897*, p. 19–26.

BIBL. W. Frank and others, eds., *America and Alfred Stieglitz*, Garden City, N.Y., 1934. National Gallery of Art, Washington, *Exhibition of Photographs by Alfred Stieglitz*, 1958 (catalogue, with biographical essay by Doris Bry, chronology, bibl.). Museum of Fine Arts, *Alfred Stieglitz. Photographer*, Boston, 1965 (essay by D. Bry revised and enlarged from preceding). B. & N. Newhall, "Alfred Stieglitz," in their *Masters of Photography*, New York, p. 60-75. D. Norman, ed. *Stieglitz Memorial Portfolio*, New York, 1947 (excellent reproductions). D. Norman, *Alfred Stieglitz, Introduction to an American Seer*, New York, 1960 (repr. from *Aperture*, VIII, No. 1). H. Seligmann, *Alfred Stieglitz Talking*, New Haven, 1966.

STRAND, PAUL
PUBL. *Photographs of Mexico*, New York, 1940 (20 photogravures, 2d ed., 1967); *Time in New England*, 1950 (ed. by N. Newhall); *La France de profil*, Lausanne, 1952 (text by Claude Roy); *Un Paese*, Turin, 1954 (text by C. Zavattini; *Tir-A'Mhurain*, London, 1962 (text by B. Davidson).

BIBL. N. Newhall, *Paul Strand*, New York, The Museum of Modern Art, 1945 (bibl.). B. & N. Newhall, "Paul Strand," in their *Masters of Photography*, 1958, p. 102–17. F. Vrba, *Paul Strand*, Prague, 1961 (text in Czech and English).

TALBOT, WILLIAM HENRY FOX
PUBL. *Some Account of the Art of Photogenic Drawing*, London, 1839 (repr. from *Athenaeum*, Feb. 9, 1839); "Photogenic Drawing, Further Discoveries," *Literary Gaz.*, Feb. 23, 1839; *The Process of Calotype Photogenic Drawing*, London, 1841 (repr. from *Proceedings*, Royal Soc., IV, 3, p. 12–16); *The Pencil of Nature*, London, 1844-46 (illus. and text repr. in *Image*, June, 1959); *Sun Pictures in Scotland*, 1845 (illus. only); appendix to G. Tissandier, *A History and Handbook of Photography*, 2d ed., 1878.
BIBL. B. Newhall, "William Henry Fox Talbot," *Image*, June, 1959. D. B. Thomas, *The First Negative*, London, Science Museum, 1964. A. H. Booth, *William Henry Fox Talbot, Father of Modern Photography*, London, 1965.

THOMSON, JOHN
PUBL. *Illustrations of China and Its People*, 4 vols., London, 1873–74; *Street Life in London*, 1877 (with A. Smith; 29 of these plates are reproduced in *Brit. Jour. of Phot. Annual*, 1965, p. 99–107).
BIBL. R. Doty, "Street Life in London," *Image*, Dec., 1957, p. 240–45.

TOURNACHON, GASPARD FÉLIX. See NADAR (pseud.)

VACQUERIE, AUGUSTE
BIBL. P. Gruyer, *Victor Hugo, photographe*, Paris, 1905.

VOGEL, HERMANN WILHELM
PUBL. *Die Photographie farbiger Gegenstände in den richtigen Tonverhältnissen*, Berlin, 1885 (French transl., 1887).
BIBL. J. M. Eder, "Biography of H. W. Vogel," in his *History of Photography*, New York, 1945, p. 462–64.

VROMAN, ADAM CLARK
BIBL. R. I. Mahood, ed., *Photographer of the Southwest: Adam Clark Vroman, 1856-1916*, Los Angeles, 1961 (essay by B. Newhall).

VUILLARD, EDOUARD
BIBL. J. Salomon & A. Vaillant, "Vuillard et son kodak," in catalogue of exhibition at L'Œil, Galerie d'Art, Paris, 1963; and Lefèvre Gallery, London, 1964.

WEDGWOOD, TOM
BIBL. Sir H. Davy, "An Account of a Method of... Making Profiles by the Agency of Light... Invented by T. Wedgwood," *Jour. Royal Institution*, 1802, I, p. 170–74. Repr. in R. B. Litchfield, *Tom Wedgwood*, London, 1903.

WEEGEE (pseudonym of Arthur Fellig)
PUBL. *Naked City*, New York, 1945; *Naked Hollywood*, 1953 (with Mel Harris); *Weegee's Creative Camera*, Garden City, N.Y., 1959 (with Roy Ald); *Weegee by Weegee*, New York, 1961.

WESTON, BRETT
BIBL. F. H. Halliday, "Brett Weston, Photographer," *Camera Craft*, Mar., 1940, p. 113–22. M. Armitage, *Brett Weston Photographs*, New York, 1956. Amon Carter Museum, *Brett Weston Photographs*, Fort Worth, Texas, 1966 (essay by N. Newhall).

WESTON, EDWARD
PUBL. *Photography*, Pasadena, Calif., 1934 (pamphlet; incisive statement); *California and the West*, New York, 1940 (text by C. W. Weston); *My Camera on Point Lobos*, Yosemite National Park, Calif. & Boston, 1950; *The Daybooks of Edward Weston*, Rochester, N.Y., & New York, 1961–66 (2 vols.).
BIBL. *Aperture*, Vol. VI, No. 1, 1958 (Weston issue, ed. by N. Newhall). M. Armitage, *The Art of Edward Weston*, New York, 1932. *Fifty Photographs [by] Edward Weston*, 1947. B. Newhall, "Edward Weston in Retrospect," *Popular Phot.*, Mar., 1946, p. 42–46+ (description of Weston's technique). B. & N. Newhall, "Edward Weston," in their *Masters of Photography*, New York, 1958, p. 118–33. N. Newhall, *The Photographs of Edward Weston*, New York, The Museum of Modern Art, 1946. N. Newhall, ed., *Edward Weston Photographer; The Flame of Recognition*, Rochester, N.Y., 1965 (also in *Aperture*, Vol. XII, Nos. 1-2, 1965).

WHITE, CLARENCE HUDSON
PUBL. "The Progress of Pictorial Photography," *Annual Report of the Pictorial Photographers of America*, 1918.
BIBL. P. C. Bunnell and C. H. White, Jr., "The Art of Clarence Hudson White," *The Ohio University Review*, VII (1965), p. 40–65.

WHITE, MINOR
PUBL. "Equivalence: The Perennial Trend," *PSA Journal*, July, 1963, p. 17–21; "Happenstance and How It Involves the Photographer," *Photography*, Oct., 1956, p. 40–45; "On the Strength of a Mirage," *Art in America*, Spring, 1958, p. 52–55; *Camera* (Lucerne), Aug., 1959, p. 5–23 (autobiographical statement, 23 reproductions); *Zone System Manual*, 2d ed., New York, 1963; *Aperture*, 1952–present (quarterly, edited by M. White).

WILSON, GEORGE WASHINGTON
BIBL. G. Peterich, "G. W. W.," *Image*, Dec., 1956, p. 220-23.

ZOLA, EMILE
BIBL. J. Loize, "Emile Zola, photographe," *Arts et Métiers Graphiques*, No. 45 (1935), p. 31-35.

Index

by Lucy R. Lippard